ROUTLEDGE LIBRARY EDITIONS:
JAPAN

JAPAN

JAPAN
The Hungry Guest

G. C. ALLEN

Volume 23

Routledge
Taylor & Francis Group
LONDON AND NEW YORK

First published in 1938

This edition first published in 2011
by Routledge
2 Park Square, Milton Park, Abingdon, Oxon, OX14 4RN

Simultaneously published in the USA and Canada
by Routledge
711 Third Avenue, New York, NY 10017

Routledge is an imprint of the Taylor & Francis Group, an informa business

First issued in paperback 2013

British Library Cataloguing in Publication Data
A catalogue record for this book is available from the British Library

ISBN13: 978-0-415-58527-9 (hbk)

ISBN13: 978-0-415-85235-7 (pbk)

Publisher's Note
The publisher has gone to great lengths to ensure the quality of this reprint but points out that some imperfections in the original copies may be apparent.

Disclaimer
The publisher has made every effort to trace copyright holders and would welcome correspondence from those they have been unable to trace.

PLATE I

BENKEI BRIDGE, TOKYO

JAPAN:
the Hungry Guest

by

G. C. ALLEN

Brunner Professor of Economic Science, University of Liverpool

"*You said you must stop,*
Because your horse was tired:
I said I must go,
Because my silkworms were hungry."

ARTHUR WALEY (*trans.*)

GEORGE ALLEN & UNWIN LTD

LONDON

FIRST PUBLISHED IN 1938

PRINTED IN GREAT BRITAIN BY
UNWIN BROTHERS LTD., WOKING

TO

MY WIFE

PREFACE

NO one who has had the good fortune to live in Japan has ever failed to be profoundly influenced by his experience, for the country exercises a fascination, which cannot be resisted, over the minds of all who come to her, even of those who are her most bitter critics. From the time of my first arrival in Japan about sixteen years ago the country has held for me an interest which has deepened with the years, and I have felt for her people an affection which has never cooled. I returned to England in 1925, after holding an appointment for three years in a Government College at Nagoya, and shortly afterwards my general impressions and the results of my studies of economic conditions were embodied in a book entitled *Modern Japan and Its Problems*. In 1936 I paid a second visit to Japan, at the request of the Bureau of International Research of Harvard University and Radcliffe College, mainly for the purpose of collecting data for the study of the development and organization of Japanese industry. The results of these researches are published in America. Apart from my detailed investigations into industrial conditions, during the months I spent in Japan I had an opportunity of comparing many aspects of Japanese life in 1936 with those I remembered from my former residence in the country. I renewed old friendships and made new ones, and I had discussions on many political and social questions that interested me. The information provided in this way, and the impressions which I gained, were of utmost help to me in my efforts to trace the tendencies in Japan's social, political, and economic life with which this book deals.

The book has been written since the outbreak of the war with China, and Japan's actions during this time have been the object of widespread condemnation. An author cannot hope to escape completely from the effects of this heated atmosphere, especially in these days of propaganda. But I have tried to write objectively and without prejudice, and I hope that in recording the facts I have not been influenced either by my affection for the Japanese people or by my personal views about Japanese foreign policy. Here and there I have not hesitated to evaluate tendencies and events, nor to express my own judgments. But I hope that I have left the reader in no doubt about what are inductions from the observed facts and what are interpretations or criticisms dependent upon my own opinions and outlook.

Many Japanese friends and acquaintances have contributed information and have admitted me to intimacy with much that is peculiar to Japanese life. I can record my indebtedness to only one of them—to my late friend, Mr. Takeshi Matsumura. For several of the photographs I should like to thank Mr. A. Morikawa and Mr. J. Bewsher. My wife has given me invaluable help and criticism at every stage in the writing of this book.

G. C. ALLEN

March 1938

CONTENTS

ILLUSTRATIONS

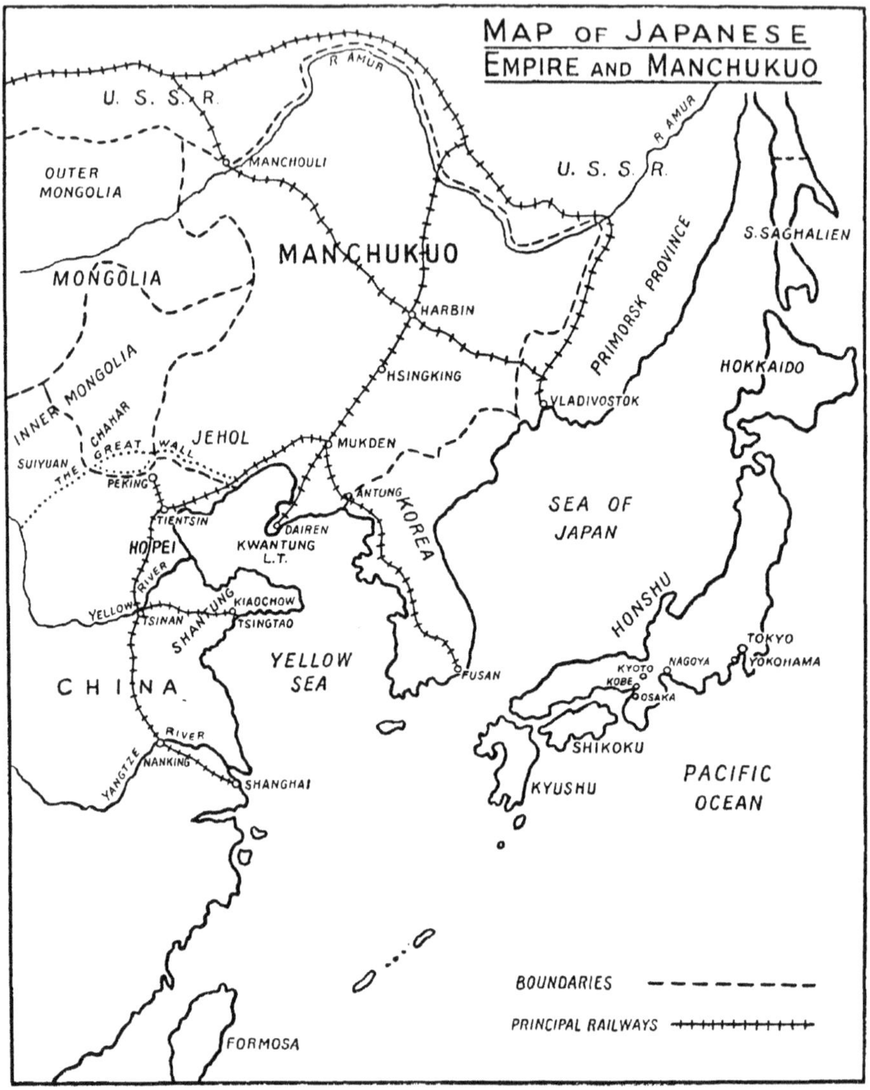
MAP OF JAPANESE EMPIRE AND MANCHUKUO
U. S. S. R.
R. AMUR
OUTER MONGOLIA
MANCHOULI
MONGOLIA
MANCHUKUO
HARBIN
HSINGKING
INNER MONGOLIA
CHAHAR
SUIYUAN
THE GREAT WALL
JEHOL
PEKING
TIENTSIN
MUKDEN
ANTUNG
DAIREN
KWANTUNG L.T.
HOPEI
YELLOW RIVER
TSINAN
SHANTUNG
KIAOCHOW
TSINGTAO
KOREA
FUSAN
VLADIVOSTOK
PRIMORSK PROVINCE
S. SAGHALIEN
HOKKAIDO
SEA OF JAPAN
HONSHU
TOKYO
YOKOHAMA
NAGOYA
KYOTO
KOBE
OSAKA
SHIKOKU
KYUSHU
PACIFIC OCEAN
YELLOW SEA
CHINA
YANGTZE RIVER
NANKING
SHANGHAI
FORMOSA
BOUNDARIES
PRINCIPAL RAILWAYS

CHAPTER I

INTRODUCTION

A MAN who has lived and worked among a foreign people must always feel uneasy when he is confronted in his own country with the sweeping generalizations in which their qualities are commonly summarized. A laudatory account brings to his mind persons of whom such eulogies are ludicrous and everyday occurrences which reveal precisely contrary qualities to those described. Adverse criticism of the people recalls to him friends and acquaintances whose worth gives the lie to their critics, and incidents which show none of the discreditable characteristics these condemn. So he stands, poised aloof and irresolute, unable to take sides—a lukewarm friend, a critic without the sharp sword of dogmatism. A man who has lived happily in Japan and has formed friendships among the people has an especially difficult task when he tries to set down honestly his views about the country and its inhabitants. For since Japan has a civilization very different from our own, and since few Englishmen have made intimate personal contacts with her people, writers are tempted to subsume under a few sweeping generalizations all those multitudinous individual differences which distinguish the members of any nation. The Japanese are thus treated in our Press and on our platforms more summarily than are European nations with whom we have closer contacts and whose civilization and ours have common foundations. Those who have lived in Japan know that such generalizations are misleading, and they resent them accordingly. Yet when they try to correct the common impression, they know that they, too, must generalize, and that they cannot avoid giving a partial account of the people, an account coloured by their own individual experiences and by their own limited judgment of what is significant.

In the last resort the artists are more successful than most other writers in conveying a correct impression of the people. Lafcadio

Hearn and the gently ironical author of *L'Honorable Partie de Campagne* have provided the West with pictures that bear the stamp of truth, although it is easy to refute the details. The artists' success may be attributed in no small degree to their freedom from political partisanship. Unfortunately, much of the writing about the Japanese to-day is done by persons who, consciously or unconsciously, have allowed their opinions to be influenced by their political allegiances or their views about national economic advantage. Since 1931 the Japanese have been prominent in world politics, and they have emerged as exceedingly successful competitors of Western nations in world trade. Consequently, Western writers have been inclined to consider them in their capacity as political or commercial rivals, even when they have been dealing ostensibly with other aspects of national life. For this reason the Japanese have appeared as sinister figures among the peoples of the world to some, and clothed in the virtues of heroism, energy, and constructive capacity to others.

Many circles not otherwise congruent in this country are united in viewing the Japanese with suspicion and dislike. The conservative-imperialist looks upon Japanese territorial expansion in Asia as a threat to British political interests in China and a growing danger to the British Empire fringing the Pacific shores. Mr. Shaw explained that by the term "traitor" an Englishman means one who is not entirely devoted to the English interests. It is not therefore difficult for an Englishman who believes that Japan presents a threat to the security of the Empire, to ascribe to her people the more deplorable personal qualities. But Japan has not merely been moving in a direction which is leading to a clash of political ambitions; she has also been sending her goods into markets previously served by the British manufacturers. So from another quarter she is assailed as a nation which is undermining the standards of life of Western peoples; and odium is also cast upon her because, it is said, her success has been achieved at the cost of lowering the standards of life of her own workers. Those circles in which some vestige of the old liberal economic and political traditions is still preserved might have been expected to reply that, harmful as cheap Japanese exports may be to established British industries, Japan, nevertheless, confers a benefit on impoverished Asiatic consumers by supplying them with those goods, and that it is irrational and ungenerous to deny them that benefit. This answer has indeed been given. It has not, however, found a large and appreciative audience, even among the liberally minded in this country, because the Japanese have gained in those very quarters to which they might have addressed themselves for support, an evil reputation, even before the present conflict with China broke out, on account of the exploits in Manchuria and Shanghai, and their breach with the League of Nations.

Recent events have greatly confused the old political allegiances in this country. If Japan had not pursued a political course abhorrent to liberal political opinion in the West, then her economic expansion and its effects on world markets and on Western producers would have stood alone as a clear issue. In that case, liberal opinion must have rejected the crude and ignorant criticisms that were made of Japan because of that expansion. But as it was, their abhorrence of Japan's political action led liberally minded people to acquiesce in the condemnation of her economic development, and even to seek further excuses for their attitude in their charges of "sweated labour" or "social dumping." The internal political situation also has developed in a way that liberal opinion deplores; for the period of territorial and economic expansion has been the period in which the progress of Japan towards democratic institutions has been checked, and violence and assassination have characterized her own political conflicts. Thus Japan seems to have allied herself with the irrational and barbarous forces in the present-day world, and humanitarianism has come to regard her as an enemy. Her recent alinement with the dictator-states has confirmed this view.

Japan has, moreover, been ill-served by her friends in Western countries. A brief study of Japanese conditions within the last few years can lead to a sympathetic understanding of the causes which led to the tragic events in Manchuria and China and released the forces of fanaticism within Japan herself. To understand the springs of action is not, however, to make the action itself any less deplorable or less disastrous for the progress of civilization. Many friends of Japan pass too easily from sympathy with her problems and difficulties to support of her policy of aggression in Asia. Some of those who view international relationships as a conflict between rival imperialisms for the exploitation of the weak, argued after 1932 that Great Britain should ally herself before it was too late with the ascendant power of Japan, and should divert Japanese attention from British territories and interests on the Pacific shores by giving diplomatic support to her in her expansionist policy in North China. Others whose political attitude is less explicit suggest that for Great Britain to condemn Japan for her recent policy is hypocritical, since the building of the British Empire can provide parallels for most of the actions of Japan. These writers sweep aside the fact that Japan was committed by treaty to avoid actions that were commonplaces of imperialism in the past, and conclude that, after all, the adverse criticism of Japan, though apparently based on moral grounds, owes its origin to a more selfish reason, the threat of Japan to British imperial interests. The "satiated" Powers, it is said, are trying to thwart Japan's expansion in their own interests, and to mobilize the moral forces that lie behind the League to assist in preserving the *status quo*. Japan's territorial expansion has been necessitated by the over-population of Japan Proper and the threat of Russia to her existence as a Power. Great Britain, so it is said, should sympathize with her difficulties and support her policy. But while it is true that the storm of criticism directed against Japan owes its force largely to selfishness and fears of Western Powers, yet these arguments cannot move those who believe that it is dishonourable to sacrifice the weak to the necessities or ambitions of the strong, especially when this country has sworn to protect the integrity of the former.

Many "friends," moreover, are incapable of perceiving the moral difference between territorial expansion and commercial success in foreign markets. They repeat the official Japanese propaganda which declares that since Japanese goods are excluded from markets, the only way of occupying the growing population and supplying the necessary raw materials is by acquiring territories in which Japan will find new markets. Now, it is possible to argue that commercial expansion in foreign markets and territorial expansion in Asia are *practical* alternatives for Japan. But it is absurd to suggest that these alternatives are moral equivalents, that each can be equally condemned or justified. If Japan is able to satisfy the wants of certain peoples for goods at lower prices than those charged by former suppliers, this constitutes a net gain to the world. But there is a wide difference between supplying Eastern people with goods they are anxious to buy and imposing on some of them a form of government which they dislike.

These political and economic questions will be considered in detail later in this book. They are mentioned here because it is important to realize the extent to which judgments about the qualities of the Japanese people have been influenced by the political views of speakers and writers in Western countries. Those who condemn recent Japanese policy think of the people as harsh and unscrupulous aggressors without respect for contracts or for justice. In the past their life had charm, and they were sensitive to beauty in art and nature; but these qualities have been choked by ignoble military ambition and commercial greed. The "friends" of Japan who excuse her policy speak of a nation of loyal and heroic patriots united in devoted and unselfish service to their State, great alike in war and in the arts of industry, preserving in the midst of their mighty practical achievements the flavour of a Japanese tradition of living. Although there are some dissentients, both groups are inclined to hold that the Japanese are distinguished by fierce energy and exceptional capacity in the pursuit of their aims. None of these judgments is entirely false; but how odd it is for anyone who has made friends among the Japanese, who has shared personal joys or griefs with them, and who has been irritated, amused, and touched by the ordinary chances of life among them, to be confronted by these generalized descriptions of the people he has known. The sinister or the heroic figures that are drawn by some political writers or journalists seem to have little in common with the few friends or the crowd of acquaintances who have crossed his path. And, if he is to be honest, he must try to describe the Japanese, not as members of a nation whose Government is pursuing this or that policy, and who in their collective capacity seem to have certain political ambitions and be willing to pursue certain measures for their realization, but rather as a group of persons, all with qualities of diverse kinds, yet linked by common traditions and by adherence to common standards of social conduct.

CHAPTER II

NIPPON SEISHIN[1]

"'Tis true ther is no balance to weigh these goods and ills nor any measur of them, like as of colour and heat in their degrees; they are incommensurable in kind."

ROBERT BRIDGES

IT is difficult to put forward any proposition about the Japanese character without the feeling that a contrary proposition could be easily defended. This is as it should be. The qualities of seventy million persons cannot be summed up in a few sweeping generalizations when a considerable proportion of the seventy millions consists of persons of character and virility, and when the society to which they belong has been subjected to many strong and divergent influences. Yet there are some broad characteristics which distinguish the Japanese from Westerners. A very intelligent Japanese friend once said to me, in effect: "We read what Europeans write about us, and we marvel at their confident judgments. We do not really know whether their views are correct or no; for we are not an analytical race, and a detached, intellectual examination of our qualities, or of anyone else's, is quite beyond our powers, and is, indeed, repugnant to us. So we are inclined to accept what others say about us." This statement, I believe, brings out an important contrast between Japanese and European habits of mind. In no country, of course, are analytical powers practised by the mass of the people. But in Europe intellectual tradition since the Greeks has created this habit of mind among the educated classes, and from it scientific achievement has proceeded. The Japanese, nourished upon a different intellectual diet, have still little appreciation of the Western way of viewing a problem, especially if the problem is in the field of human relationships. To them detached

[1] *The Japanese Spirit.*

analysis seems almost indecent. Even the serious judgments of the learned are often based mainly upon emotions. When the question is one that affects the society or nation, then the Japanese is inclined to answer it by reference to his feelings of loyalty or his sense of social obligation. Certain things are true, certain lines of action are to be applauded, because he *feels* that they are so; and if he writes down his views, he casts them in the form of an emotional appeal rather than of a logical argument. For this reason, the writings of Japanese upon a particular political or social situation often appear, when translated, to be not merely ingenuous, but, to use a favourite term, "insincere." Nowhere else in the world is the phrase that releases hidden stores of emotion more powerful than in Japan. It may end a school strike, cause mutinous troops to hold their hand, or convert the communist to a "proper" view of society. Japanese propaganda is childish because the appeals are addressed not to the intelligence of the foreign audience but to an emotional complex which is universal in Japan but not possessed by the foreigner. There are, of course, many individuals to whom these generalizations do not apply; but they make up only a small proportion even of the educated classes.

The lack among the intelligentsia of a scientific habit of mind, the result, presumably, of the intellectual tradition of the country, is confirmed by the present isolation of the Japanese scholar. Academic workers in the West have frequent personal contacts with their fellows in other countries, and they can exchange ideas with one another in languages which have common roots. But the Japanese who concern themselves with the Western apparatus of thought are able to familiarize themselves with the latest developments of their subject only through reading in languages which have been the expression of civilizations and mental habits entirely different from their own. The intellectual traffic, too, is all one way. A Japanese scholar can only seldom hold converse in Japanese with a foreigner working in the same field, and if he wishes to give the West the benefit of his own ideas he must communicate them through the imperfect medium of a language not his own. Again, if a European scholar finds his environment uncongenial, it is not impossible for him to transfer himself to a more sympathetic atmosphere. For example, many German scholars displaced by the Nazi persecution have found a haven in the United States or in England, where they are accepted as partners in the pursuit of knowledge by the scholars who are nationals of those countries. But if a Japanese is guilty of an offence against the political or social canons of his country, where can he find a haven? Even if he could secure a livelihood in a foreign country, he must abandon his own civilization and enter one with entirely different traditions. The barrier is a harder one to cross than that which faces any European who takes up residence in England or the New World, and only a man of the strongest convictions and of heroic mould is likely to run a course which brings him in conflict with his own society. The Japanese scholar is, thus, much less detached and cosmopolitan in his outlook than are those of the West. The large view and the far-reaching speculation are not to be expected of him. But the lack of objectivity which is sometimes said to characterize the Japanese worker in the social sciences must not be attributed to cowardice. Objectivity is more difficult for him to attain, partly because of the differences in his intellectual training from that of Western scholars, and partly because of the greater social pressure to which he is subjected. Some actually manage to attain it in spite of these handicaps.

Up to fairly recent times there was a considerable degree of academic freedom in Japan. During the post-War wave of liberalism books expressing "advanced" or "leftist" opinions were popular in Japan, and there was little hindrance placed upon free discussion of social and political problems in academic circles. Jurists who had strong leanings towards democratic legal and constitutional methods had a large following, and were surrounded by enthusiastic bodies of students. In the college in which I taught, lecturers examined, without being criticized, the economic and political doctrines of the Marxist and socialist schools. A propagandist play, with pacifist leanings, was written and performed by the students before an eager audience of townspeople; and although sometimes the police interfered in student conferences and contests, this was strongly resented as an infringement on liberty. The students, on the whole, were critical of imperialism and were far more interested in social problems than in international politics. At Waseda University the students went on strike as a protest against the proposal to form a society for the study of military subjects. The officers appointed to the schools and colleges to conduct the military training of students were very unpopular and frequent changes had to be made in their personnel. Many students called away to military service after graduation did not hesitate to express to me, though a foreigner, their objections to it on grounds of political principle.

When I returned to Japan in 1936 the position was very different. Free expression of "leftist" views had become very difficult for the students and their teachers. Although the bookshops still contain plenty of Marxist and socialist literature in European languages, its presence is largely accounted for by police ignorance of its contents, and foreign books are often banned on political grounds if they have come under official notice. Foreigners who can read the works of Japanese scholars say that the treatment even of such subjects as archaeology is becoming tendencious, and lecture-courses to instil the "Japanese Spirit" into the public are given even by scholars of some reputation. While in Japan I was approached by some of my old students, now officials in the Ministry of Education, in the hope that I might tell them something about the organization of adult education in Great Britain. They were exceedingly surprised to learn that an attempt is made here to treat objectively even such subjects as economics and political science. One of them asked naïvely: "Surely, if workers are given accurate information about the economic position, they become Marxist and revolutionary?" It was clear that in his view "education" for the working class should be directed to the encouragement of their "patriotism" and the inculcation of contentment with their lot. He referred to Germany as a country where these lofty educational ideals received their most satisfactory expression. There are many educationists who have genuinely lost their belief in rational humanitarianism. One professor of my acquaintance who ten years ago was a pacifist in his outlook on international relations and who, on his first visit to London, deplored the indifference of the Highgate population to the location of Karl Marx's grave, has now gone over to the "patriots." Others have become cynical; and many who view bitterly and with despair the present political and cultural tendencies have to remain discreetly silent. Some men of liberal outlook can still speak brave words. A friend who is a keen internationalist said that he and his fellow teachers with the same outlook can still do something to influence their students; but that they have to be very cautious.

A strong tendency has lately developed towards mystical and irrational explanations of political or social phenomena. The Japanese who were once inclined to apologize for the peculiarities in their outlook or way of life now emphasize them as indications that they are a race apart. A short time ago a dam collapsed and the released waters overwhelmed mining villages in the neighbourhood. It was shown that the disaster was brought about by faulty construction and the firm to which the dam belonged contributed a million yen towards the relief of the bereaved families. A business man informed me that this action was likely to be misjudged by foreigners. It was not to be regarded as compensation, as it would be in an individualistic society, but rather as a gesture to show the sympathy of the firm for those of its members who had been involved in the catastrophe—it was a willing assumption of a common sorrow. This, I was to understand, was a point of view peculiar to Japan. Now it is perfectly true that there is less emphasis on pecuniary motives in Japan than in Western countries and probably, also, a deeper sympathy between rich and poor. But nowadays this distinction is being exaggerated for the purpose of eulogizing the national "spirit." Actually, the firm's generosity is probably to be explained by its fear of provoking the popular criticism which in the last six years has been directed against many of the great business families. Again, many business men like to explain the recent industrial advance, not in terms of improved technique, lowered costs, or changes in the rate of exchange, but by reference to the superior spiritual qualities of the Japanese to those of Western nations. One of the most frequent radio broadcasts consists of talks about the Japanese "spirit," and even social reformers like to distinguish between the "spirit" of Japan and that of Western countries, and to explain international conflicts in these terms. Now nationalism in nearly every country expresses itself in such language; but outside Japan this kind of mysticism is reserved for home consumption. It may be useful in awakening the members of a nation to a sense of their common purpose. But even the Germans and the English scarcely expect other nations to take seriously their claims to spiritual superiority, unless these claims are supported by rational argument and evidence. A great mass of Japanese propaganda for foreign consumption, however, is couched in mystical language which can have only a local appeal.

Strong national feeling has, of course, played an important part, in Japan as elsewhere, as an agent of unification, and patriotism is in the modern world one of the most powerful instruments for giving coherence to an otherwise distracted people. But the emotion may be rightly or wrongly directed. It is liable, unless carefully controlled, to overcome reason, kindliness, and humanity. This has happened to a large extent in the Fascist countries, and although Japan has not yet sunk to their levels her life, too, is being corrupted by this once wholesome emotion which has begun to fester. We have seen that scholars and educationists have begun to lose their personal integrity under the influence of nationalistic feeling. Administrative and political life is slowly being infected also. Thus a minor official with a grudge against a superior may, on slight grounds, prefer a charge that he is lacking in patriotism and cause him to be replaced. Many arbitrary acts performed by ignorant and fanatical minor officials pass unchallenged by their superiors because the latter fear that their patriotism may be impugned. For instance, an official may refuse to supply quite harmless data to foreign consular officials, and his departmental chief may hesitate to reprimand him because by doing so he would make himself vulnerable to attack. Gangsters and murderers often escape with light sentences if they are able to plead that their actions were directed towards patriotic ends, as when their victims are unpopular statesmen, politicians, or business men. Political crimes thus often go unpunished, and a feeling of insecurity is engendered in the whole of society. Men who are likely to be the next targets are forced to equivocate and to make a pretence of holding ideas that they really scorn.

The extraordinary powers possessed by the police have, in times of political trouble, an unhealthy influence on society. In theory the police are the mentors and helpers of the people—a kind of secular village priest, and the best of them do much for the people in their charge. But actually they exercise very wide powers of control and prohibition. They supervise the publication of all printed matter; they can prevent the reporting in newspapers and periodicals of any matters which come under the control of the public procurators and of the Ministers of War, the Navy, and Foreign Affairs. Public meetings must be announced to them before they can be held. Certain shops and businesses are under their supervision, such as inns, public bath-houses, pawnshops, stalls, licensed houses, and private employment exchanges. They take charge in case of accidents like fire, flood, and explosion. They inspect buildings, and they are in charge of public morals. Even the prevention of the spread of epidemics and measures to ensure pure food come into their province. Experience has shown that in no country can such great power be entrusted to the police without careful safeguards which are lacking in Japan. There all the police come under the direct administration of the State; there is no local government control over them. They are administered in the name of the Emperor by the Minister of Home Affairs. So the protectors of the people often become their tyrants. A very respectable Japanese citizen who had lost some money in a burglary said that he did not propose to call in the police; it was worth the amount he had lost to keep them away. I have seen them lose their tempers and become unnecessarily violent when trying to direct crowds which were, as always in Japan, exceedingly good-natured and amenable. They walk into public meetings and force speakers of whom they disapprove to be silent, and there seems to be no effective appeal against their autocratic behaviour. They decide what books should be banned on the grounds of their "dangerous thoughts." A short time ago when a Japanese painter ironically placed in the foreground of his picture of the new and massive modern Parliament building a modest Japanese-style dwelling-house, the police ordered that it should be removed from the gallery where it was displayed on the grounds that it was subversive political propaganda. They are justly disliked by the people as a whole. It is probable that no single reform would do more to sweeten social and political life and to stimulate the individual towards the promotion of public welfare that has seriously lagged in Japan than would a thorough reorganization of the police force.

From early times the *soshi* or gangster has been a figure in Japanese politics and public life. He has not become such a menace in Japan as in the United States and some other countries; but many disgraceful actions can be put down to him. *Soshi* can be hired by the more disreputable political societies to "beat up" their opponents, or by unscrupulous manufacturers to damage the property of competitors. One of their most recent activities was to assault some missionaries who were sheltering an unfortunate girl who had escaped from a licensed house.

In the life of every country there are elements of which the civilized patriot is ashamed, and the defects that have been noted here are not designed to suggest that Japan is worse than any other country, but only to indicate where some of the major faults lie. And it must not be imagined that foreigners alone have perceived them. No one can live among the Japanese for any length of time without realizing that desire for reform and for the abolition of the worst abuses is strong. At present reformers are not vocal. But there are thousands of them who have not forgotten the finer aspects of their own civilization and who do not despise the best that the West has to offer to their country. They are revolted at the radio propaganda with its unending laudations of the "Japanese Spirit" and at the crude assertions of superiority which are found so frequently in newspapers and political speeches. Japanese tradition is indeed hostile to this vulgar parade of excellences. As a Japanese friend said to me: "There is too much said about the Japanese spirit nowadays. Although one feels that it exists, one cannot define it, and it ought not to be spoken about as it is." There are men working in obscurity for ends that have nothing to do with the more vulgar manifestations of national pride; men whose influence for good is great because in them the power of self-abnegation, characteristic of the race, is allied to noble purposes. They are found in all branches of national life—in teaching, art, letters, administration, and business. When the ranting of the vulgarians and the nationalists dies down, their voice may be heard. Should disaster overtake the nation as a result of present courses, there are not lacking men with the skill and imagination to lead it back to nobler paths.

Imperialistic tendencies have not passed unchallenged, and there are many Japanese in all walks of life who still cling to democratic ideals. The foreigner can get little impression of the weight of this liberal opinion, but he finds occasional expressions of it in unexpected quarters. "I hate war and all this military preparation," said a young Japanese official of a large company, when we encountered some troops on the march. "There is always in this country plenty of money for the Army, but very little for the social services," a civil servant in the Home Office declared bitterly. "We call it the Tomb of Democracy," said another civil servant as we passed the new Parliament building in Kojimachi, Tokyo. When I ventured to say that peace was endangered because in all countries there were men who resented the claims that civilized living made on them, a Japanese replied: "They are especially numerous here." There was dismay at the end of 1936 when in signing the Anti-Comintern Pact, Japan seemed to be aligning herself with the Fascist Powers. "Many of us feel very much disturbed about this agreement," I was informed, "but the people here are not consulted about political affairs. These are arranged for us." At the beginning of 1938 a considerable number of university professors were arrested on the charge of "dangerous thinking." A colleague of theirs attributed their arrest to the fact that they had been critical of Government policy. "The Minister of Home Affairs," he said, "is Admiral Suetsugu. Admirals do not understand that criticism fulfils a necessary function in a modern State." These remarks were made in the course of casual encounters, and are all the more significant in view of the shy reluctance of the ordinary Japanese to venture to criticize his country to foreigners. Those who have intimate friends among the Japanese know that liberalism is still alive in the country. Indeed, there is still a good deal of the nineteenth-century Radicalism that has almost entirely died out elsewhere. John Stuart Mill's works have a considerable vogue in the universities, and Japan is perhaps the only country where his *Principles of Political Economy* is still extensively used as an economics text-book.

The Japanese do not produce many men of outstanding intellectual ability, and as a nation they are neither profound nor quick in mental activity. Throughout their modern history foreign observers have declared from time to time that this or that defect in character or intellect would prevent any striking national development. Yet they have made astonishing progress. The main quality responsible for this success has been their will-power which, once their ambitions have been fired, has enabled them to overcome their natural inclination to let things slide, and their tendency to meet difficulties with a fatalistic shrug of "*shikataganai*."[1] Though handicapped by their language and by their physique, they have shown enormous energy in achieving their aims. They work slowly at intellectual or at business tasks, but tirelessly and almost incessantly. Some of them, for example, without ever having left

[1] "It's inevitable."

Japan, have a good knowledge of English, a very difficult language for them to acquire. This knowledge has often been attained by extraordinary effort. One Japanese of my acquaintance used, during his student days, to rise early in the morning and go to Tokyo Station in the hope of meeting foreigners from the trains whom he could help and at the same time obtain the benefit of conversation with them. The business man's hours are those of the English manufacturer in the early nineteenth century, and the long week-end is unknown. The students at schools and universities are driven very hard, and in the farms and workshops labour seems endless. Once a Japanese has grasped a new method or idea he is indefatigable in carrying it out. Although conservative in so far as his own traditions are concerned, he is at an advantage, in some respects, in coming to various manifestations of Western civilization without the inhibiting influences that long experience of them may engender. He is, thus, always attempting things which are imperfectly comprehended or seem beyond his grasp, and yet, although mistakes are made often, he does not at any rate fail through timidity or excessive caution.

Modern Japan is much concerned with material achievement; but this does not mean that the impulse behind these ambitions comes from a nice calculation of gains and losses. For the Japanese business man is not disingenuous in trying to relate his own worldly efforts to spiritual promptings or to the mystical destiny of his nation. Alfred Marshall realized this when he said of the Japanese: "Their quick rise to power supports the suggestion made by the history of past times that some touch of idealism, religious, patriotic, or artistic, can generally be detected at the root of any great outburst of practical energy."[1] In this they are not, of course, peculiar; the connection between religious enthusiasm and the development of modern capitalism is a commonplace of Western economic history. And it is for this reason that modern Japan recalls many features of our own early industrial era. There are the same abounding energy and determination; the same idealiza-

[1] *Industry and Trade*, p. 161.

tion of business success; the same belief in the duty to work hard; and in many business circles the same simple and unostentatious way of living that were found among the great nonconformist manufacturers and merchants. There is, of course, something of the same hypocrisy and the tendency to draw a veil of high-sounding phrases over the uglier facts associated with industrial development.

Where the Puritan manufacturer could find his spiritual refreshment in his religious devotions and activities, the Japanese has his aesthetic tradition. This tradition is the source of much that is graceful and of enduring value in Japan. A Japanese may devote his leisure moments to landscape gardening, to scroll painting, to the composition of verses, to the study of Noh drama, or to the decoration of porcelain. Even if he has no talent in these arts he can obtain repose in other and more popular forms of entertainment. The Japanese restaurant appeals to the aesthete, and as the seasons pass, he can share with the multitude the quiet pleasures of moon-viewing, or visit the places famous for maples or cherry-blossom. Of course, there are some who obtain little pleasure from these festivals or who use them as occasions for carousal; but sensitive appreciation of an aesthetic kind is widespread.

Among the educated classes this natural taste is fostered by a conscious desire to free themselves for a time from besetting material cares. "We meet here one day a fortnight to practise scroll-painting under a master so that we shall remember that profits are not everything," said a successful business man and journalist in Tokyo. A sea captain, without any self-consciousness, wrote for me on a fan the verse which he had composed on the subject set for the annual Imperial Prize Poem. A working man encountered casually on the hills above Kyoto said that many of his fellows spent their time foolishly in drinking, but he and some of his friends liked in their leisure hours to come to the place where he met me and look at the hills. A doctor said that when his working day began he became immersed in the round of duty and was little better than a machine; so he rose early and spent

A STREET IN NAGOYA FIFTEEN YEARS AGO

FACTORY-SHRINE AT THE MITSUBISHI AEROPLANE WORKS

an hour in contemplation or in reading philosophy, and for that hour he felt himself to be a personality. Thus the harassed and ambitious Japanese does not find spiritual solace, as did the business man of our own corresponding economic era, in religious exercises, nor in voluntary public service and political and philanthropic activities as the English business man has tended to do in later times, but rather in the practice of an art, in aesthetic appreciation or contemplation. It is to this quiet haven that he repairs when the world presses upon him too closely.

In this he is but carrying out an old tradition of his race. *Bushido*, as a way of life, held two opposing principles. One was concerned with social and personal relationships; it enjoined unflinching loyalty to a superior and complete self-abnegation. But there was a gentler side, which pointed away from practical effort and from the tireless pursuit of duty. At times the *samurai* could withdraw into the fortress of his own soul and seek to express in painting or verse something of the sweetness or sorrow of existence and the melancholy that lies over nature and the fate of man. As he saw his cause in ruins a famous *samurai* wrote:

Sunset upon my path
And for mine inn to-night
The shadow of a tree
And for mine host
A flower.

The Japanese apply the term *furyu* to describe the quality of spirit, at once sensuous and melancholy, that is cultivated by these sophisticated and yet simple aesthetic exercises. This quiet spirit is indeed far removed both from the strenuous world of practical personal achievement and from the heated atmosphere of nationalist passion and ambition.

Aestheticism alone, however, is not sufficient to provide a moral basis for national life, and like most nations since the War, the Japanese have been suffering from serious psychological disturbances. Perhaps more than most, they have been distressed by the lack of any great organizing idea, and so they have been swept by ideological fashions which have left an intellectual chaos. The reasons for this are not difficult to discover. Westernization has brought not merely new productive technique and new kinds of economic activity, but also changes in the system of living and in outlook. New ideas in the field of art, politics, and morals have swept across the country and have shaken the old foundations of Japanese life; but as the soil in which these ideas originally germinated was of different composition from that in Japan, they have seldom struck deep root before they, too, were choked by others. Material things can be easily transplanted and can quickly be accommodated to the needs of another civilization. But ideas and institutions wither in an unfamiliar environment or become distorted beyond recognition. Just as it is impossible fully to understand the conclusions of any school of thinkers unless one has studied the development of their system of thought, so institutions which are the result of a historical process lose their meaning when they are wrenched from their setting and hurriedly imposed upon another society. In another chapter this point will be illustrated by reference to Japan's political history, and the architectural and artistic chaos that is found wherever the Japanese attempt to practise Western forms will be described presently. Here we may refer to manners and social ideals.

America has had a most profound influence on manners and the general outlook of the younger people of the cities. Japanese with a conservative outlook or those who are sensitive to the delicacy and refinement of their old ways of life are, it is true, repelled by the crudities which they associate with America. The family of a Japanese friend of mine who has spent many years in America often tell him that his manners are now so blunt as to make him indistinguishable from a Western barbarian. But many of the younger people are greatly attracted by the novelty of the life that the films present to them, by the toys and mechanical tricks which America is so skilled in producing, and by the freer and more boisterous conduct permitted in that country. A young

Japanese who had paid a brief visit to California thought it delightful that young men and girls were allowed to lie about the parks in each other's arms. "In Japan," he added wistfully, "the police would at once take steps to prevent such behaviour, and so deprive Japanese youth of a most pleasant pastime." The young girls of Tokyo model themselves on the film stars, and avidly read the "movie" magazines; jazz has a great attraction for them. Everyone wants a camera and a wireless set, and if he can get a foreign one it adds greatly to his prestige. Some of the business men deliberately assume the brusque and direct manners of their American counterparts, and these manners fit the Japanese man exceedingly ill. One of them complained to me of a certain foreign-style restaurant in Tokyo because, he said, the waitresses persist in bowing in Japanese manner when the guest enters. Many serious-minded young men with a liberal political outlook are favourably disposed towards Americanization because it stands for individual freedom and is hostile to their oligarchical system of government. The films, the American magazines, American business men, tourists, missionaries and school teachers, Japanese business men who visit America and students who are trained there, and, finally, the Japanese born in America, all help to spread the new way of life. The majority of those who are affected by Americanization, however, are quite ignorant of the fundamental aspect of the civilization of which the manners, equipment, and social and political outlook are but the manifestations. Sometimes a Japanese flavour is added, as happens with jazz music, and although this is not always unpleasing, the result is to increase the confusion of Japan's national culture to-day. The Japanese girl who is graceful in her *kimono* and *obi*, often seems pert and cheap in her artificial silk near-Western dress. The "nice, pure tea-room," or the café advertising its "fine Brazil coffee and soft jazz record" is often merely vulgar. An exaggerated importance is attached to American trivialities.

The ordinary conservative Japanese, who is repelled by these changes, comes to associate political liberty and spontaneous and frank manners with other manifestations of Americanization that are vulgarizing and corrupting his country. The forces of political reaction are thus strengthened, and the more generous tendencies in Japan's social life come to be regarded with suspicion because of their undesirable concomitants. In 1936, when it was announced that Japan had been chosen as the seat of the Olympic Games for 1940, the enthusiasm of the young Westernized Japanese was unbounded, and seemed quite disproportionate to the importance of the event. But these Japanese, of course, believed that this would mark a stage of progress towards their ultimate goal. An Army leader, however, who was suspicious of international gatherings of this kind and who felt that these sports in which women competed were scarcely consonant with ancient Japanese ideals, was critical of the proposal, and said that his countrymen, and especially his countrywomen, might make themselves ridiculous in this venture. Thus, in the Japanese mind, some quite trivial event in the world of sport or entertainment is linked with deeper social and political conflicts.

The intrusion and the as yet imperfect assimilation of Western ideas and manners have meant the destruction of those conventions and canons of behaviour which are necessary for the economization of energy in all civilizations. The Japanese are unsure of themselves, not merely in their relations to foreigners, but in their relations one to another. So, although hand-shaking now is common in the cities, a missionary who shook hands in public with one of his women-helpers was bitterly attacked by one of his flock for his indecent gesture. On the other hand, a general was taken to task by circles of modern Japanese because he allowed himself to be seen off at the station by his favourite *geisha*.

The break-up of the older social conventions would not be so serious if the Japanese possessed any generally accepted ethical principles or religious ideals to which an individual could refer the new problems of conduct that are confronting him. These, however, they seem to lack. Confucianism and *bushido* which were satisfactory as guides to the privileged classes in the old days are of limited value to-day. Buddhism may be a solace in misfortune, but it does not apparently provide the Japanese with principles with which they can face the new world. *Shinto* is powerful, and is of tremendous importance in the preservation of the family system and of devotion to the Emperor and the State; but it contains no body of abstract ethical ideas. The influence of Christianity is not growing and makes no wide appeal, chiefly because its ethical teachings are obscured by the historical accretions which have meaning for the West but to which the Japanese are naturally indifferent. It is perhaps not surprising that among the Japanese Christians those who seem to have reached most successfully an assured moral basis consist of the small circle of Quakers. The decay of doctrinal religion in the West has still left intact, in many countries, the body of moral ideas associated with it, but in Japan the older religions or systems have no message adequate to the present day, and, except among a few intellectuals, Christian ethics make little appeal because they are not associated in the Japanese mind with any historical emotional experience. For the ordinary chances of life, no doubt the older Japanese creeds and codes are sufficient, and aestheticism comes to their aid. But for grappling with new and bewildering influences and as guides to individual judgment in a chaotic and rapidly changing social situation, they can give little help. The Japanese are conscious of this and they are searching for help. For instance, I was asked by a Minister of State whether I thought that the Buchman Group Movement might not have some message for the Japanese! The rise of new religious movements during the last decade, such as *Omoto-kyo*, and the way in which these spread like wildfire among the masses of the population, are symptoms of the general spiritual unrest and dissatisfaction. Most of these religions are of a primitive kind, and are purely emotional and fanatical. They have alarmed the authorities and from time to time they have been suppressed without difficulty. But the fact that a new one springs up quickly and is eagerly embraced by millions almost as soon as an earlier one has been suppressed, shows that they are of utmost significance.

In the first post-War decade the emotional dissatisfaction in intellectual circles and among the city workers made radical, and even Marxist, ideas extremely popular; but since 1931 there has been a recrudescence of Nation-worship. This has been the method followed by Germany and Italy to provide an escape from ideological bankruptcy, and in Japan, no less than in those Western countries, it has involved the brutalizing of national life. It was doubtless the easiest way out of her difficulties. In Japan there has been no tradition of individual liberty, no recognition of the rights of private judgment and no general acknowledgment of a loyalty to universal ideals which are far removed from the State or its purposes. Japanese society is held together by family and group loyalties and, above all, by Emperor-worship. The Japanese is much closer to his nation than is the individual in other countries. The more liberal ideas which were coming in from the West were struggling in the post-West decade for recognition and the struggle had not been unsuccessful. But they had no secure foundation in the hearts of the people and it was not difficult to overthrow them by appeal to more primitive and irrational ideals. They are not dead by any means, but for the moment they have been overshadowed. The worship of fierce tribal deities, in Japan as elsewhere, has been reinstated and the failure of loftier ideals grounded in reason to supply an emotional satisfaction has thus resulted in a setback to humanitarianism.

CHAPTER III

INFINITE VARIETY

"and now will the Orientals make hither in return
outlandish pilgrimage: their wiseacres have seen
the electric light i' the West and come to worship;
tasting romance in our unsightly novelties
and scientific tricks."

ROBERT BRIDGES

VISITORS to Japan in the early part of the century were delighted (or amused) by the contrasts and incongruities presented by the everyday life of the people. Even those Westerners who knew her best loved to dwell upon the quaint juxtaposition of things traditional and things modern. It seemed likely, however, that the former would pass away as Western influence increased, and that future ages might see Japan efficient, tidy, and comfortable, but without the old picturesque charm. Yet, if the changes in some of the aspects of her life have been far-reaching, the persistence of the traditional in other aspects is equally remarkable. The streets of the great cities have been paved; taxis have driven away most of the rickshaws; large concrete "buildings"[1] now house the banks, offices, and departmental stores; foreign food, clothes, and amusements every year become increasingly popular. Still, the contrasts between these innovations and the solid core of ancient habit are as striking as ever they were.

During the last two decades there have been great changes in social customs and conventions. It was rare in the early post-War years to see a Japanese woman in foreign dress; but now many of the young girls who go for their *gin-bura*[2] have taken to Holly-

[1] This term is used in Japan to describe large foreign-style buildings which are used for offices, banks, apartment-houses, etc.

[2] A stroll along the Ginza, Tokyo's chief street.

wood fashions, as well as those who are employed in offices and foreign-style restaurants. In the smaller provincial towns this development has still not gone very far among adult women, although nearly all children possess foreign-style clothes for school wear. Like other Western innovations, this habit of dress is likely to spread steadily; for foreign-style clothing, in which the Japanese standard of taste is very low, is much cheaper than the qualities of Japanese-style clothes which would be worn as an alternative.

Again, in the capital, it is quite common to see young men and girls together in the foreign-style cafés which have become very numerous, whereas ten or fifteen years ago social convention would not have permitted it. The changing position of women is shown, too, by the appearance of apartment-houses for women engaged in teaching or clerical work in Tokyo. The development of flat-life is, indeed, one of the most noticeable changes in the capital. A few years ago apartment-houses were almost unknown; but lately they have become very numerous. Most of them are tenanted by middle-class families; but some have been built by the authorities for working-class families and others in connection with slum-clearance schemes. Yet although these "buildings" are of ferro-concrete, and externally of Western design, the flats themselves are usually adaptations of the Japanese domestic interiors. The floors are covered with *tatami*; the rooms divided off by *fusuma* and *shoji*; and there is the usual *tokonoma*.[1] So far, apartment-houses are common only in Tokyo; but their rapid development in that city is of great social significance.

One of the most charming and peculiar of Japanese institutions is becoming modified by Western influences. The *geisha* have learned to fox-trot and play golf with their clients, and the Shimbashi *geisha* have a theatre where, from time to time, they give public performances of plays and dances—a sharp break with their tradition of entertainment, which is private and personal in character. The popularity of foreign-style dancing has led to the rise of public dance halls. As convention still does not permit young men to

[1] *See* Glossary for these terms.

take girls to such entertainments, unless they are betrothed, professional dancing-partners are provided. Conservative Japanese are revolted at this form of entertainment, and from time to time efforts are made to suppress it. In Nagoya and Osaka, for example, dance halls are forbidden by the police. Sometimes one wonders if people financially interested in older forms of nighttime diversion are also in part responsible for this suppression. But ballroom dancing does not mean the same thing, even to the "modern" Japanese, as it does to the Westerner. There seems to be neither spontaneous gaiety nor an exhibition of *les figures si tristes et les derrières si gaies* about the dance hall. The fox-trot has become a ritual in Japan. As the partners move round the room, serious and intent, they remind the onlooker of the religious dances that are still performed in the temples at Nikko or Nara. As in the case of Western clothing, some of the popularity of these forms of entertainment can be attributed to their cheapness when compared with the cost of traditional kinds.

Since most Japanese live still in houses of traditional style, they have naturally not acquired much real understanding of the use of Western domestic equipment in foreign-style buildings nor any feeling for Western decorative schemes. Most of the Western-style buildings are furnished according to the worst canons of Victorianism. The walls are covered with garish wallpapers of brainless design; the chairs are upholstered in plush and adorned with antimacassars; carpets and curtains are usually hideous; and the pictures are bad beyond belief. In the public halls and in hotels and offices the heavy hand of the German-inspired decorator is evident. As to the exteriors of the large foreign buildings, a cautionary guide to Tokyo or Kyoto would not suffer from lack of material. The visitor passes from severe Greek temples of later-banking era to office-blocks of the iced-cake period, then to hotels and public buildings in the modern, despairing, child's-box-of-bricks style, and finally seeks refuge in Tokyo's Imperial Hotel, like a Hollywood idea of the mysterious East. In the quarters where the wealthy live, it is not unusual to find a charming Japanese house surrounded by a hideous wall of whiteish bricks, or to see through a lovely gateway of traditional style a "Tudor" villa that would be uneasy even in a London suburb. Yet fifty years ago the Japanese could build the Nara Hotel, where the native architectural style and modern needs are gracefully brought together. But it must be remembered, again, that whereas the Japanese can satisfy cheaply their extremely low standards of taste and quality in Western-style building and decoration, adherence to traditional canons of construction and decoration is very expensive.

If there are more architectural atrocities now than there were fifteen years ago, there are, fortunately, more Japanese who deplore them. People of discrimination are indignant at the intrusion of ugly examples of Western taste, and at the corruption of their own artistic forms by vulgarians to whom ostentation is synonymous with beauty. A young friend at Kyoto told me how bitter was the resentment felt in the locality at the enterprises of an Osaka millionaire who had done his best to ruin one of the streets by two hideous "buildings," and an architect showed me with scorn some of the more unfortunate efforts of his wealthy compatriots to adapt Western styles to their domestic needs. This criticism, coming from Japanese themselves, suggests that the present phase is only temporary. They are still struggling with unfamiliar media. The mistakes which they have made can be put down to the exuberance of people working in an artistic tradition which they have not yet come to understand. The Japanese could, if they wished, cite many examples of the ludicrous efforts that Westerners have made in devising Oriental buildings or decorative schemes. To use a chamber utensil as a soup container, a practice once followed in a Nagoya café, is not more to be ridiculed than to display a Japanese back-scratcher or some other humble article among the ornaments on a mantelpiece in a Western house—a sight that has astonished many a Japanese visitor.

In some directions, moreover, the Japanese are already showing skill in adapting Western materials to their peculiar needs and in infusing something of their own spirit into Western forms. To give an instance of a trivial kind: they are fond of enclosing part of their garden in close bamboo fencing. When for cheapness they substitute corrugated iron, they use material which has been manipulated so as to give the effect of the knotches on the bamboo and skilfully painted in a delicate green tint. Even at a short distance it is often quite difficult to detect the substitute. Again, the arches beneath electric railway bridges are sometimes used as dwelling-houses or shops. But even though the environment is so unsympathetic, it is not unusual to see a small restaurant built into one of the arches with a delightful façade of traditional style, and often with a tiny landscape garden in front of it.

The huge departmental stores which have become a prominent feature of the chief cities during the last decade, though superficially identical with those in other lands, yet have some hint of Japan's own way of life. The foreign-style restaurants, cafés, and hotels are externally similar to those of America; but the service is unmistakably Japanese. A taxi-driver who took me for a long drive in the picturesque Hakone district had a powerful American car and was dressed like a garage hand anywhere. But when my journey came to an end, he lingered a few moments to apologize to me for the inadequacy of his poor vehicle. As soon as one penetrates below the surface of Western forms and institutions one finds an unfamiliar spirit. For example, on great liners or buildings, or outside modern factories, there is usually a *Shinto* shrine. The manager of an up-to-date clock works, when complimented on his new factory shrine, said, only half in jest: "Yes, business has picked up quite a lot since we had that." At another factory I noticed that the shrine was closed. This, I was told, was because of the interference of the police, who had not yet decided whether the chosen tutelary god could be numbered among the myriad *Shinto* deities. A favourite haunt of students and of the liberal intelligentsia in Tokyo is the Ruskin Tea Room. This is furnished in Victorian style and is thickly adorned with Ruskin's letters and manuscripts and with pictures of Coniston. It is run as a hobby by a member of a famous business family in the culture-pearl trade. In the autumn of 1936 this family closed its pearl factories for three days so that the employees might offer prayers for the spirits of the oysters killed in the course of this trade. Incongruities such as this are numerous as ever, and add much to the delight and colour of Japanese life.

A professional speculator on the Stock Exchange, educated in England and very modern, in his own estimation, when excusing himself from accepting an invitation gave as his reason the necessity for taking part in a family gathering at the ancestral shrine. The next day he might well have attended a Rotary Club lunch, or played golf like any of his counterparts in Western countries. In Tokyo, with all its American taxis and crowded buses and trams, one still sees the night-watchman going the rounds of his ward, carrying his paper lantern and clashing two strips of wood to notify the householders of his presence on watch. The ground-floor of a certain popular restaurant in the heart of that city resembles a European café, or tea-room, and here Western-style drinks and refreshments are served by waitresses in Western dress, while jazz records are played on a radio-gramophone. The first floor, however, has the appearance of an old village in miniature, and in little rooms of Japanese style guests are supplied with *suki-yaki* and can feel that they are ages removed from the bustling twentieth-century capital below. In the most unlikely settings one comes across unexpected touches of ancient charm. Many of the cities are hideous with box-like concrete buildings, with galvanized iron roofing, with rickety poles supporting a tangle of wires. But behind the scenes there still survive details that are surprisingly beautiful. And although the new factories, offices, apartment-houses, warehouses, and banks strike the eye in the great cities, their very prominence is caused by the contrast of their setting; for round them crowd thousands of the low wooden shops and dwelling-houses. Outside the great cities, indeed, life in its outward aspects has altered little. Except for an occasional large factory, the buildings are all of traditional style and the domestic life of the population, their food, clothing, and amusements are still mainly those of past times. In spite of the rapid growth of the great modern centres, the bulk of the population remains in rural areas or in small country towns.

Life in Japan, even in the great cities, still retains something of its parochial character. Just as domestic life is without seclusion or privacy for the individual, so public life is marked by a complete absence of reticence about the personal qualities and activities of the leading figures. The Japanese love gossip. The idea that the private lives of public men are matters that concern themselves alone would bewilder a Japanese. The Press is full of frank discussions of the life, personality, and conduct of prominent persons. Such and such a politician when young was inclined to indulge in heavy drinking or debauchery, but has now reformed. Another is known to his intimates by an unflattering nickname because of his odd appearance. The law of libel scarcely ever seems to be invoked. The English convention that our public men are personally above reproach and that criticism should be directed solely against the political principles or the policies they advocate is not observed in Japan, where it is easier to vilify the character of a statesman or business or military leader than it is to criticize the principles for which he stands. Indeed, a policy is often challenged not by a direct attack, but by the discovery and publication of something reprehensible in the private lives of those who advocate it. Some years ago, for example, when a powerful group wished to oust a certain Minister of Commerce and Industry who was following a policy to which they objected, they succeeded in their aim, not by showing the defect in that policy, but by bringing to light a passage in a book written years before by the Minister, revealing that he did not hold the fashionable view of the constitutional position of the Crown. In recent years certain of Japan's great business houses were the subject of such outspoken comment in the Press as would have led in England to actions for libel; but nothing of the kind happened in Japan. It is well known that the stringent English libel laws mean that justifiable criticism often has to be emasculated and that they often prevent abuses and corruption from being brought to light. In Japan, on the contrary, one is provided with a good example of the disadvantages of exceedingly lax laws of libel.

A Japanese visitor to England stayed for some time with an English family. When he returned to his own country he told his friends that it was impossible for him to live happily in an English household because English etiquette is so strict. That a Japanese, whose life is believed by Westerners to be guided at every stage by formal rules of conduct, should pass this judgment upon the conventions of a people who consider that they have long given up elaborate manners, is amazing. The example that was given to illustrate his contention adds to the Westerner's bewilderment. The Japanese visitor, while out alone one day, met an acquaintance and, enjoying his company, took him to dinner in a restaurant. He returned some time after the hour at which the family usually dined, and, to his embarrassment and shame, he found that they had held back dinner until he arrived. He was astonished to learn that a guest was expected to return to his hosts' house at the usual meal times, or at least to inform them if he proposed to be absent. Now this procedure seems so obviously correct to us as to raise no question of formal etiquette. Yet to the Japanese it seemed just another of those countless rules which he was always unexpectedly encountering. No Japanese housewife expects her husband or his guests to inform her when they are likely to turn up for a meal, or, indeed, whether they will want her to provide one when they do appear. In any case, the dinner hour is very elastic and no one is bored at having to wait while a meal is being prepared. Yet it would be a shocking breach of manners if a guest arrived without a present, and a host would not spare himself in showering attentions upon his guest and in making him feel that the whole household was concerned solely with providing for his needs. It is not difficult to see, therefore, that intercourse between Westerners and Japanese, except when there are intelligence and tolerance on both sides, is likely to be disturbed by more or less serious breaches of courtesy which are quite unrealized by one or the other.

In fact, Japanese social life is marked by a curious mixture of informality and strict etiquette. Elaborate forms of greeting are still adhered to. The guest is expected to pay formal compliments to the host about the *tokonoma*. Extraordinary care is necessary in dress, which must be varied according to the season of the year, the occasion and the social condition of the wearer. It would be ludicrous, for instance, for a woman to wear in the autumn a *kimono* and *obi* of which the designs were spring flowers. It is essential that men should wear a frock-coat on public occasions. When summer reaches its official end the men at once cease to wear white suits even if the weather remains hot. The exchange of visiting cards is always expected when an introduction is effected. The conductor on a bus or train apologizes formally for having kept the passengers waiting whether the vehicle starts punctually or not; at the end of the journey he thanks them for having ridden in it and asks them to see that they have left nothing behind. Even the lift-girl calls "O-machido sama"[1] before she operates it. The unfortunate owner of a house that has been destroyed by fire is obliged to make a round of calls upon his neighbours to thank them for having assisted in putting the fire out. In the more conservative places it is still necessary for the head of a household to leave cards with all his acquaintances at the New Year, and some men have been known to spend a whole day in performing this social duty.

Yet the Japanese are informal just where Europeans practise the greatest formality and reserve. In the bath house, they crouch in the common bath, talking and laughing with their neighbours In the inn, each party expects to have a private room for its meals; but this room will later serve as the bedroom for the entire party, and the guests all meet in the bath where the aristocrat and his servant will chat and joke as equals. Then, clad in *yukata* (bath robes), the guests will be waited on by maids who may join easily

[1] "I am sorry to have kept you waiting."

in the conversation. They may engage *geisha* to sing and dance and amuse them. Yet, while the *geisha's* art is the product of a most elaborate training, and while they provide a very formal entertainment, they become members of the party, calling the guests *Onésan* (brother), and indulging in highly personal witticisms, for they are no respecters of persons. Even in foreign-style restaurants and hotels the relations of the staff to the guests seem to have nothing of the formality and aloofness that is met with in England. The passengers who enter the trains in their neat suits remove all their outer garments if the weather is hot and sit comfortably in their underwear, sometimes even with a block of ice tied with a towel upon their heads. Once the students of the college at which I was teaching were caught in a thunderstorm on their way to lectures. When I entered the lecture room I was greeted by the sight of some fifty students naked except for the cushion on which they usually sat. There is, to the foreigner, a comical element even in the most solemn and dignified of their occasions and institutions. When I visited the law courts in Tokyo my mentor pointed out to me with some awe the room of the leading high-court judge. Immediately outside the august door there was a clerk busily making toast on a *hibachi* (fire-box). At the hearing of one of the most important cases in the criminal courts, I was startled to see the judge turn in his seat, clear his throat noisily, and spit accurately into a cuspidor.

Some foreigners go so far as to say that, while the Japanese are careful in observing their own formal rules of etiquette, they have no real *politesse de cœur*. But, of course, every nation has habits which, though taken for granted by its own members, are objectionable to foreigners. A Chinese who had lived for some years in England was asked whether he found English people barbarous. With a tolerant smile he answered: "Well, your shopkeepers are very polite." Japanese who have some acquaintance with England are appalled by the smells of our crowds. The most sensible thing for a foreigner to do is to ignore the manners that are repugnant to his upbringing or to set against them the agree-

FAMILY TAKING A WALK

MIDDLE-SCHOOL BOYS

able habits which are prominent in the country of his sojourn. Thus, if he is shocked by the hawking and spitting of the Japanese men he can reflect that every Japanese, even the slum dweller, takes baths and is personally clean, and that he may move in a crowd without being troubled by the smells that offend him in a football crowd or a tram car in (say) an English industrial town. This can help to console him for the stench of the public conveniences or the carts that carry away the night soil. If he is disturbed by the gaping of the ignorant crowds, he can calm himself by remembering that, outside the ports and large towns, Westerners are still unfamiliar to the ordinary Japanese, that they appear very tall and strange creatures, and that their curious habits and dress excite a real interest. Further, the wonderment is often tinged with admiration. And he can doubtless recall many instances in which Japanese, heroically overcoming their shyness, have volunteered to help in a difficulty at inconvenience to themselves, or have shown him some small courtesy. If he is jostled in the tram car, he can at least applaud the extraordinary good nature and cheerfulness of the crowds.

Within their own family circle or group of friends the Japanese are full of fun and indulge readily in buffoonery and punning, and throw off all self-consciousness. But towards strangers, especially towards foreigners, they suffer from an overwhelming shyness. It is not uncommon, for example, for a Japanese to turn away in embarrassment when approached by a foreigner wishing to be directed somewhere; he is frightened of appearing foolish before his friends in case he cannot understand what the foreigner is talking about. I remember a policeman who walked quickly in the opposite direction, after a glance of diffidence and alarm at his compatriots, when he saw me approaching with obvious intent to ask him the way. This self-consciousness or fear of losing dignity often causes Japanese to act childishly and brusquely when they are really most anxious to help a stranger. The people as a whole are modest, unassuming, and patient, but of course they have their vanities. These, though sometimes irritating, are generally disarming because of their *naïveté*. A university student who had attached himself to me while I was walking in the country, in the hope of practising his English, led me up a hillside to a point from which we could see a few shabby wooden buildings in a little gravel playground down below. "There," he said proudly, "is my Alma Mater." It was the village primary school!

Whatever faults the Japanese may have, meanness or lack of kindness are certainly not among them. To those to whom they feel that they owe an obligation or hospitality, they give of their time, energy and substance without counting the cost. Among the lowliest, hospitality is given in the grand manner. No country could be more agreeable for the tourist. Outside the ports there is no touting, in spite of the development of the tourist industry. No Japanese hotel servant ever makes it obvious that he expects a tip for his services. Poor men will often give help to the stranger as host for guest and are insulted if offered any recompense. He will seldom be cheated and he need have little fear of the pilferer. In the English restaurant the management announces that it is not responsible for losses sustained by patrons who hang their belongings on the coat racks. In a Japanese café the customers, in summer, even take off their jackets and hang them up, without removing money or valuables from the pockets. If anything should be stolen, the honour of the house would demand that the proprietor should make restitution to efface the disgrace.

During my recent visit to Japan I experienced many instances of how the natural kindness, generosity, and courtesy of the nation break through the veneer of xenophobia which attempts are made to create. Business men are warned against revealing any sort of information about Japan's economic position to foreigners, who are to be regarded with great suspicion. But when in contact with an individual foreigner, they cannot maintain the high level of "patriotic" fervour and exclusiveness that is expected of them, and they fall back easily into friendliness and hospitality. Once the first bridge has been built they go out of their way to give the foreigner the data he needs. It is interesting to see the fine qualities native to the people struggling with the narrow nationalism that is being imposed on them.

Women are treated in public with less consideration in Japan than in Western countries. They carry the parcels, walk behind their husbands, and are served with food after the men of the household. These customs are the expression of the accepted obligation of the Japanese wife to serve her husband. But women are not without power. The Japanese wife usually takes complete charge of the family income and expenditure; she often plays an important part in running the family business; she spends a high proportion of the income on clothes; and although she must be self-effacing in public, she can usually exercise considerable influence upon family affairs in private. Close acquaintance with a number of Japanese families has not left me with the impression that the Japanese woman is oppressed or miserable. To a considerable extent the outward conduct of husband and wife is the result of a desire to keep up appearances, rather than of any feeling of superiority or subordination, just as the habitual courtesies paid to women in the West are often merely the outcome of obedience to a formal code. A Japanese who carries his wife's parcels or treats her with more than indifference in public would be regarded as effeminate or uxorious. His conduct would excite ridicule, and both he and his wife would feel foolish. Yet the husband, without loss of dignity, can carry the baby.

Until she approaches marriage the middle-class Japanese girl has considerable freedom. When her family think that it is time for her to marry, it is true that she becomes subject to much constraint and that she has to observe an etiquette which limits her freedom of movement. But every girl can be certain of finding a husband. She does not have to degrade herself by scheming for a prospective suitor's affections, or by an insincere pretence of indifference. As a result, the Japanese girl's manners are charming and natural. Though she may be silly and empty-headed, there is no flirtatiousness nor coyness about her. When she is married she must be prepared, like all Japanese of both sexes, to sacrifice herself to the interest of the family group of which she has become a member. But, as a mother she gains prestige, and, as a wife, she can exercise an important influence on her husband's affairs. As we have seen, custom still requires that the wife should play a subordinate part in social life. Thus, a man entertaining his friends will usually invite them to a restaurant where they will be entertained by *geisha*, and his wife will not be present. But in the larger towns other kinds of amusements are becoming very common. The husband and wife together visit theatres, foreign-style restaurants, and cinemas, generally accompanied by their children. The practice of taking children everywhere introduces a homely note into the public places they frequent. For instance, when a party comes into the dining-room of a foreign-style restaurant, the waiters bring forward high chairs for the very small children and a waitress smilingly takes charge of the baby. At the theatres, one corner of the auditorium often contains a large cot where the mothers can leave their babies during the acts. At first this seems amusing, but after all, it shows an extraordinarily sensible and logical adaptation to needs. The sudden transformation, on marriage, of an irresponsible Japanese girl into a serious and intensely practical housewife has often been commented upon by observers well acquainted with domestic life. Although the sphere of a Japanese wife may be more narrowly limited than that of her Western counterpart, she is extremely competent in that sphere. She takes charge easily of difficult situations as they arise. When the news of the great Kwanto Earthquake (1923) came through, the women in other parts of the country lost no time in bewailing the fate of their relatives. Groups of them immediately set about preparing consignments of clothes and other necessities for dispatch to the devastated areas.

The view that the Japanese are lacking in public spirit deserves a little attention. It seems odd that people who are obliged to subordinate so completely their individual interest to that of their family, group or nation should even be said to lack this attribute. Yet the Japanese citizen is extremely slow in taking political action for remedying an abuse; inconvenient and selfish practices persist because no one takes the initiative in getting them abolished. Every foreigner in Japan has been struck by minor examples of this. Cyclists leave their bicycles strewn all over the pavements in the cities, so that pedestrians often have to move into the road in order to pass. It does not seem to occur to the cyclists to arrange their machines more conveniently, nor to the public to organize a protest. I once witnessed a curious scene. A galvanized tank which was being taken to a scrap merchant had fallen off a cart unnoticed by the driver, and it remained in the narrow road where it impeded the traffic and, indeed, was exceedingly dangerous. Shopkeepers came out to watch the traffic as it carefully skirted the obstacle, and passers-by stopped to gaze. None thought of removing it. Finally a policeman came along and did what was necessary. This gives the clue to the whole Japanese attitude. Authority comes from above. It is not for the members of the public to take the initiative in remedying abuses or to adopt practices that will be mutually convenient. Let the police tell us what to do, is the ordinary point of view. Since the police have not yet thought of forming the public into queues for buses or trams, no queues are formed. This characteristic is exceedingly unfortunate for social progress. Many evils and abuses continue to exist, not because the Japanese are insensitive to them nor because they desire to preserve them, but because their removal awaits action by authority. Most of the social improvements that have occurred in England during the past century have been initiated by groups of individuals who have led "movements" or formed societies which at length have compelled the State to act. Some instances of this kind of movement in Japan exist; but they are ineffective on the whole, and social reform societies do not seem capable of organizing powerful campaigns for social amelioration. Yet, curiously enough, the Japanese have a great capacity for acting in functional groups and authority is susceptible to such action. Thus, when the Minister of Commerce and Industry authorized the raising of the price of petrol a few years ago, the taxi-drivers of Tokyo immediately took all their taxis to the Department and tooted vigorously outside it until the Minister gave way. But really effective action by disinterested bodies of people who are anxious to promote social betterment is rare.

CHAPTER IV

THE STRUCTURE OF SOCIETY

"*. . . and so they set forward, every one after their families, according to the house of their fathers.*"

NUMBERS II. 34

SOME curious misconceptions exist both among Japanese and Westerners concerning the differences in their respective social organizations. It is commonly asserted that whereas in the West the individual is the social unit, in Japan it is the family group. This supposed contrast is then made to serve as a basis for generalizations about differences in the social institutions and social ideals of East and West. Some writers emphasize the dominant place of self-interest and materialism in European and American society, and the importance of the concept of individual rights in the development of social and political institutions, whereas Japan, they say, is distinguished by the subordination of the individual to the welfare of the family, group or State, and by a scant regard for calculations of personal loss or gain. As a first approximation to the truth, this view may be accepted; but it cannot be regarded, without important qualifications, as a really satisfactory interpretation. The Japanese in discussing this matter are inclined to confuse the legal and political aspects of a country's life with its social structure, and to assume that the social relationships described in the works of utilitarian philosophers are identical with those existing in modern Europe. Now it is true that law and politics in the West are concerned with the individual citizen and his rights and duties, and for the enlargement of knowledge about certain economic processes it is convenient to assume the existence of an atomistic society. But man is a social being in the West as in Japan. There, as everywhere, his life has its roots in the family, and he pursues his ends in association with his fellows in various kinds of groups and, finally, in the State.

For the vast masses of the people in all countries, the family is the institution which has most reality for them, and most influence upon their conduct. Everywhere the family provides its members with help in times of difficulty and they in turn recognize and accept obligations towards it. But, of course, the nature of this institution differs from time to time and from country to country. The modern English family exhibits important contrasts to the French, American, or German family, and is different to-day from what it was two hundred years ago. It is, therefore, misleading to suggest that Japan differs from Western countries because she possesses a family system, or because the family is the unit of Japanese society. A more correct statement is that the Japanese family as an institution possesses peculiar features that distinguish it from the family in Western countries, although the peculiarities seem much more striking to an Englishman or an American than they do to (say) a Frenchman or a Jew. Again, it is natural that the Japanese should feel when he reads the works of Anglo-Saxon political or economic theorists that the vision of social relationships underlying their arguments bears no close identity with his own social experience; for since he has no theoretical constructions of his own, he does not realize that these theorists concern themselves deliberately with particular aspects of reality and do not pretend to embrace the whole of social life. They abstract from reality in order to give an account of some part of it, an account that is true only within a particular chamber of reference. The confusion that has attended these discussions demonstrates the failure of even well-educated Japanese fully to appreciate analytical processes of thought.

The distinguishing features of the Japanese family system have often been set out and need not detain us long. First, the family plays an even more important part in the life of a Japanese than of a European. In the country districts where the patriarchal family survives, it is common for a household to consist of three generations and to include also other relatives by birth and adoption. Even with the town-dwellers where this kind of household is no longer typical, the ties between a group of relatives are much closer than in Anglo-Saxon countries, and recall the clan-relationships of earlier times. The resources of a family group are mobilized to assist a member in distress to a greater extent than in the West, and the responsibilities of a member towards the group are more onerous. Important discussions concerning the career or education of a member are still commonly decided by a family council. When a young man or woman reaches marriageable age, a consort is selected by the family, often with the help of a professional go-between,[1] and the consent of the family group is necessary before a marriage can be dissolved. At one time the pressure of the family on its members in these matters was stronger than it is now. Under the influence of Western ideas and of new methods of life, the wishes of an individual have more weight in the selection of a husband or wife than was formerly the case, and nowadays a family would rarely force a girl to marry a man to whom she had a strong objection. In the same way, divorce, which frequently followed the failure of the wife to produce an heir, seldom takes place for that reason at the present time. But even now marriages are often not registered with the civil authorities until a year after the performance of the religious ceremony; and they can be easily dissolved during that period. It is unthinkable that any girl, other than the *geisha*, should remain single long after she has reached marriageable age, and, therefore, elderly spinsters are rare. Unmarried women missionaries in country towns are often assumed to be the concubines of the male missionaries whom they are helping. A Japanese girl expressed amazement to learn that an American lady who was

[1] The existence of the go-between exerts a considerable check on the deportment and public behaviour of many Japanese girls who might otherwise be glad to avail themselves of the increasing freedom and opportunity to consort with young men in social amusement. A professional go-between cannot risk his reputation as a successful maker of suitable marriages and will view with disfavour any conduct or rumours of conduct that is not seemly or in accord with conventions for Japanese women.

teaching her had never been married. "Haven't you even been sent back?" she asked (that is, returned to her family after a trial period).

Love is still regarded as a dangerous basis for marriage in many circles, since a mutual infatuation may undermine the loyalty which is owed first and foremost to the family group as a whole; but this attitude is less usual now than it was when three-generation households, in which such a conflict could more easily arise, were common. It still survives, however, in the ridicule which is shown towards couples who exhibit marked affection one to another. It is still exceedingly bad form for a husband to treat his wife in public with anything more than courtesy, and a friend once confided to me that he was unable to take his wife out with him in his motor car very often, because, if he did, people would laugh, and his family would lose face. There is naturally a considerable contrast in these respects between the conventions observed in Tokyo and the ports, where Western influences are strong, and in other parts of the country, where the older traditions still persist without much modification. In the moral codes of the Japanese, filial piety and the duty to parents are emphasized more than the virtues of comradeship and loyalty between husband and wife. It is a commonplace of anti-Japanese propaganda that this often results in girls sacrificing themselves by entering houses of prostitution in order to relieve their distressed families—a sacrifice that receives social applause. Other critics say that the family system destroys initiative and robs the Japanese of the joy of spontaneous personal and social relationships. "We have little joy in our home life," a Japanese once said to me. On the other hand, admirers of Japanese institutions declare that the family system removes the necessity for extensive social services, and provides a valuable discipline and a training in the art of social compromise and co-operative effort.

A Westerner can scarcely evaluate the advantages and disadvantages of the Japanese family system any more than a Japanese can assess the virtues and defects of those in Western countries. But observation from outside suggests one or two tentative conclusions. One cannot, of course, judge the Japanese family system by considering only its unpleasant features. At its worst, it involves intolerable restrictions upon personal freedom and development; filial piety may be exploited by unscrupulous parents, such as those who are occasionally reported as having not only sold a daughter to a licensed house, but also as having used the money so obtained in debauchery; and the help that families provide for their members may serve to excuse the negligence of the State to provide adequately for the social needs of the poor and weak. But the majority of the Japanese are kindly and tolerant in their social relationships, and mutual affection and consideration are by no means absent, even in "arranged" marriages. Except among the *moga* and *mobo*, who are not very attractive types, the Japanese social life outside the family is lacking in freedom and spontaneity because of the position which women occupy, but inside the home family life is not vastly different from that found elsewhere.

The family, as already shown, is being modified as in other countries by the influences that everywhere attend the development of modern industrialism; but many of its most important features are being preserved because of its association with *Shinto.* The worship of ancestors is still carried on, even in households that are nominally Christian. The first duty of a wife is to provide heirs who will perpetuate the family and will make offerings to the spirits of the dead. At the *O-Bon* festival in summer, the members of each family gather together to worship the ancestors who are supposed on that day to return to the family shrine, and even the most modern and sophisticated city dwellers take part in this festival. The emotions which are bound up with these practices are very real and powerful, and are likely to prevent the strong ties which bind the members of the family group together from being relaxed under the strain of modern ways of living.

The Japanese family system is not difficult for the Westerner to understand; for the European family system in earlier times, especially in the classical civilizations, differed from it in no important respects.[1] But Japanese social classes and the institutions that stand midway between the State and the family are not easy to appreciate or comprehend. Some writers point out that in Tokugawa times society (apart from the Court and the Court nobility) was made up of four classes, or rather "estates" in the sociological sense; namely the military and administrative class (*daimyo* and *samurai*), the farmers, the artisans and the merchants; and they sometimes go on to argue that, in spite of the upheavals of the last sixty years, this classification still corresponds to the more significant divisions in Japanese society, and that contemporary social conflicts can be interpreted in terms of these groups. This conclusion, with certain qualifications, may be accepted as a first step towards the understanding of the social structure, although, without explanation, it may easily lead to an unduly simplified view of the course of social development since the Restoration (1868). It must be realized, for instance, that the rigid divisions between these classes, which came into existence in the early years of the Tokugawa régime, had broken down long before its overthrow.[2] The impoverishment of the *samurai*, for example, and the increase in the wealth of the merchants led to inter-marriage between these classes, to the purchase of *samurai* rank by merchants, and to the degradation of many *samurai* into the ranks of artisans and farmers from whom they became indistinguishable. Some of the *daimyo*, long before 1868, had set up trading enterprises and factories in the hope of increasing their revenues, and these were managed by their retainers. On the other hand, wealthy merchants to whom the *daimyo* were indebted could often dictate the policy of the clan governments. In the first half of the nineteenth century thousands

[1] Professor Zimmern's interesting comparison between the Greek and Japanese social organization (see *The Greek Commonwealth*) is well known. The *hetaira* is shown to correspond to the *geisha* and the Greek wife to the *Okusan*.

[2] The Tokugawa era stretched from 1603 to 1867. For information about the social changes of that era, *see* E. Honjo, *The Social and Economic History of Japan*.

of farmers deserted their holdings and became artisans or labourers in the towns.

It cannot be said, then, that even before the modern era, Japan possessed a rigidly stratified society, that families always followed the calling or preserved the status to which it had "pleased God to call them," or that the functions exercised by the different classes persisted unaltered from generation to generation. Since the Restoration, as will be seen later, society has become still more fluid. In one respect, however, the traditional classification is useful in throwing light on the nature of political conflict in Japan. Although particular families, or individual members of those families, have frequently changed their social status, wealth and occupation during the last century, and although class divisions of the kind familiar in the West have appeared, the four "estates" themselves have preserved something of their identity, with modifications of their character. And political conflict still depends upon groups based on the traditional "estates," rather than upon the kind of class division which is to an increasing extent the source of conscious group action in Western Europe. This points needs a little elaboration. In England, the changes of the last century and a half have led to the virtual disappearance both of the aristocracy, as an order possessing a special economic and political significance, through its union with the wealthy industrial, commercial, and professional classes, and also of the peasant class through the agricultural revolution. The main social cleavage to-day, as it affects political activities, is between the owning class, which is allied with the upper administrative and professional classes, on the one hand, and the wage-earners, with whom can be grouped the small shop-keeping and lower-salaried classes, on the other. In other words, differences in income, security, and independence are the main determinants of class in English society. Partly because the boundaries of classes are blurred and changing, and partly for historical reasons into which it is unnecessary to go, this society is distinguished from others by an all-pervasive snobbishness, its most unlovely feature. This snobbishness has been strengthened by a class system of education and is perceptible in most fields of public activity from the Services to sport. But social snobbishness has not prevented the development of political democracy and the wide diffusion of political initiative. It is true that the main power is still exercised by the upper strata of the owning classes. Those who have been most skilful in the selection of their parents and have been to the right schools can still expect to fill positions of authority and influence. But other classes have gradually claimed a considerable share of power in government and industry, not merely through the extension of the franchise and the rise of the trade unions and the Labour Party, but through the part that workers are able to play in local government, in the magistracy, and in official bodies such as trade boards and other types of wage-bargaining machinery. These developments and their effects on the economic position of different classes have been sufficiently gradual to avoid provoking the governing orders to terror-stricken resistance, and sufficiently rapid to check the resort of other classes to revolutionary violence.

Although class divisions do not by any means coincide with political alinements, they are tending in that direction, and to-day the major political conflict is between those who wish to preserve the existing social and economic arrangement and those who desire drastic changes in it in the interests of the workers. So far, however, the conflict has taken place according to the rules of constitutional procedure, and this has been possible because of the restraint and caution exercised by the contestants. Progress has been achieved without resort to violence by a series of working compromises, and social stability has been preserved without stagnation. For our present purpose, the two facts about the English situation which are of significance are, first, that the chief social and political divisions are determined by differences in income, and second, that the skill in constructive compromise, the tolerance and the common sense which dignify the greater part of public life in England, should be the concomitant of the snobbishness which is a ludicrous feature of English social life in all classes.

Japan presents a marked contrast. The Westernization of the

country is, of course, creating classes that bear some resemblance to those in Europe; but the emotional dispositions associated in Europe with those classes have not yet appeared in Japan. Snobbery, though it exists, is not a prominent feature of life in that country. Intercourse between classes is easier than in England, and there is much greater uniformity of manners. The Japanese servant treats his master with respect but yet with familiarity; he shows neither the obsequiousness that is met with in Europe nor the brusqueness and indifference of the American. And the master, though he may be exacting, does not attempt to adopt a distant attitude to his servants. In a restaurant or hotel, the servants chatter and joke freely with the guests whom they are serving, although they use polite forms of address. In a large English industrial undertaking it is usual for the directors and higher executives to have one dining-room, the clerical staff another, and the operatives a third. But it is quite common in Japan for everyone to sit down together in the same mess room; frequently even separate tables are not provided for the officials and directors, who take any place that is available among their workers. "There's no Mussolini or Hitler here," said a young Japanese manager who was showing me the common mess-room in a great factory in Nagoya. A wealthy confectioner and some of his friends once took me round his factory; at lunch time we went to a little café, also owned by him, where his products were sold. We ate the meal provided there for ordinary customers, and the proprietor called for the bill at the end of it; no hint was given of his identity and no suggestion made that his party should receive special attention. In the British Army the distinction between the officers and the other ranks is emphasized by striking differences in the quality and cut of the uniforms and in degrees of ostentatiousness of other equipment. In Japan no such striking contrast can be observed. Of course, people of some classes look down on people of other classes. Some of the older families with a tradition of culture and refinement despise the *narikin* or *nouveau riche*. An old servant of mine who came from a town family used to refer contemptuously to the people of the neighbouring village as *mura-mono* (village things). But these attitudes are very seldom obvious in the outward demeanour of the Japanese, and it is not an exaggeration to say that, from a social standpoint, they are far more democratic than Anglo-Saxon nations.

A particularly good illustration of this pleasant quality is provided by the educational system. There is no special provision of schools and colleges for different social classes as in England.[1] Children from all social classes attend the primary schools and there is nothing that corresponds to our varieties of schools at each educational stage conferring different degrees of social prestige on their pupils. A friend to whom I mentioned this was surprised that I should have found it a matter for remark. Though he was a well-to-do man, he saw nothing surprising in the fact that the people who were now his servants and the local farm workers should have attended the same primary school as he. The common experience provided by an educational career in which children of all types are mingled, especially in the primary grade, adds enormously to the sense of community that the nation possesses, to the sympathy among people in different callings and with different incomes, and to the absence (in general) of an overbearing and arrogant demeanour among people in authority and of obsequiousness among those who serve.[2] One important factor which may be said to be both a consequence of this social intermingling and also a cause that makes it possible, is the absence of such marked differences in the habits (even, unfortunately, bad ones such as spitting) and manners of people in different income groups as are evident in the Western world. Especially important is the high and almost universal standard of personal cleanliness in Japan. Nearly all Japanese, as already pointed out, like to take

[1] The Peers school is the chief exception.

[2] This seems to apply only to Japanese in their relations with their own countrymen. According to all accounts they are just as overbearing in their treatment of subject peoples as are Europeans or Americans. The demeanour of the police also provides an exception to the general rule; but this is a matter of function, not of class.

frequent baths. After the Earthquake (1923) the first demand of the people of Tokyo was for the reconstruction of the public bath houses. In factories where work is dirty, the men take baths before they go home. Consequently, people of all ranks can mingle together without offence to each other's sense of smell. Bathing is, of course, a very recent innovation into Western countries, if one excludes the pre-Christian civilizations, and the same uniformity in this matter cannot yet be expected. But it is probable that such a development would do much to remove social barriers in this country. Another consideration which must not be neglected is the emphasis placed by Japanese tradition on simplicity. The Japanese seem to demand little in the way of material comfort. Even though changes are being introduced by the rise of industrialization, yet ostentatious expenditure even by the very wealthy is frowned upon not merely by the poor and envious but by powerful circles. Bitter criticism in the Press is often levelled against the extravagance of particular rich persons, who may have to adopt strange subterfuges in order to gratify their wants.

From a political standpoint the significant categories in Japanese society are not classes as determined mainly by differences in income, but functional groups that have been derived from the old "estates." There are, first of all, the peasants and small landlords; secondly, the small manufacturers and shopkeepers; thirdly, the great industrial and merchant families with their managers and executives; and finally the groups that have replaced the old administrative and military class, namely, the bureaucracy, the Services and the intelligentsia. This classification is satisfactory only up to a point. It clearly does not cover the whole of the Japanese population; each of the four main groups has important sub-divisions; and from time to time political movements arise which depend upon alliances between one or other of the major groups. But it does include the groups that exercise the greatest influence on Japanese policy, and each of the major groups does embody a tradition which marks it off from the others, although of course legal inequalities no longer exist.

The peasantry and the small rural landlords, with whom may be grouped the fishermen, are the repository of the customs and traditions of old Japan. These people pursue a calling which is still far less affected by Western technique and new habits of life than any other occupation. Many ancient handicrafts are still carried on by the peasantry as a by-employment. The peasants provide the bulk of the soldiery. The Westernization of the country has, in their judgment, done little for them and has, in fact, damaged their interests. They look with suspicion on the town dwellers, especially the large city capitalists, whose activities have done so much to transform the economic life and outlook of the people as a whole. Among them survives in its most significant form the old Japanese family system, and the religious emotions and ceremonies associated with it. They are very poor, burdened with debt, and doomed to ceaseless labour. Their pleasures must, perforce, be of the simplest kind and are chiefly connected with the ancient festivals and ceremonies of their land. There have been bitter disputes between the tenant farmers and the small landlords; but both have essentially the same outlook as they confront the other groups in Japan. The position of both has deteriorated in consequence of the rise of modern industry, and both are intensely conservative and hostile to the innovations that have affected the habits and manners of the urban population.

The small manufacturers, merchants, and shopkeepers who are found in the large and small towns, as well as in the villages, make up a group which is also hostile to the large financiers, merchants, and industrialists on whom they are often dependent, or with whose enterprises they are in hopeless competition. Although many of the small manufacturing trades are turning out Western-style products and are making use of machinery, yet this group as a whole feels that it has had little material benefit from the introduction of Western civilization. At the same time, while many persons in it have been drawn from peasant families, yet their interests and outlook are not identical with those of the peasantry. For one thing, they are mostly urban dwellers, and for another, some of them have suffered as a result of the attempts of the peasants to create their own co-operative purchasing and selling organizations. Some small manufacturers manage from time to time to develop their businesses and to become fairly large employers of labour; but the majority are little more than out-workers earning piece-wages. This group is very large, second only in size to the peasant group.

Then, forming a plutocracy, come the great merchant, industrial, and financial families, the *Zaibatsu*, each of which embraces in its scope many kinds of manufacturing trades, commerce, transport, and finance. Practically all the large-scale modern enterprises are concentrated in a small number of these families. They and the able men they have called into their service have a profound influence on the economic and political development of the country. The State depends on them to carry out its schemes of economic development in Japan Proper and the Empire and to finance its political ambitions in Asia and elsewhere. They are the object of criticism by the spokesmen of both the groups already discussed and also by democratic critics of monopoly. They are enterprising, quick to adopt the latest technical advances that the West has to offer, and eager in the extension of their power and wealth.

Finally, there is the group which exercises the main Governmental functions. This is made up, first, of the military and naval leaders, drawn mainly from the old *samurai* cliques and embodying the ancient military tradition of *bushido*. They have provided the statesmen who have been most prominent in Japan's modern history. There is rivalry, and sometimes hostility, between the Army and Navy cliques; but these disagreements are of relatively little significance in view of their fundamental similarity of outlook. Within this ruling group, also, are the bureaucrats. These comprise not merely the civil servants in our sense, but also the governors of the semi-official banks, the administrators of the great public concerns like the South Manchuria Railway, and ministers of State other than those drawn from the fighting Services and the political parties. The bureaucrats, too, are in the tradition of the *samurai* who administered the fiefs for the *daimyo*, and originally most of them came from *samurai* families. But the area from which they are now drawn has been widened, and the majority begin their career by entering the civil service after examination at the end of their university studies. The literary, artistic, and learned people also fall into this broad group.

Although these different groups have preserved something of their identity, this does not mean that each has pursued its own course in isolation from the others. Between the members of the merchant group on the one hand and members of the military and bureaucratic group on the other, there have been numerous important alliances, both of a political and family nature, which have been exceedingly important in determining the development of political life. Prince Saionji, the last surviving *Genro*, is the uncle of the present head of the Sumitomo firm; Mr. K. Takahashi, the late Minister of Finance and one of the chief ornaments of the bureaucratic clique in modern times, was financial adviser to Yasuda, another great *Zaibatsu*. A merchant house is reported to have given financial support to a certain important political group which a few years ago gave violent expression to the discontent of the peasants. Members of the Army cliques have from time to time had close links with Mitsui, and members of the Navy cliques with Mitsubishi. But most of these alliances between groups or sub-groups were the result of manœuvrings for positions of advantage and do not represent a coalescence of conviction or interest. Thus, Marquis Inouye who backed Mitsui in the early Meiji times found it useful to have the financial resources of that family at his disposal in carrying out his political schemes, while Mitsui obtained valuable Government contracts and was able to buy Government properties at low prices because of his support. Count Okuma found Mitsubishi's help of great value in his efforts to build up a strong mercantile marine and to create a political party for furthering his various political aims. At the same time Mitsubishi increased in power and wealth through the turn that he gave to economic policy. These cross-currents are bewildering, and more will be said about them in Chapter V; but they have not been of such a nature as to divert the main course of these streams. It is important to realize, however, that the ruling oligarchy does not represent the interests of a particular social class; various sections of it derive their support from and reflect the wishes of the other groups, although the peasant, artisan, and small shopkeeper groups are only intermittently politically conscious.

There seems no place in the categories given above either for the aristocracy or for the workers in modern enterprises.[1] Of the aristocracy it can be said that, as in England, it does not now comprise a class with special interests or functions. The descendants of the old *daimyo* and of the Court Nobles sit, it is true, in the House of Peers, and a member of the Tokugawa family was until recently President of the House. But they are not now among the wealthiest people in the country, nor do they derive their incomes from any special source, as the English nobility did from the ownership of large landed estates. Most of them appear to have been merged in the various divisions of the administrative and military class. Some have followed careers in the Army; others have served as diplomats and, thus, have fallen into the bureaucratic class. A number have contented themselves with social, artistic, and literary interests. They have all, with few exceptions, been overshadowed by the "new men" that the Meiji Restoration threw up; the outstanding figures among the titled nobility of the last sixty years, Prince Ito, Prince Matsukata, Count Okuma, Prince Yamagata, and many others, have all been men who were born in unimportant *samurai* families and rose by their genius to positions of eminence. And this new titled nobility was merely part of the governing group; it did not become a separate caste; and of the individuals who composed it some were part of the military or naval clique and some of the bureaucratic clique. The industrial-worker group and its problems will be considered in a later chapter.

[1] It should be noted also that there is no large rentier class in Japan. This fact has an important bearing on the social and political attitudes discussed above.

This account of the major groups leads naturally to a description of a very prominent feature of Japanese social life as a whole. Japanese, like other peoples, promote their purposes by association with their fellows who have similar interests or points of view. But the groups to which every Japanese belongs make a claim on him that is more exacting than that experienced by the Westerner, and it is the group which provides leadership and to which loyalty is owed. The history of a political or social movement in Japan must be written not in terms of individuals of strong convictions or exceptional genius or insight, but in terms of groups. The term *batsu* or clique is used in a large number of combinations in accounts of Japanese political and social life. The Satsuma-*batsu* (or Satsuma clique which for a long time dominated the Navy), the Choshu-*batsu* (which used to direct the Army), the Zai-*batsu* (plutocracy or money-cliques, which are supreme in large-scale business); all these and many other cliques or groups are the realities of Japanese politics and, indeed, of Japanese life in general. The loyalties felt towards his group by every Japanese are intense. While a public opinion in our sense scarcely exists in Japan, or is at any rate weak and inarticulate, the group is nevertheless a powerful instrument for the expression of the will of its members. Thus, the Japanese Government pays little heed to widely diffused antagonism to its general policy, such as may be expressed at the polls; but it is exceedingly susceptible to pressure from coherent groups or to manifestations of group displeasure at some particular action.

Again, in business life, the officials of a great family concern feel towards it some of the emotions that are elsewhere excited by a Church, a city, or a college. They are stamped as Mitsui men, or Sumitomo men, and they feel that not merely their self-interest, but their whole active life is involved in their service. This is not, of course, peculiar to Japan; but the emotion is more general and more fervent there than in most other countries. Yet devotion to a particular family business does not mean that exceptional regard or respect is necessarily felt towards individual members of the family for whom the executives are running the business. The member of the family who is nominally at the head of a particular business kingdom is often a very much limited monarch. The ministers who really exercise control never attempt, however, to usurp the throne. The chief of them usually have around them a band of subordinates and a group of supporters, and each group intrigues against others in the hope of promoting the policies that it favours. But should a policy prove unsuccessful or bring disaster on the kingdom, the dominant group is quickly swept away and its leaders, however lofty and powerful their positions may seem to be, will have to surrender their power. The managing director of the Mitsui Bussan Kaisha, whose successful expansionist policy had created hostility to the House of Mitsui and was partly the cause of the murder of Takuma Dan, the chief executive official, in 1932, was relegated immediately to an unimportant position in the firm to whose development he had greatly contributed. The policy of the Army, also, is determined by the same kind of manœuvring among groups or factions representing different interests or policies. The great *Genro* (elder statesmen) of the Meiji era were not so much leaders in our sense as the spokesmen of the groups to which they belonged, and corresponding examples could be given in every walk of life.

The cohesion of Japanese national life owes much to this capacity for group action. The groups provide an agency for the expression of the wills of the members who compose them and for the mobilization of sections of public opinion. It has often been pointed out that a Japanese in authority, though he may apparently derive his power from above is, in fact, controlled very largely by the opinions and wishes of his group of subordinates. Even in schools and colleges it is exceedingly difficult for the staff to pursue any policy of which the students disapprove, and an expression of that disapproval often leads to the resignation of the offending professor or principal. Sometimes the rivalries of different factions lead to disorder and become a danger to the State; but generally the conflicts take place within the bounds set by considerations of the welfare of the larger whole. The struggles between different factions in the Army or in a great business house, though often bitter, are seldom carried to a point where the institution to which all owe service is endangered; and in the conflicts between the military, the bureaucrats, big business and other groups, through which national policy is determined, each group has to remember that its own ambitions must not run counter to those of the State. There are, of course, occasions when these higher obligations are forgotten; but they are fewer than might be expected in a system in which struggles among rival factions are not regarded as unavoidable misfortunes, but are a necessary ingredient.

If the ruling groups in Japanese society have been derived to a large extent from the "estates" that existed in Tokugawa times, this does not mean that the individuals who compose each of them have been drawn from a narrow circle of families. Almost exactly the contrary is true. Each ruling or influential clique has been recruited from persons with very diverse origins. Thus, of the four great *Zaibatsu*, two were great merchants in feudal times, one was a money-lender of less renown, and one was of *samurai* origin. Two others, of secondary importance, but still very powerful, were founded by peddlers. Their leading officials have come mainly from the ranks of *samurai* or from country families. Some wealthy business men, outside the ranks of the *Zaibatsu*, began their career as primary school teachers and in very humble circumstances.[1] Of the *Genro*, the survivor, Prince Saionji, was of noble birth; but most of them came from the lower ranks of the *samurai* or even from the families of commoners who had acquired the rank of *samurai*, like Prince Ito who was the son of a peasant. Among the bureaucrats the same diversity of origin is seen. Mr. Hirota, the present Foreign Minister, is the son of a stonemason. Mr. K. Takahashi, the famous Finance Minister, was the son of a painter and a serving-maid, and, after adoption into a family, he worked for some years as a temple servant. General Araki, the

[1] *See* Seiji Noma, *The Nine Magazines of Kodansha*, for a fascinating account of the career of a well-known magnate in the world of popular journalism.

PLATE IV

[*Reproduced by the courtesy of the N.Y.K. Line*

JAPANESE ROOM ARRANGED FOR SLEEPING

leader of the Army extremists, was born in a poor *samurai* family in Kyushu.

There is nothing remarkable about this phenomenon. The Meiji Restoration from one point of view can be regarded as a revolt by the poor *samurai* of the "outside" clans[1] and certain merchants against the privileged classes, and a new ruling oligarchy had to be created from the formerly weak and depressed groups. The new era required the creation of a fresh system of administration and gave vast opportunities for the development of industry and commerce. Men who had little but their own genius and energy naturally came to the front in these circumstances. There can be little doubt that the extraordinary rapidity of Japan's development since 1868 is largely to be explained by the way in which careers were thrown open wide to talent and energy. Nepotism was at a discount. This does not mean that appointments were or are made in Japan solely on questions of merit. The membership of a clique that happens to be influential is often a passport to high office, but that membership is not always gained solely by birth or as a result of family connections. Some loss of stability may have attended this system of promotion and even some loss of personal integrity among public men. A man who owes office to membership of a clique may find it difficult to resist the course of action demanded by that clique even when it is dishonourable, and the careerist was naturally favoured by the circumstances of the new era. For these reasons, perhaps, the grosser forms of corruption have been prominent in Japanese public life. But from the standpoint of national vitality and enterprise, whatever the disadvantages that have attended Japanese cliquism, so far these have been less detrimental to vigorous leadership than are those associated with nepotism and class exclusiveness. When the present régime is older and the period of national expansion draws to a close, the same corruption and inefficiency that marked the end of the Tokugawa era may again become prominent.

[1] That is to say, the clans that were excluded during the Tokugawa era from a share in the central administration.

CHAPTER V

THE GOVERNMENT OF THE PEOPLE

"Of all the engine-work of state,
Of commerce, laws and policy."
MATTHEW ARNOLD (*after* HORACE)

". . . whether we do not divide upon Trifles, and whether our Parties are not a Burlesque upon Politics?"
GEORGE BERKELEY

IN the development of Western civilization a distinction has been recognized between the duties that a man owes to the State and those that his own conscience enjoins. Socrates is honoured because he placed his devotion to justice and truth above the gods of the tribe and the city. Christianity has kept before us the gulf that separates the things that are Caesar's and the things that are God's. The rise of totalitarian States in Germany, Russia, and Italy is seen by those who are faithful to the noblest traditions of European civilization as a return to primitive barbarism. Now modern Japan does not recognize this fundamental distinction; and the ordinary Japanese can scarcely conceive of a good man who at the same time sets himself against the purposes of the State. Some writers have even boasted that in the Japanese State these two claims are reconciled or are harmoniously combined into a single loyalty and devotion. They speak of the Japanese nation as consisting of a great family with the Emperor at its head. The Emperor cannot be tyrannical or arbitrary, for he acts towards his subjects as a father towards his children; while the people feel towards the Emperor the veneration and honour that children have for their father, and in his service they realize their own best ideals. The Emperor is thus not merely a convenient constitutional instrument, whose power is to be defined by law and precedent. His relationship to his people is an emotional, not a legal, relationship; Japanese society cannot be conceived of without it. Moreover, the Emperor is divine, a descendant of the Sun-goddess. Just as the head of an ordinary Japanese family is the repository of the traditions of that family in his lifetime and attracts to himself from the other members a devotion owed to the whole line, so the Emperor embodies the historical experience of the race and is revered accordingly. He thus draws to himself not merely the emotion associated with the State and the family, but also that which is usually paid to a Church or the founder of a religion.

He has not always occupied this position nor excited these emotions. For long centuries he lived in seclusion, while ambitious lords governed the country. It is true that they are supposed to have ruled in his name; but this was often merely a convenient fiction. Nor, from the controversy that attended the revival of *Shinto* in the eighteenth century does it appear that his divine attributes were commonly accepted by scholars and administrators. It was not until the modern era that he was universally recognized as enjoying the lofty position that he now occupies, although it is now said that his power during the feudal era was not extinguished but only in abeyance. Thus, a Japanese cannot discuss the position of the Emperor in terms of constitutional practice or political theory; but only in terms of theology.

Since the Japanese are not a logically minded race and since they have a liking for constitutional compromise, the full implications of the Imperial status have not always been realized or insisted upon. Other religions, including Christianity, have flourished alongside *Shinto* in the last sixty years, although their tenets are inconsistent with the totalitarian political theory of Japan. The majority of Japanese are, of course, Buddhists; and they have maintained these beliefs and the religious practices associated with them without ceasing also to be Shintoists. In some parts of the country *Shinto* shrines and Buddhist temples are found together, and at present one of the leading advocates of extreme nationalist doctrines is a Buddhist priest of the Nichiren sect. Even many Japanese Christians see nothing inconsistent in ancestor-worship, and they take part without uneasiness in the religious observances associated with the Emperor. Until recently, no question of religious persecution arose in modern times. So long as Christian families paid formal reverence to the Emperor and to the national shrines, this was enough. But the clouds are now massing ominously. The rise of nationalist feeling and of xenophobia in recent years has led to a more precise definition of the Emperor's position. The view that had been developed by leading liberal jurists that sovereignty resides in the State, and that the Emperor in his constitutional aspect is an organ of the State, has been condemned as heretical, and Professor Minobe, its famous exponent, has been violently attacked and has had to give up his seat in the House of Peers. The Emperor, it is now asserted, is the embodiment of the State and the source of all power. The double allegiance which Christianity brings with it cannot be permitted to his subjects. At present, only the extremists have advocated that this argument should be pushed to its logical conclusion; but the extremists are steadily gaining a firmer grip on the governmental machine. Japanese Christians fear that their religion may soon be proscribed and that they themselves may be subject to a persecution which will recall the terrors of three centuries ago. If this happens, the Japanese will have taken another step towards the position attained by the States that have advanced furthest towards totalitarianism, Russia and Germany.

Since 1889 the Imperial power has been exercised through organs established by the written Constitution granted in that year, or through extra-constitutional bodies which depend upon custom and precedent. Constitutional government in Japan, however, has never implied a representative system, and its character can be understood only in relation to the political history of the country and to world conditions at the time when the Constitution was drawn up. The Japanese people at the time of the Restoration were not politically conscious and power rested in the hands of a small group of leaders, drawn mainly from *samurai* of the Choshu and Satsuma clans, whose efforts had led to the overthrow of the Shogunate.[1] These were the men who, acting in the Emperor's name, were determined to place Japan in a position of equality with the Western Powers which had menaced her integrity. An important stage in the development of their country was the abolition of the extra-territorial rights and of the unfavourable trade treaties which those Powers had wrested from her, and one method of attaining the goal was to demonstrate that the new Japan was following a course of action of which the Powers approved. Now parliamentary government in the last quarter of the nineteenth century was synonymous with civilization, and the replacement of an arbitrary system of government by one modelled in broad outline on those of the great democratic nations of the West was naturally to be regarded as an impressive and laudatory achievement. A desire to stand well in the eyes of these nations and so to raise the political status of Japan was, then, a powerful reason for the establishment of a constitutional system of government; the high prestige of the West and of the institutions associated with it also lent support to this new venture.

The statesmen who framed the new Constitution, however willing they might be to make a conciliatory gesture to the world, had no intention of grafting on Japan a democratic representative system. Even if they had wished to do so, the experiment must have failed in view of the political inexperience of the masses. Consequently, the method of government which they set up bore little resemblance in practice to the parliamentary systems of the West. For one thing, the Constitution had not been wrested from the Emperor as a result of struggles for the limitations of his prerogatives. It was granted freely by him for "the promotion of the welfare of his subjects and for the development of their moral and intellectual functions," as the preamble to the Constitution itself states. In other words, the restrictions imposed by the Constitution on the exercise of Imperial prerogatives were restrictions which the Emperor himself initiated. The Constitution thus has

[1] *Shogun*, or military governors, had been the *de facto* rulers of the country for many centuries before the restoration of Imperial Power in 1867.

a more inviolable character than that possessed by those of the West. Proposals for amending the Constitution can come only from the Emperor, and any attempts by others to alter it are treasonable and impious. In our own time, this view of the Constitution as divinely inspired has had a result that the statesmen who drew it up can scarcely have foreseen. They were doubtless guided by a desire to check the growth of democratic forces; but in recent years the danger has been rather of a revolution from the right leading to the establishment of a military dictatorship. The nature of the Constitution has furnished the opponents of this step with a powerful weapon: is it not impious, they say, to abolish what the divine Emperor Meiji granted to his people?

The Constitution has other peculiarities which have profoundly affected the nature of Japanese government. It provided for the establishment of a Diet of two Houses, the House of Peers, composed in a fashion rather similar to that of the Upper House in the Parliament of Imperial Germany, and the House of Representatives which has been elected since 1926 on a basis of universal manhood suffrage. But in certain important matters, the powers vested in the Diet were narrowly limited. It cannot initiate any constitutional change; and it is excluded from any control over the Imperial Household, even in matters relating to the succession or to the institution of regency. Here the Emperor exercises his prerogative on the advice of the Minister of the Imperial Household, the Privy Council, and the Lord Privy Seal. None of these Ministers or Counsellors is responsible to the Diet. Further, the supreme command of the armed forces is exercised by the Emperor through the chiefs of the general staffs of the Army and Navy, who are directly responsible to him, and parliamentary interference in this field is also excluded. Various bodies, of which the chief is the Supreme War Council, have been established for advising the Emperor in military and naval affairs; and these organs are independent of those which advise him over general affairs of State. This dual control over policy is not peculiar to Japan; but, as in other countries where it exists, it has been a frequent source of conflict and disorder. Again, the Diet has little influence over foreign relations. The Emperor concludes treaties with foreign Powers upon the advice of the Cabinet; but here another organ of State, which is independent of parliamentary control, intrudes itself. The Privy Council, which is appointed by the Emperor on the advice of the Prime Minister, from among distinguished bureaucrats, Army and Navy chiefs, and diplomats, has the power of advising the Emperor about the ratification of treaties and can thus exercise a considerable influence in the field of foreign relations. The Council also has no inconsiderable powers of supervision over the executive through its power of amending draft ordinances or bills sent to it by the Cabinet, and it has, on at least one occasion, forced the resignation of a Ministry which enjoyed the confidence of the Diet. It is through their control over finance that most legislative bodies have achieved a dominating position in the government of democratic countries; but it is symptomatic of the weakness of the Japanese Diet that its power in this respect should be narrowly restricted. The Constitution itself decrees that should the Diet fail to pass the budget, then the Government shall proceed to carry out the budget of the previous year.

The Emperor himself is not responsible for any of his acts, and in general affairs he exercises his prerogative on the advice of Ministers who compose the Cabinet. But these Ministers are not responsible to Parliament, nor are they necessarily drawn from the strongest party in the House. Their constitutional responsibility is to the Emperor alone, and they must bear that responsibility even if they are acting with the advice of the Privy Council. In practice, as we shall see in a moment, the Diet in the post-War decade was able to exercise some control over the Cabinet, and there was in those years a general belief that the time was approaching when a Cabinet which did not enjoy the confidence of the Diet would be unable to hold office. But these hopes have received a set-back and that time now seems very distant. In the same way, the doctrine of collective ministerial responsibility for the acts of the Government was coming into favour in the years just after the War; but conservative jurists have always opposed it, and the controversy now has little practical significance. The application of the principle of collective responsibility to Parliament is scarcely possible so long as the curious dualism in the control of policy that has already been commented on persists. From the early days of constitutional government the right of direct access to the Emperor was enjoyed by the chiefs of the general staffs of the Army and Navy; but gradually this right has been extended to the Ministers of War and of the Navy also. The other ministers, of course, tender their advice through the Prime Minister. The selection of a War Minister, moreover, is restricted to a General or Lieutenant-General, and of a Navy Minister, to an Admiral or Vice-Admiral; and these officers must be still on the active list. Thus, no Prime Minister can form a Cabinet if the military and naval cliques refuse to provide candidates for these offices. At any time a Cabinet may be wrecked by the withdrawal of military and naval support, and at any time the Service ministers can consult and advise the Emperor without the knowledge of their ministerial colleagues.

The Japanese system of government clearly cannot be ranged among the democracies. At the beginning of the century it was defined in the following terms which are still appropriate, although "the advanced principles of modern constitutionalism" are not a very obvious ingredient.

> The Emperor holds the sovereign power, not as his own inherent right, but as an inheritance from his Divine Ancestor. The Government is, therefore, *theocratical.* The Emperor rules over the country as the supreme head of the vast family of the Japanese nation. The Government is, therefore, *patriarchal.* The Emperor exercises the sovereign power according to the Constitution, which is based on the most advanced principles of modern constitutionalism. The Government is, therefore, *constitutional.* In other words, the fundamental principle of the Japanese Government is *theocratico-patriarchal constitutionalism.*[1]

[1] Baron Hozumi, *Ancestor-Worship and Japanese Law*, pp. 87–8, quoted in T. Takeuchi, *War and Diplomacy in the Japanese Empire*, p. 9.

As policy is controlled neither by a Cabinet responsible to elected representatives, nor by an autocratic dictator, the problem of where power actually resides must next be considered. For many years after the establishment of constitutional government, authority rested with a small group of *samurai* who had been responsible for the emergence of new Japan. These formed an extra-constitutional body known as the *Genro* or elder statesmen, and with one exception (Prince Saionji) they all came from the two great clans of Choshu and Satsuma, which had played the chief rôle in the overthrow of Tokugawa.[1] These *Genro* were at once the leaders and also the spokesmen of the clans to which they belonged. Up to 1901 a member of this body was always chosen as Prime Minister, on the advice of the others, and for some years after that date a *Genro* from time to time filled that office. But later on their chief function became that of recommending the retiring Prime Minister's successor from among persons outside their own ranks. They were consulted by the Emperor on matters of grave import; and they exercised a general supervision over policy. The *Genro* were not unanimous in the policies they wished the State to prosecute, nor in their views about the personnel of which the Governments should be composed. Saionji, who favoured the liberalization of the State, was sometimes at odds with Yamagata, the arch-militarist, notably in the quarrel over the programme of military expansion which led to the fall of the Government of which Saionji was premier in 1912. There were differences of opinion also between the Choshu *Genro* and the Satsuma *Genro*; and within the Choshu ranks Yamagata disputed with Ito, the creator of the Constitution and of Japan's civil administration. Each of these great *Genro* had protégés whom they raised to high office. Admiral Yamamoto was supported by the Satsuma *Genro*. Prince Katsura as Prime Minister carried out the military programme of Yamagata; and Saionji, before he, too, became numbered among the *Genro*, owed

[1] Prince Saionji was descended from a family of Court nobles who formed a class distinct from the *daimyo*, the rulers of the fiefs into which Japan was divided in "feudal" times.

his eminence to Ito's support. As already shown, several of the *Genro* fortified themselves by alliances with certain of the *Zaibatsu.*

At first, the Governments created by the *Genro* were drawn entirely from the nobility, the bureaucrats, and military and naval chiefs, most of whom were connected with the Satsuma-Choshu (*Sat-Cho*) cliques. As time went on, however, they found that Governments composed in this fashion met with opposition from the elected representatives in Parliament. Some deference had to be paid to the political parties formed among these representatives. The parties were originally created in the early years of Meiji by *samurai* of the smaller clans who were excluded by the *Sat-Cho* combination from high office, and when the Diet was formed they tried to overcome their disabilities by using such power as the Constitution had given them to force the cliques to take notice of them. It is significant that Hara, the first commoner to become Prime Minister, began his career in the civil service as a clerk in the Foreign Office, but gave up his appointment in order to become a party politician when he found promotion blocked because he did not belong to the favoured clans.[1] The most influential of the *Genro*, Prince Ito, was at first opposed to the growth of the political parties; but the Constitution gave an opportunity for their development which could not be prevented. Further, although the Diet could not control the Government, yet it had been given certain powers in the exercise of which it could embarrass the governing cliques, and the politicians were not slow to exploit their "nuisance value." So, from the late nineties certain of the bureaucrats, including the *Genro*, began to create working alliances with the parties. Prince Ito and his protégé, Prince Saionji, were instrumental in the development of the Seiyukai Party, which was opposed by a party led by Count Okuma, who was an "outsider." Other alliances between *Genro* and the parties existed from time to time. The parties had no "platform" and stood for no definite political principles, although certain individuals who composed them did, such as Ozaki the liberal democrat. Without much

[1] U. Iwasaki, *The Working Forces in Japanese Politics*, p. 83.

exaggeration it can be said that the politicians sold their support to various *Genro* and the bureaucratic and military cliques which the *Genro* led, in return for a share in the spoils of office. Each Government had patronage to bestow in the form of governorships of the semi-official banks, prefectural governorships, and positions in important Government commercial undertakings, and these offices were granted to its supporters in the Diet.

After a time, "big business" began to take a hand. The great financial industrial houses that are known as the *Zaibatsu* strengthened their influence over the Government by supplying the parties with funds. Elections were very expensive in Japan, because of the scale on which bribery was practised, and those who furnished the necessary money could exercise pressure on the parties. A *Zaibatsu* closely allied to a party could, in this way, give policy a twist to his advantage, and could hope to ensure that when a Government supported by his party was in office, valuable contracts would come his way. Business rivalries among the different *Zaibatsu* were thus carried into the political arena. It is commonly said that Mitsui was and is allied to the Seiyukai. Mitsubishi originally financed Okuma's party, which in the early years of the century was known as the Kensei-honto.[1] The alliances created between bureaucrats and the parties were, however, often short-lived, and from time to time the former dispensed with party support and formed Governments that had no connection with them. A brief review of political history during the early part of this century will throw some light on the way in which government was conducted.

In 1900 Prince Ito had made his alliance with the Seiyukai in order to strengthen his hand against his rival *Genro*, Prince Yamagata, who leaned rather on the House of Peers. The House of Peers was not divided on the same party lines as the House of Representatives, and it supported the bureaucrats. The other chief

[1] The history of Japanese political parties is difficult to recount briefly because of frequent splits and regroupings and because of changes in the names of the parties.

party, the Kensei-honto, led by Okuma, and not allied to any *Genro*, was in a weak minority. Ito, however, made the mistake of asking the Emperor for an edict on two occasions in order to hamstring his rival, and as Japanese political tradition is hostile to the practice of using the Emperor's name to support a sectional interest, he lost prestige and had to retire from politics in 1901. Saionji, his protégé, succeeded him as head of the Seiyukai, and he and Prince Katsura, Yamagata's henchman and fellow clansman, appear to have arrived at a compromise by which the premiership was held alternately by these two men. This lasted until 1912 when a new phase began.

In the years immediately before the Great War Japan's financial position was weak and difficulty was experienced in maintaining the yen at parity. The Saionji Cabinet, which held office in 1912, decided upon a policy of retrenchment. The military clique of Yamagata, however, was always restive under Governments which depended in any measure on party support and it was anxious to extend the size of the army in Korea. It, therefore, required the Minister of War, who was of course a member of the clique, to retire, and it refused to supply any candidate for the office. So, Saionji had to resign, although he was backed by the larger party in the Lower House. The Navy clique (Satsuma), however, was not pleased with the success of its rival, the Choshu clique, and refused to supply a Navy Minister for the new Government which Prince Katsura formed. Katsura ultimately obtained his Ministry by asking for an Imperial edict, and he tried to gain support in the Diet by coquetting with the rival party. But he had damaged his prestige by his use of the Emperor's prerogative, and a good deal of public feeling was aroused against him by the Seiyukai, who declared that the political influence of the *Genro* and the clans was unconstitutional. But when Katsura fell the Seiyukai were quite willing to support Admiral Yamamoto's premiership, although he was a member of one of the cliques (Satsuma); for Yamamoto was prepared to compromise with them. A small group of Seiyukai politicians led by Ozaki stood out for a Government responsible to the Diet, and a party split consequently resulted. When Yamamoto tried to damage the influence of the Army clique by widening the qualifications of Service ministers to include generals and admirals on the retired list, the Army clique withdrew the Minister of War and the Government fell. Kiyoura, a Choshu man, who tried to form a Government to succeed Yamamoto, failed to do so because the Navy clique, resentful of the blow that Choshu had struck at their member, would not supply a Navy Minister.

This quarrel between Choshu and Satsuma placed the *Genro* in a difficulty and they were forced in 1914 to recommend as Prime Minister Okuma, who had the confidence of the minority parties and was one of the few experienced statesmen outside the *Sat-Cho* ranks.[1] Okuma, in the ensuing election, received the powerful backing of Mitsubishi and of the intelligentsia associated with Waseda University, which he had formed. But this Government was too much like a party Government and insufficiently attached to the dominant cliques to please the *Genro* for long, and it was finally overthrown by Yamagata, who placed his protégé, Count Terauchi, a Choshu general, in office. The bureaucrats and militarists had again triumphed, and for two years their rule continued. Terauchi's Government came to an end, however, through one of those outbreaks of popular disapproval which are rare in Japan, but to which, if they are associated with some particular grievance, the Government and the ruling cliques behind it are exceedingly susceptible. The rise in prices during the Great War had brought hardship to the poorer classes, and in 1918 the celebrated rice riots broke out. In Japan a Government, or anyone in authority, must accept responsibility for any disorder that may occur, and so Terauchi had to resign. The *Genro*, who were im-

[1] Okuma had left the Kensei-honto in 1907, and that party had joined with other small groups in forming the Kokuminto in 1910. Prince Katsura, after his fall from office, flirted with the politicians and formed in 1913 the Doshi-kai which many members of the Kokuminto joined. This party supported Okuma's Government, and in 1915 it absorbed other small groups and became the Kensei-kai.

pressed by this display of popular feeling, felt that it was an occasion for concessions, and called Hara to office. Hara was the leader of the Seiyukai and was the first untitled politician to head a Japanese Government. It now seemed that the day of parliamentary government had at last dawned; but this was an optimistic view, for Hara only retained office by placating Yamagata, especially in connection with the maintenance of large armed forces in Siberia.[1]

Yet power had undoubtedly shifted. It was not that a democratically elected legislative Chamber was securing control over policy; but rather that the old *Sat-Cho* groups were losing their hold while new groups were rising in power. Men who were born outside the favoured clans had achieved prominence; the economic development of the country had increased the influence exerted by business groups; and in the early post-War years opinion among the intelligentsia and the politically conscious section of the urban population was turning strongly in favour of the replacement of an oligarchic system by one that bore a closer resemblance to that of the great Western democracies. The majority of the *Genro* with great prestige had by now passed away, and the death in 1922 of Prince Yamagata, the bitterest foe of parliamentary government, left as his sole successors Prince Matsukata, who was interested mainly in financial administration, and Prince Saionji, who was strongly inclined to liberal views.

The political parties, however, had no firm foundation in the sentiment of the electorate and stood for no body of political principles to which they could appeal in support of their policies. Through the relationship of the Service Ministers to the Cabinet of which they formed part, every party Government necessarily occupied an equivocal position. After the murder of Hara in 1921 the parties proved incompetent to form strong Governments, and a number of bureaucratic Ministries were created. It was significant of the trend of the times that the Kiyoura Cabinet, formed solely among members of the House of Peers in January 1924, provoked strong resentment and was forced to dissolve Parliament

[1] See Chapter XI.

as a result of a "no confidence" address presented to the Emperor from the House of Representatives. In the subsequent elections the voters upheld this action, and so compelled the Ministry to resign. In pre-War days, although the House had power to compel a dissolution by this procedure, the parties seldom benefited by it because the Government could, by coercion and bribery, largely determine the composition of the new assembly.

After a short eclipse, therefore, parliamentary influence was re-established, and a coalition Cabinet led by Viscount Kato, the leader of Kenseikai, came into office in the summer of 1924. The seal appeared to be placed on the triumph of Parliament by the passing of the Manhood Suffrage Act in 1925 in spite of the opposition of the Peers, and later by a revision in the constitution of the House of Peers by which the number of noblemen in that assembly was reduced. Bureaucrats and Army and Navy nominees still continued to fill some ministerial offices, but the cliques which they represented had definitely lost ground. The military were even obliged to consent to a progressive decrease in budgetary appropriations for the Army. Moreover, in order to stem the tide, they now had to identify themselves more closely with the parties. Thus, General Tanaka, the Choshu protégé of Yamagata, in an effort to weaken the Government, became President of the Seiyukai and persuaded them to break up the coalition. But the Government remained under the premiership of Kato, and on his death, of R. Wakatsuki.

The Kenseikai Government, financed largely by Mitsubishi, and favouring a liberal foreign policy, clashed with the bureaucratic and military cliques in one of their strongholds, China. Throughout the parliamentary history of Japan the major issues of foreign policy have been decided in joint conferences of the *Genro* and the Cabinet in the presence of the Emperor and his personal Ministers. Thus, in this field as in defence, parliamentary control has always been very weak. The military and naval cliques, moreover, have always concerned themselves very closely with Chinese affairs; their general staffs have their own agents in China; and they have always exerted a great influence on the Foreign Office in regard to that country. Baron Shidehara, the Kenseikai Foreign Minister, took advantage of the temper of the times to free himself from this control and to pursue a "conciliatory" policy which was by no means to the liking of the Services and the Conservative bureaucrats and members of the Privy Council. An opportunity for overthrowing the Government came when it drew up an emergency imperial ordinance necessitated by the financial crisis of 1927. The Privy Council rejected it on constitutional grounds, although measures similar to those it provided were sanctioned when the succeeding Government introduced them, and the Government collapsed. Yet General Tanaka who formed the next Ministry, though a Choshu military oligarch, was obliged to base his Government, formally, at any rate, on a political party, the Seiyukai of which he was President.[1]

Tanaka was the advocate of a "positive" policy in China, and it was on his instructions that troops were sent to Shantung and Manchuria in connection with the Tsinan incident. Tanaka was bitterly attacked both in the House of Representatives and in the country for his handling of this affair; but this criticism failed to turn him from his course, or even to induce him to give information about his policy. It was not until apprehensions were aroused among the Peers and the Privy Council concerning the policy, that Tanaka was finally induced to modify it. Tanaka's Government was brought down in 1929, partly through general disfavour of his handling of the Chinese situation, and partly on a constitutional question.

These events seem to show that while in the post-War decade it was no longer possible for a Government which was independent of a political party in the Lower House to continue in office, yet the Cabinet was far from being responsible to Parliament. The Prime Minister was still selected by the *Genro*, although in this

[1] After its fall from office in 1927, the Kenseikai absorbed a small group of politicians who had broken away from the Seiyukai a few years earlier, and it then came to be known as the Minseito.

choice the *Genro* could not ignore the wishes of Parliament. The life of the Cabinet still did not depend on its maintenance of a majority in the House of Representatives, for Tanaka's Government in 1927 was a minority Government, and when he fell he had a majority in the Lower House. The Privy Council still retained its power of destroying a Government of which it disapproved, by an adverse ruling on a constitutional issue. The House of Peers, moreover, which is not divided on the same party lines as is the House of Representatives, can bring great pressure to bear on a Ministry. While it tends to support a bureaucratic Government against the House of Representatives, it may be a formidable opponent to a Government which is closely associated with the Lower House. In other words, while the *Genro* and *Sat-Cho* combination had lost the dominating position, and while politics could no longer be regarded in terms of an internal conflict within those groups, the major political power still continued to reside in various military and bureaucratic cliques which expressed themselves through *Genro*, the Privy Council, the Peers, the General Staffs, and the personal advisers of the sovereign. Nevertheless, that the trend was towards responsible government in our sense was clear, for the Lower House could no longer be ignored or treated as a mere tool of the military cliques. The encroachment of the political parties reflected the growing power of great business interests in Japan which was itself a symptom of the industrial and financial development that had occurred during the century. In so far as these interests stood for a more liberal foreign policy, especially towards China, a more benevolent domestic policy and a more rational outlook on affairs than the older cliques, it may be said that Japan had made an advance towards democratic ideals. But it must be remembered that the mass of the people had only a spasmodic influence on policy, and, indeed, only an intermittent interest in it, and that, moreover, the business interests behind the parties were not sharply divided from the bureaucrats and militarists, but, rather, they were allies of the less imperialistic and reactionary members of those groups.

It does not follow, of course, that political parties, just because they depend largely on the support of particular economic interests, are incapable of formulating a policy which appeals to the disinterested judgments of electors; for it may happen that at times the policy that will promote a particular interest is also one that derives its validity from some universal political principle. The doctrines of the English radicals in the nineteenth century were none the less tenable because they provided the new manufacturing class with weapons against the landlords. In Japan, however, democratic principles of government were an importation from the West. A few men came to cherish them; but they were alien to the mass of the people, and there were no widely held political principles to which policy could be referred. Thus, there was lacking a well-informed electorate with political convictions derived from a long experience of self-government, and capable of criticizing the acts of their representatives and of checking their rapacity. The Constitution was a gift from above. It was not won as a result of a long struggle for liberty which had become part of the national consciousness. The bureaucratic nature of local government meant that there was no counterpart in Japan to the valuable school of administrative experience in which English politicians learn their first lessons. The struggle of the parties in the Diet to wrest power from the bureaucracy and militarists was not the outcome of a strong and organized movement for reform in the country, although the support of the electorate might from time to time be obtained. So the politicians tended to play for their own hand or for the interests that financed them. "In recent years the Diet has come to be an organ not primarily to perform constitutional functions of legislation and of supervision of the executive, but one through which political parties seek to obtain the powers of the Government. Hence, the parliamentary interpellations and debates centre not around great questions of national policy . . . but around technical or non-consequential matters. . . ."[1] In these circum-

[1] T. Takeuchi, *op. cit.*, p. 59. This point is well illustrated by the tactics of the Opposition (the Minseito) during Tanaka's administration (1927–9). The

stances, though the power of the parties increased, the integrity of their members diminished. Corrupt practices became very common; and the devotion of many of the party leaders to the service of big business by which they were financed was cynically accepted as a matter of course.[1]

Minseito opposed the signing of the Pact of Paris by this Seiyukai Government on narrow constitutional grounds (although it had no objection to the purpose of the Pact) solely in order to embarrass its opponents. Again, it demanded the publication of the report on the circumstances of Chang Tso-lin's assassination (in which Japanese authorities were suspected of being implicated), and it bitterly attacked the Seiyukai Government for its refusal to meet this demand. Yet when the Minseito Government came into office shortly afterwards, it was as adamant in opposing the publication of the report as its predecessor had been.

[1] Mr. K. Takahashi's failure as leader of the Seiyukai after Hara's assassination in November 1921 was attributed by a Japanese writer to his being "too good." *Japan Year Book*, 1933, p. 156.

CHAPTER VI

FIELDS, FACTORIES, AND WORKSHOPS

"Beschäftigung, die nie ermattet,
Die langsam schafft, doch nie zerstört."
SCHILLER

BEFORE the beginning of the Showa Era (1926) the economic life of Japan excited very little interest in the West. The artistic, religious, and political history of the country was the subject of serious study and of journalistic comment; but finance, industry, and trade received only cursory treatment. During the last ten or twelve years, however, eyes have been drawn to this hitherto neglected section of Japanese life, and there has appeared an enormous number of books, articles, and official reports in Europe and America which purport to describe the activities of the Japanese in the ordinary business of life, and especially to explain the causes of the great expansion of foreign trade and industry that has occurred in that country. Some of the detailed information provided by these studies has penetrated into the public consciousness of Western countries; but the general picture is still exceedingly confused in its composition. This is largely because the attention given to Japanese industry in the Press has been spasmodic, for interest has been aroused only on occasions when Japan's industry, through some special development, has happened to impinge on the markets of Western countries. Obviously, to regard as significant only those trades which are the rivals of Western manufactures is to give a distorted picture of the country's economic life.

When the Japanese cotton industry first became a serious rival to Lancashire in Oriental markets and information about that industry became available, the impression was created that most of it was conducted by huge concerns and plants, and this organization was held to contrast favourably with the sectional character of the British cotton trade. The impression was strengthened by the knowledge, communicated by business men who had dealings with the Japanese, that a large part of Japan's industry, trade, and finance was dominated by a few great business families. Japan, it seemed, had a rationalized and highly integrated economic life. But while it appeared that she had, in spite of her short industrial experience, attained the stage of what is sometimes called "monopoly-capitalism," other features of her economic life that became known suggested rather that she was still subject to conditions that recalled our mid-Victorian era. It was not merely the long hours of labour in the factories and the absence of collective bargaining that placed Japan in that stage of development. There were also the furious energy and buoyant optimism of the Japanese business man to whom long week-ends were unknown and who saved a large share of his profits for reinvestment. "Capitals are increased by parsimony," had said the prophet of the new age in England; he is not without honour in present-day Japan. Later, when miscellaneous manufactured goods poured into English and American homes through the cheap stores, information reached us that these came from thousands of tiny workshops where people toiled from daybreak to late at night without proper manufacturing equipment for the pittance allowed them by merchants who controlled the trade. This suggested an even earlier era in our industrial history. Then after the political assassinations of the last few years, the newspapers and the broadcasters told us that these were associated in some way with the antagonism felt by the rural masses towards the great business families who were in political alliance with the bureaucracy; we heard that nearly half the Japanese population consists of small peasant farmers, many of whom had been ruined by the fall in raw-silk prices.

All this seems very remote from the country depicted by tourists or by writers on Japanese culture and art, or by those who have tried to explain to us the ordinary life of the people. For these observers tell us of a domestic life very different from our own, of strange traditions handed down from the remote past, of widespread sophistication of taste that requires for its satisfaction beauty and individuality in articles which are the common necessities of daily existence. Since the Greeks, we are told, there has been no people among whom aestheticism has been more widely diffused than it is among the Japanese, and the craftsmen who satisfies everyday demands must be an artist. Then, when the war with China broke out, there arose the vision of a ruthless and ambitious State which for half a century had been bending the energies of the people into pursuits which would contribute to political power and was now bringing under its control the greater part of the country's economic life. Which view is correct? Is the economic life of Japan typified by the artist-craftsman? Or by a "sweated" outworker or a "garret-master"? Or by a primitive peasant? Or shall we find the best prototype of the modern Japanese in the pages of Samuel Smiles? Or should we look rather to the American trust builders? Or must we think of Japan as possessing a "planned" Fascist economy?

These questions are very difficult to answer. For stages of development that are widely separated in Europe seem to be telescoped in Japan. Features commonly associated with "monopoly-capitalism" or a Fascist economy are prominent; but so are features associated with the full flush of economic liberalism. Again, the huge factory, the giant business house, and the tiny workshop are there together; but the last is not a mere survival and the others not exceptional creations of a few geniuses or megalomaniacs. An idea of the quantitative importance of some of the chief members of the economic structure may be given by a glance at figures showing the occupational distribution of the population at the last Census.

The table (page 95) shows that Japan is far from being a highly industrialized country; for half of the occupied population is engaged in agriculture and fishing. Even if we take account of the male occupied population only, we find that nearly 44 per cent. of it is found in these two ancient industries. The structure of this part of Japan's economic life recalls in some degree that of Europe before the industrial revolution, although there are some important features that are peculiar to Japan. There are very few large landed proprietors (if the Imperial Household which owns the forest lands is excepted). Indeed, in 1934 nearly a million persons other than cultivators were recorded as owning agricultural land, and this means that their average estate is less than seven acres. It is estimated that there are only 4,000 persons with estates larger than 124 acres and that the average estate of these relatively large proprietors is 306 acres, the area of a moderate-sized farm

Persons employed in all Occupations in 1930
(*in thousands*)

Occupation	*Numbers*
Agriculture	14,082
Fishing	565
Mining and Quarrying	314
Manufacturing	5,707
Commerce	4,858
Transport and Communications	912
Public and Professional Services	2,002
Domestic Service	794
Others	66
	29,300

in England. Of the farm households, which number 5,600,000, just over one-third are peasant proprietors; just over a quarter are tenants; and the remainder consist of farmers who own some of the land they till and rent the rest. The holdings of all these farmers are extremely small. Over one-third of the farm households have less than 1·23 acres and the average size of the farm is only 2·61 acres.[1] Much of a typical farmer's holding is in scattered strips. The main crop is rice, grown in paddy fields, which make up 53 per cent. of the cultivated areas, with barley or some other cereal as a winter crop. On the upland fields there are wheat and other

[1] For further information about the recent condition of the agricultural classes, *see* articles in the *Far Eastern Survey*, January 1st, 1936, July 7th, 1937, and September 1st, 1937.

cereals, mulberries, fruit, and vegetables. There is very little livestock, except in Hokkaido. The work of cultivation requires protracted and tedious manual labour. "Teasing their narrow plots with hand and hoe," the peasants make little use of mechanical equipment, with the exception of electric pumps for irrigating the rice fields and simple treadle machines for threshing. Each rice plant has to be transplanted by hand during the course of its growth, and reaping is by the sickle.

Although a superficial glance would suggest that the farmer had been little affected by the impact of the West, and although the nature of his labour and preoccupations remain in essence unchanged, yet he has not escaped from the influences of the last half-century. While the rice fields have remained his chief care, he has had to adapt himself to new economic conditions. Before the opening of Japan to Europeans, he grew cotton on the upland fields; but when cheap supplies came in from abroad he had to abandon this crop. Instead of it he began to grow larger quantities of wheat and other crops, especially of mulberries; for the rising foreign demand for silk gave him an opportunity of supplementing his income by rearing silkworms—he calls them his "hungry guests"—which are fed on mulberry leaves. Lately, when demand for silk fell, he was forced to make further adjustments, and he has been devoting his labour to an increasing extent to fruit and poultry. He has not lacked ingenuity in discovering new uses for his land. In Shizuoka, for example, he has found a way of growing strawberries all the year round on the hillsides facing south.

Yet he is exceedingly poor. When feudalism was abolished a heavy land tax was substituted for the dues formerly paid to the *daimyo*. The keen competition from many different types of user for the limited area of suitable land means that agricultural rent is high. For rice land this takes the form of a payment in rice, and between 1931 and 1935 this payment represented on an average from 46 per cent. to 60 per cent. of the crop.[1] In a few

[1] *Far Eastern Survey*, July 7th, 1937, p. 157.

PLATE V

ENTRANCE TO A JAPANESE RESTAURANT

A CHARCOAL SHOP

areas, notably Tohoku,[1] the landlord provides seeds and equipment as well as the land in return for the rent; but generally this is not so. The remainder of the crop is often consumed by the peasant's family; but part of it may be sold and cheaper cereals bought with the proceeds. For his upland fields the farmer usually pays a money rent and the crops raised on them are marketed. The peasant households are also the seats of some of the old manufacturing industries which cater for traditional needs. In Kyushu, for example, peasants cultivate rushes and weave from them the covers for *tatami*, the floor covering in Japanese houses. In other areas they produce traditional kinds of pottery. But the main industry located among the peasantry is silk-raising, to which reference has already been made. About two million peasant families are concerned in this trade, which is the source of one of the chief export commodities. The survival of a large peasantry has been bound up with the remarkable growth of a great demand for raw silk from the United States and this provides many peasant households with one of their chief sources of money income. The fall in this demand since 1929, with the collapse of American "prosperity," brought ruin to thousands of peasants and has been the source of much of the recent social and political tension in Japan. Moreover, it is not unconnected with the international troubles of the Far East.

There are other trades in which the peasants take part. Some families in the coastal areas spend part of their time in fishing. The womenfolk used to weave the common cloth of which the ordinary cotton *kimono* was made in their homes on hand looms. But this trade has diminished in the last twenty years and they now go to work in small factories and workshops in neighbouring towns and villages. The large textile mills recruit most of their labour from the daughters of peasants. It is well known that these girls are housed in dormitories provided by their employers; they send back part of their earnings to their families; and after a few years, when they have reached marriageable age, they return to

[1] Tohoku is in the extreme north of the main island.

the farm with "leaving allowances." Some of the men, too, find work in the towns for a period of years. In many Japanese industries there is a demand for seasonal labour that is satisfied by the rural workers; these industries include fish canning, tea gathering, preparing and packing, and *sake* (rice-wine) brewing.

In spite of these diverse sources of income, the family income of the peasant is pitifully small. The Minister of Agriculture and Forestry has provided some figures illustrative of this condition. In 1929 the average gross family income of a sample of tenant farmers came to only 781 yen from agricultural crops and 236 yen from other sources, 1,017 yen in all. From this some 400 yen had to be deducted for rent and taxes.[1] By 1934 income from crops had fallen steeply and the peasant was much poorer. There has been some improvement since that time; but the level reached in 1929 has not yet been regained. The peasants, moreover, are heavily indebted to usurers and merchants, and the average debt per farm household is now estimated at 800 yen. In spite of the development of co-operative credit societies and semi-official mortgage banks, the farmer normally has to pay from 8 to 12 per cent. interest on this debt. There can be little wonder, then, that the peasants are "restive," that landlord and tenant disputes are frequent, and that unions of tenants have been formed to press for an amelioration in their conditions.

The landlords, in so far as they receive rents in rice, share with their tenants the burden of falling agricultural prices. It is the landlord, moreover, who usually pays the land taxes which, after the Restoration, replaced the feudal dues formerly owed to the *daimyo*. These taxes are very heavy, and it was calculated in 1934 that a landlord with an annual rent-roll of 1,000 yen would have to pay over half of it in taxation.[2] In many cases he has also been obliged to reduce his tenants' rents in the last decade. Like the peasant, he has been induced to seek sources of income other than the land. He acts as a local merchant and financier and he some-

[1] *Japan Year Book*, 1936, p. 471.
[2] *Far Eastern Survey*, July 7th, 1937, p. 157.

times establishes manufacturing enterprises in the village. In most of these activities, however, he is under the control of large merchants and financial interests on whom he depends for capital and for the distribution of the products which he produces or sells. His bargaining position *vis-à-vis* the larger interests is weak at the best of times, and since 1929 he has been menaced by two important tendencies. With the financial assistance of the Government the peasants, especially those with the larger holdings, have been active in the promotion of co-operative societies which, through the provision of joint buying, selling, and finance, have seriously damaged the interests formerly concerned with these functions. On the other hand, the great trading companies, especially Mitsui Bussan Kaisha, until recently were invading the business in certain agricultural and marine products, like eggs and seaweed, which was hitherto conducted exclusively by small local merchants. Thus, if conflicts between tenant and landlord have become more acute, these two classes in some measure share in a common distress upon which a common hatred of the great business groups has been nourished; for they and their policies are regarded as the source of these misfortunes.

The depression since 1930 has certainly led to a fall in the standard of life in the rural prefectures. It would be wrong to suggest, however, that over (say) the last thirty years the rural population has failed to share at all in the improvement in material welfare that has taken place in the country as a whole. A quantitative estimate is difficult to make; but the opinions expressed to the writer by an official of the Social Affairs Bureau throw some light on the situation.[1] Thirty years ago in a village in Saitama prefecture—some fifty miles from Tokyo—the vast majority of the families ate *waru-meshi* (low-grade cereals); very few of the boys in the primary school possessed *hakama* (an article of formal Japanese male attire); and scarcely any could afford to buy foreign clothes in addition to their Japanese dress. Now, except for two or three families, rice has become the staple diet and nearly all the

[1] The Social Affairs Bureau is a department of the Home Office.

children of the villagers have *hakama*, and most of them have foreign-style clothes as well. This, of course, is in a rural area near to one of the great urban centres; in the remoter districts, especially in Tohoku in the far north of the main island, there has probably been no improvement. But it is not, of course, the absolute decline in standards of living which has produced the social troubles, but rather the fact that the country families have lagged behind the townspeople in the advantages secured from Japan's increased productivity.

Naturally, the depression in agriculture is leading to a decline in the proportion of the rural population to the total. Although the birth-rate is higher in rural districts, yet recent Censuses show that the bulk of the increase in the population is being absorbed by the cities. Young men and young women are leaving the farms for urban employment, and whereas formerly this was a temporary movement, recently many of them have settled down permanently in the cities. Since 1929 a huge volume of labour has flowed into the urban labour markets from the overpopulated countryside, and has naturally had a depressing effect on industrial wages. The migration has produced a marked contrast in age-distribution between urban and rural prefectures. The former have an abnormally large proportion of persons between fifteen and thirty-five; while the population of the latter is composed of an abnormal proportion of children and persons in the older age groups.

At the foundation of Japan's economic system, then, lies this peasant agriculture, not untouched by modern influences, but still preserving in its tiny farms and its methods of cultivation conditions that have come down from a remote past. Even when we leave agriculture and move into the orbit of manufacturing industry, we still seem to be among forms of organization that are associated with earlier times. If we exclude building and public utilities, there were in 1930 just over four and a half million people engaged in manufacturing industry and some 315,000 in mining and quarrying. Of the numbers in manufacturing industry about half were in workplaces with under five persons, and about 70 per cent. were in workplaces with under fifty persons.[1] To these numbers engaged in small-scale manufacturing trades should be added many other persons (classified in the Commerce group in the Census) who are working in little shops where goods are made as well as sold. Measured in output, the importance of these small-scale industries is less than would appear from the proportion of total employment which they afford. Some of the workers are only intermittently employed in the trades within which they are classified; there is much under-employment in the little shops; and in most of them labour is less effectively used than in the large factories. Still, with all these qualifications, one can conclude that the major part of Japan's manufacturing industry is conducted in very small workplaces.

These small-scale industries are of very different types. First, there are the trades which satisfy the everyday needs of the people. In Japan Westernization has not yet destroyed the traditional habits of consumption, and these habits have been strongly influenced by the national cult of aestheticism. Consequently, articles of common use must be in accord with this aesthetic tradition. For instance, although the main components of a Japanese house are standardized, the interior fittings and decorations have an individuality that cannot be given by machinery. Moreover, since the main wooden members and the sliding screens (*shoji*) are unpainted, their construction demands a high standard of workmanship. The furniture is scanty and the ornaments few; but style and quality are required for them, even in a simple home. Ordinary domestic utensils—rice bowls, lacquer trays, and cups—are of traditional design and all have some artistic merit. A considerable proportion of the male city dwellers wear foreign-style clothes when at work, and the children, also, wear Western dress at school; but they all wear Japanese attire for the hours spent at home, and the vast majority of women do so all the time. Now this dress is for the most part made of cloth woven and finished in small quan-

[1] Cf. T. Uyeda, *The Growth of Population and Occupational Changes in Japan, 1920–1935* (Japanese Council, Institute of Pacific Relations), p. 14.

tities of each pattern or design. Most of the food eaten in the home is peculiar to Japan, and much of it is bought by the housewife in a prepared state. These goods are not of a kind that can be produced by mechanical methods in large factories. There are exceptions, of course. For example, the greater part of the supply of *tabi* (Japanese socks) is turned out by huge factories that have adapted machinery and modern methods of organization, such as the conveyor system, to their production. For the most part, however, the demands can only be satisfied by the manual skill of the craftsman, either because, as with pottery and china wares, the product must possess artistic merit, or because, as with the *tatami* (floor covering), the material cannot easily be manipulated by machines. A host of trades conducted in tiny workshops has grown up to cater for these wants.

The demand for prepared foods is served by small producers who prepare the bean-curd (*tofu*) and rice-cakes (*mochi*) and either take them to the houses of their customers or sell them in little shops. Every district has numerous producer-vendors of this kind to supply the housewife's needs, and everywhere there are small manufacturers turning out the simpler kinds of durable consumers' goods for local sale. The more elaborate goods required in the Japanese home are the product of groups of craftsmen located in a traditional centre of their production. Silk and cotton fabrics for Japanese dress, pottery, shrines, fans, *hibachi*,[1] and lacquer ware are all turned out by small-scale trades with an elaborate organization. The silk trade may be taken as an example. A typical silk piece-goods merchant in Kyoto, the commercial centre of the trade, may have a small factory of his own; but he obtains most of his supplies from other sources. Usually he has connections with large numbers of local merchants in the various silk-weaving districts, each of which often specializes on some particular type of fabric. The Kyoto merchant orders his requirements from these

[1] The *hibachi* is the ordinary heating apparatus used in a Japanese home. It takes the form of a container, made of metal, pottery, or wood, in which charcoal is burnt.

local merchants, who then buy the raw silk and give it out to groups of weavers. In localities where more highly standardized fabrics are made, the weaver may have a fair-sized mill with about fifty looms. But in other areas the fabric is woven in the home or by small manufacturers with under ten looms. Although looms driven by electric motors are now becoming common, handlooms are still typical of districts engaged in the upper branches of the trade. When the fabric comes into the hands of the Kyoto merchant, he sends it out again for dyeing, finishing, and embroidery work to other small specialists; and some goods may go out thirty or forty times before they are ready for the market. There are many variations in detail from the organization just described; but in broad outline these are typical methods. A good deal of the narrow cotton cloth used for Japanese dress is produced in much the same way, although the organization is rather less elaborate. The high-quality pottery trade also is conducted by craftsmen who impart to their products a style and individuality that the Japanese demand. All the famous *mei-butsu* (speciality) trades, for which the Japanese have long been renowned (such as the lacquer trade), are carried on in small units of production, and most of them are dominated by merchant employers, who finance the producers, co-ordinate their activities, and market the finished goods. These are the trades characteristic of a country that demands grace and beauty rather than abundance. They are becoming less important, and some are even declining absolutely through the influence of Western standards of consumption. But, in the aggregate, they still form a large section of the Japanese economy and they are likely to survive so long as Japan resists Americanization of taste which is their chief enemy.

There are other small-scale trades very different in type, namely, those which supply the populations of Japan and other Asiatic countries with inexpensive manufactured goods of kinds which are familiar to the West, and which fill the cheap stores of the United States and Britain with minor comforts. The goods include such things as knitted wares, rayon fabrics, some of the broad-width cotton fabrics, bicycles, electric lamps, pencils, rubber shoes, metal smallwares of all kinds, and toys. The workplace in these industries is usually a small factory with under fifty hands, or a little workshop that is sometimes merely part of the dwelling-house. The organization typical of many of these manufactures is found in the bicycle trade, especially the branch of it that produces cheap export goods. In the Osaka district hundreds of small workshops or factories of medium size specialize on some part or component of the bicycle. One makes the frame, another the handlebars, a third the hubs, a fourth the rims. All these producers work on contract for a merchant who sometimes supplies materials and even makes advances to equip the workplaces with machinery. The parts are taken to the merchant's warehouse, are then often sent out to small shops for enamelling, plating, and other finishing processes, and they finally return to him for assembly. There are a few big factories producing dearer bicycles for the Japanese market; but even these buy many of their semi-finished parts from small specialists. This organization is not unlike that found in the bicycle trade and other metal industries in Great Britain some fifty years ago.

The hosiery trade affords another example. The larger merchant houses have their own factories; but they all get the bulk of their supplies from little factories or shops in country districts. Some of these producers have power-machinery, some merely hand knitting machines. They receive the yarn from the merchant and each specializes on hosiery of a particular kind. When the knitted goods come into the warehouse, they are sent out again to home workers, who sew on buttons and perform other finishing processes. Much of the electric lamp trade is carried on in the same way. Miniature electric bulbs and automobile bulbs for export, and house lamps for the home market that are sold in the cheap stores for ten sen apiece, are mainly produced in little shops which employ under twenty persons and use no machinery except a vacuum pump. Here the merchant employer plays the same part as in the industries just described. In the woollen-weaving trades which have grown so rapidly in the last six years the small units are very common. In one of the woollen centres visited by the writer there was a large merchant who had thirty producers dependent upon him. The number of looms in each of their sheds ranged between twenty and fifty. The merchant supplied these weavers with yarn and with capital both for equipment and for paying wages, and he was responsible for supervising and directing all their activities. Producers with medium mills, when trade is brisk, themselves give out part of the yarn they receive to still smaller country weavers with from one to five looms.

These small shops have been appearing in remarkable numbers during recent years. Some of them were started by workers who were discharged from larger factories during the depression and who used their dismissal allowances to establish themselves in business. Some originated with farmers who previously carried on industry as a sideline. The producers have shown extraordinary flexibility in changing over to new trades as they have become more profitable, and many workshops are well equipped with power-driven machinery. Cheap Japanese machines of the simpler type both for textile and metal work are now used, and electric power is everywhere available.

The importance of the small unit in these trades is explained not so much by technical reasons, but rather by the abundance of labour and the scarcity and narrow diffusion of capital in present-day Japan. The pressure on the labour market, caused by agricultural depression, is so great that there is nothing in the nature of standard rates of pay. The small workshops are staffed by members of a family who work long hours for very low returns and by very cheap labour from the country. It does not pay an entrepreneur to risk capital in setting up a factory when he can obtain his supplies so cheaply from numerous small dependent suppliers. Yet some of these small producers—in the more rapidly growing trades—are extending the scale of their businesses. In the prospering bicycle trade and woollen trade, where they have earned fairly high rewards, they have reinvested these profits in their businesses and are beginning to free themselves from merchant control. All this must recall the position in many English manufacturing areas in the middle of the nineteenth century.

Most of these small-scale industries are engaged in the production of finished consumption goods, and their organization stands out in marked contrast to that found in the heavy industries and in some trades concerned with intermediate or semi-finished products. In the iron and steel, heavy engineering, shipbuilding, mining, rayon, chemical, flour-milling, sugar-milling, cotton-spinning, and wool-spinning industries the typical unit is the great factory characteristic of the twentieth century. The observer ought not to be surprised to encounter this contrast. The heavy industries and the trades producing standardized intermediate goods have been the first industries in all countries to adopt, for technical reasons, the large-factory system of organization. In Japan, however, special influences have been at work. Many of the industries are those considered necessary for national power and defence —iron and steel, shipbuilding and heavy engineering are obvious examples—and they have owed their rise to Government assistance in some form or other. A Government plant has from the outset been responsible for the larger part of the iron and steel output, and at present the Japan Iron Manufacturing Company—capitalized mainly by the State—turns out over 90 per cent. of the pig-iron and about half the crude steel. Private producers in this industry have received State encouragement in the form of subsidies, import duties, and tax exemptions. The same is true of shipbuilding and certain branches of engineering and mining. It applies also to the sugar industry. So, one can conclude that the large-scale trades would not have achieved their present magnitude had it not been for the Government's policy of encouraging them. This explanation, however, does not cover all the trades that are conducted in large factories. The great cotton industry, for instance, has owed little to Government support in recent years, and there are other large-scale industries of which the same may be said.

As Japan's cotton industry is one of the greatest of her manufacturing trades, and as many misconceptions about it are prevalent in popular writings on Japan in the West, a brief account of it may not be out of place. It is often supposed that the bulk of the industry is conducted by great integrated companies with interests in all its stages including merchanting, and that the typical mills, unlike their Lancashire counterparts, both spin and weave. Moreover, the typical Japanese firm and mill, as measured in spindleage and loomage, are sometimes said to be greater than their British counterparts. These views are scarcely borne out by the facts. About three-fifths of the wide piece-goods (in quantity), and all the narrow goods from which Japanese-style clothing is made, are turned out by small and medium-sized specialist weaving sheds.[1] Some of these sheds have under ten looms, of which a fair, though declining, proportion consists of handlooms, and sheds with under fifty looms account for nearly half of all the looms in the hands of specialist weavers.[2] The bulk of the Japanese output of drills, jeans, cotton satin, flannels, and fancy cloths of all kinds is produced by such sheds, which are equipped with "ordinary" (non-automatic) looms. It is only in the production of highly standardized piece-goods for export (such as shirtings and sheetings) that the large weaving sheds which form part of combined spinning-weaving mills are predominant. These sheds, of which the equipment consists almost entirely of automatic looms, are owned by firms that produce the greater part of the country's yarn output. Large though some of these firms are, it cannot be said that they overshadow the leading concerns in the Lancashire trade. An exact comparison of Japanese with Lancashire mills and firms is, however, very difficult. Because of the type of goods on which the two industries specialize, and the type of labour available, the "combined" mills in Japan use

[1] In 1935 about two-thirds of the total value of all cotton fabrics were estimated as the share of the specialist-weavers. *See* H. Miyake, "The Cotton Industry," in *Japan Times and Mail*, September 6th, 1936.

[2] Mitsubishi Economic Research Bureau, *Japanese Trade and Industry*, p. 242; and T. Uyeda and T. Minoguchi, *The Cotton Industry*, *passim* (I.P.R., International Research Series).

ring spindles and automatic looms, whereas in Lancashire about two-thirds of the working equipment in the spinning mills consists of mules and most of the looms are of the ordinary type. Yet a rough comparison is possible, at any rate for the spinning branch. The largest Japanese firm, Toyo Boseki, has 1½ million spindles compared with about 6 million in the Lancashire Cotton Corporation. The plants that the Japanese firms control are also, on an average, smaller than those found in Lancashire. In one sense, however, the Japanese scale of operation is larger; for her spinning and weaving mills (in this section of the industry, though not in the specialist weaving branch) are much more highly specialized than is usual in Lancashire.

For the narrow range of goods on which the combined mills are concentrating, this integrated organization and this scale of operations are probably more suitable than those found in Lancashire, which has indeed lost its foreign trade in these fabrics. It is wrong to conclude, however, by reference to data covering this section of the trade only, that the Japanese cotton industry as a whole possesses an organization superior to that of Lancashire. As already indicated, for fancies and specialities the organization found in Japan is very similar to that in Lancashire, and there is a strong tendency, now that Japan is finding this type of trade more profitable, for the great combined mill to decline in relative importance and for the greater part of the Japanese cotton industry to assume the structure familiar in England. Thus, it is rash to say that Japan's cotton industry as a whole is conducted in larger units than the Lancashire industry, or that her organization is necessarily superior.

In some of the other textile industries there are some very large mills and firms. This applies, for instance, to the wool-spinning trade. Yet the great mills in this industry produce both woollen and worsted yarn and, in addition, they also weave some kinds of worsted and woollen products. In other words, they are far less specialized than are the typical Yorkshire mills, where there is a division between the woollen and the worsted branches, and in the latter, between worsted spinning and worsted weaving. In the engineering industry the same generalization holds. Here there are some very large factories—the Hidatchi factory, for instance, employs over five thousand men—but each of them usually has a very wide range of products. This lack of specialization is an indication not of superiority in organization, but rather of immaturity. In engineering, as in the wool textile trade, the development has been comparatively recent, and the demand for each kind of product is still small compared with that in similar kinds of industry in Great Britain, Germany, or America. These factors, together with the narrow diffusion of capital in Japan, supply the chief explanation of the concentration of production in certain industries within a small number of large plants each with a wide range of output. Again, in the chemical industry, although some very large firms and factories have recently developed, there is nothing comparable to the great chemical trusts of America and Europe, and the typical chemical factory is smaller than it is here.

On the whole, then, Japan's progress towards mass-production, remarkable as it has been in some industries, such as cotton spinning and rayon spinning, should not be over-stressed. Several important trades, in which for technical reasons the large unit is essential, have depended for their rise upon Governmental financial assistance. In many other industries, where the factories are comparable in size to those of Europe and America, those factories are far less highly specialized than their counterparts in the West. It is only in a few industries (notably in that part of the cotton industry which is conducted in the "combined" mills) that the technical units are more highly specialized than those of comparable size in England; and, generally speaking, the contrast can be explained by the differences in the classes of goods with which Japan and England are respectively dealing.

Even in the large-scale trades a place for the small producer can generally be found in Japan. Wherever a large factory is erected, it soon becomes surrounded by multitudes of small workshops which perform subsidiary processes. The neighbourhood of the Kawasaki Dockyard at Kobe is populous with small machinists who are engaged upon jobs given out by the great factory. A large confectionery and chocolate works near Yokohama has attracted to its vicinity numerous small shops in which packing materials are produced. In the foreign-style china trade, the higher quality export goods are made in a few factories which in size and methods of production compare favourably with similar units in the West. Yet, in the lower quality trade the white "bodies" are produced for merchants or large factory-owners by small potters, each of whom specializes on a particular type of article, and the decorating is performed by other small specialists. Some Western observers, who have remarked on the prevalence in Japan of the small unit in the manufacture of goods which in England are produced in large factories, have taken this as an indication of the relative inefficiency of many Japanese industries. But this view is as unjustified as is the contrary belief that the large "combined" mill in part of the cotton trade is a superior form of organization to the specialized mill typical in Lancashire. These contrasts in scale and organization, where they do not depend upon differences in the types of goods produced, can be largely explained by reference to the relative scarcities of the various types of labour and of capital in the two countries.

What is remarkable about Japanese industrial life is not the size or nature of the technical units but the extent to which control over modern types of industries is concentrated in a few business houses. Large-scale manufacturing industry, mining, finance, transport, and foreign trade are all dominated by a very small number of great families known as the *Zaibatsu*, each of which has an enormous range of interests. Each of the four greatest *Zaibatsu* (Mitsui, Mitsubishi, Sumitomo, and Yasuda) owns a great bank, and together they account for one-third of the total bank deposits. Their trust companies have 70 per cent. of the trust deposits; their insurance companies dominate that branch of financial business. Their trading companies conduct one-third of the country's foreign trade; three *Zaibatsu* (Mitsui, Mitsubishi, and Sumitomo) have about half the tonnage of ocean-going ships; and two of them (Mitsui and Mitsubishi) own about half the shipbuilding capacity of the country. These four families and a very few others control nearly all the large plants in the heavy engineering, mining, electrical apparatus manufacture, brewing, paper, chemical, sugar, steel, non-ferrous metal, oil-refining and dealing, and food-canning industries. Even in the cotton industry, which is relatively independent of the *Zaibatsu*, Mitsui owns one of the three large cotton importing and exporting firms and one of the six largest cotton-spinning companies, besides many small ones. The *Zaibatsu* have great investments and properties abroad, from cotton plantations in the United States to iron mines in Malaya. A good deal of the Japanese capital invested in the development of the resources of China and Manchukuo as well as of the Japanese colonies has been provided by them. They have invested heavily in Government or in semi-official concerns, such as the Japan Iron Manufacturing Company, the South Manchurian Railway, and the "special" banks. The trust builders of America would have felt at home in their society.

The trading companies of the *Zaibatsu* have close connections with many small merchants and producers. Mitsubishi has invested much capital in providing equipment or working capital for small-scale weavers in the woollen trade, and Mitsui has done the same in several branches of agriculture. So, it must not be forgotten when the small scale of much of Japan's industry is being emphasized that this is often true of the technical unit only. In a wider sense, from a commercial or financial standpoint, the small enterprises are often part of a great business and could not exist without it.

It must be explained why economic control has become so highly concentrated in Japan. When Japan began her career of Westernization (only seventy years ago) the State was determined to create rapidly the material equipment and manufacturing enterprises necessary for national power and security. There was little experience of Western methods of industry and commerce. So in building up these new manufacturing industries, banking institutions, trading companies and a mercantile marine, the State had to rely on a few family businesses. Some of these, like Mitsui, had been important for centuries and had experience of large-scale enterprise (for instance the Mitsui departmental store employed one thousand persons in the eighteenth century). The Government induced these families to serve the ends it had in mind by giving them various privileges, such as subsidies. The more able among these family businesses absorbed the enterprises of the others and so enlarged their interests. Even to-day a wealthy middle class willing to invest in large-scale industry does not exist. A large part of the savings passes into the banks and trust companies of the *Zaibatsu* who use these resources to extend their sphere of control. The State relies on the *Zaibatsu* to initiate enterprises of national importance and to provide finance for the realization of its political ambitions. The *Zaibatsu* have lent large sums to the Government in time of war and they have supplied capital for the development of territories which have become Japanese possessions as a result of war, or for the building up of enterprises that contribute to national power. At present, for instance, the hydrogenation process and aluminium manufacture are being promoted by the *Zaibatsu* with Government encouragement. From these activities the *Zaibatsu* have derived great profits and they have become important instruments of national policy.[1]

The extent to which economic enterprises are owned by the State is often exaggerated. At the beginning of the Meiji era, and even before then, the Government established many enterprises; but before the end of the century most of them had passed into the hands of the *Zaibatsu*. The Government still owns the larger part of the railway system; it derives a considerable revenue from its camphor and tobacco monopolies; and it controls certain undertakings which are considered essential for national power and

[1] For further information about the *Zaibatsu*, *see* G. C. Allen, "The Concentration of Economic Control in Japan," in the *Economic Journal*, June 1937.

[*Reproduced by the courtesy of the N.Y.K. Line*

THE COUNTRYSIDE IN SPRING

security (such as the greatest iron and steel company and certain shipbuilding yards). In the colonies and Manchuria, also, much enterprise is under the control of the Government. In the sphere of finance, the famous exchange bank (the Yokohama Specie Bank), and the Industrial Bank of Japan and the Hypothec Bank, which were designed to provide long-term loans to industry and agriculture, as well as the Central Bank, are official concerns; and through the Postal Deposits Bureau a large part of the savings of the poorer classes is brought under Government control. But in most of the manufacturing industries State-ownership is not extensive, and the importance of its official banks has been declining with the rise of the ordinary commercial banks. Still, through its association with the *Zaibatsu*, the State has been able to exert considerable influence over industrial development, although it should be remembered also that the *Zaibatsu*, through their great financial powers, can also bring pressure on the Government. They are in a sense the agents of the State; but they are not passive agents, and in the post-War decade they became a major factor in the determination of policy.

The different parts of the Japanese economic landscape have now been briefly surveyed. We have passed over the rice-fields and tiny plots of earth where the peasants pursue their primitive tasks; over the widely scattered tradesmen who serve from their small workshops the everyday needs of the Japanese consumers; over the groups of craftsmen who produce special qualities of clothing, furniture, and utensils for the Japanese homes and their inhabitants; over the multitudes of quickly rising workshops and small factories where cheap, Western-style manufactured goods are turned out for sale at home and abroad; and then over the great factories and shipyards which produce both the capital-equipment needed by this most ambitious participant in industrial civilization and the competition for national power, and also the cheap textiles which now clothe the masses of Asia. We have finally to come to rest among the great business families in whom is concentrated so much of Japan's industry and finance, and without whose skill and energy (it must be admitted) Japan could never have attained her present level of economic development. These different groups in Japan's economic society confront each other not so much as competitors in the economic sense, for they are concerned with different branches of industry, but rather as representatives of different ways of life and as the upholders of rival social philosophies. The tension that these rivalries have created has passed into political life and has exercised a profound influence upon the policy of the State.

CHAPTER VII

ECONOMIC DEVELOPMENT UP TO THE WORLD DEPRESSION[1]

"The tide of business, like the running stream,
Is sometimes high and sometimes low,
A quiet ebb or a tempestuous flow,
And always in extreme."

JOHN DRYDEN (*after* HORACE)

IN the later years of the Tokugawa era, especially after the opening of the country to Westerners, both local and central governments began to establish industries modelled on those of the West. This policy was continued by the Meiji Government after the Restoration of 1868; for the leaders realized that until Japan had herself acquired the technical equipment that had been worked out in the West, a menace to her independence from ambitious European Powers would remain. The State naturally had to take the lead in this process of Westernization, because although there were a few business families with a long experience of large-scale undertakings, knowledge of modern industrial and financial technique was not widely diffused, and the great business families themselves had to be encouraged to direct their activities into lines favourable to the Government's political aims. But while many of the new enterprises were established by the State, it did not retain the ownership or administration of them once they were firmly rooted. There were some exceptions as was shown in the last chapter. But the main function of the State was not to exercise a detailed control over industrial and commercial life, but rather to set up certain economic objectives and to assist private enterprise (espe-

[1] Part of this chapter is based upon an article by the author which appeared in *Economic History*, January 1933. The author's thanks are due to the Editor of this journal for permission to make use of the material.

cially the great *Zaibatsu*) to attain them. In other words, its aim was to create the conditions which would lead the entrepreneurs to direct and organize the economic resources of the country in the way believed to be desirable. Only in this sense could the Japan of the pre-War period be said to possess a "planned economy."[1]

If the policy of building up a modern State was to be successfully and rapidly carried out, the Meiji Government had two main problems to solve. The first was the provision of capital for new enterprises. Railways, factories, and capital-equipment of all kinds had to be constructed within a short space of time in a poor community which had hitherto devoted its resources to the satisfaction of its immediate needs. The diversion of economic activity from the production of consumption goods to that of capital goods was achieved by resort to several expedients. Funds raised by taxation were invested by the State in new industries or were given as subsidies to existing enterprises regarded as worthy of encouragement. The State used its credit to raise loans both at home and abroad which were applied in the same way. Once an industrial and commercial class had been established, the State encouraged investment by the provision of cheap credit facilities through a group of semi-official banks, by subsidies, by the imposition of protective duties, and by framing its taxation system so that it pressed lightly on the profit-earner.[2] The decade before the Great War was the period in which these stimuli were administered with greatest effect. The successful issue of the Chinese War in 1895 and of the Russian War in 1905 made the policy much easier to pursue than formerly; for the consequent rise in political prestige enabled Japan to obtain fiscal autonomy after the first war and to borrow abroad at cheap rates after the second. So, during the early years of the present century, the protection granted to Japanese industries was steadily increased, the subsidization of certain industries and of the mercantile marine was made part of

[1] Cf. Bertrand Russell's statement: "Modern Japan is almost exactly what it was intended to be by the men who made the revolution of 1867." *The Scientific Outlook*, p. 212.

[2] H. G. Moulton, *Japan*, pp. 340–3.

a permanent policy, and the Government itself invested heavily in a number of enterprises, notably the Yawata iron and steel works, and in railway development.[1] In these circumstances it is not remarkable that the period 1904–13 constituted an era of very rapid economic expansion.

But the Japanese Government of the time was by no means concerned solely with economic objectives. The creation of an economic system such as might promote the maximization of the national income was far from being its only aim. It was also concerned with political security. For this reason it had fought against China and Russia. For this reason it embarked after 1895 on the development of the resources of Formosa, and after 1905 on colonial expansion in Korea. Political domination of these regions did not satisfy the Government. Japan wished also to develop their resources so as to provide herself with the raw materials she lacked, raw materials considered necessary to her political security. Thus, although the development of rice production in Korea, according to a Japanese economist, "was originally undertaken as a colonial policy based on human love,"[2] its prosecution was certainly pressed forward in later years because the domestic rice supply of Japan proper was becoming insufficient to satisfy the needs of the growing population. Economic penetration in parts of Asia outside the Empire was undertaken with the same ends in view. The efforts to develop the coal and iron resources of Manchuria and of the Yangtse valley were part of the policy of rendering Japan, which lacks coking coal and adequate supplies of ore, independent of foreign metallurgical industries, a policy which was also expressed in the establishment of the Government's iron and steel works, already mentioned.

The pursuance of these political objectives had important reactions on the country's economic life. After the Russian War,

[1] H. G. Moulton, *op. cit.*, pp. 322–3; also S. Uyehara, *The Industry and Trade of Japan*, pp. 251, 256 *et seq.*, 284; and J. E. Orchard, *Japan's Economic Position*, pp. 169, 222.

[2] Y. Yagi, "Relations between Japan and Korea as seen from the Standpoint of Rice Supply," *Kyoto Economic Review*, December 1931.

Japan's military and naval expenditure continued to increase;[1] while economic penetration in Asia involved the Government in heavy expenses and led to the establishment of official financial institutions, such as the colonial banks and the Oriental Development Company. These diverted Japanese capital to enterprises which would not otherwise have attracted investors and for which, in many cases, there was little economic justification. The policy of developing the Formosan sugar industry, for example, directed much capital into a colonial undertaking which could never have grown to substantial proportions without official subsidies and preferential treatment in the home market.[2] These schemes necessarily placed a considerable strain on State finances. The heavy additional taxation, which had been imposed at the time of the Russo-Japanese War as a temporary measure, was retained until the Great War;[3] and large loans were raised at home and abroad to finance this political and economic expansion. Japan's national debt (excluding certain special debts incurred at this time, such as the State railway and iron foundry debts) rose from 445 million yen in 1903 to over 2,000 million yen in 1912.[4] Of this last amount nearly three-quarters consisted of foreign debt. To some observers the situation was disquieting. The Government's expansionist policy had probably raised the productive powers of the nation to a level which they could not have attained in the same space of time under a *laisser-faire* régime. But it is obvious that a policy which involves the very rapid development of economic resources under the stimulus of Governmental financial assistance is likely to lead to instability if the State should be unable to maintain its bounties, and Japan's capacity for doing this was being weakened by her heavy expenditure in the pursuit of non-economic objectives.

The other major problem was bound up with foreign trade. For

[1] A. Andréadès, *Les Finances de l'Empire Japonais et leur Evolution*, pp. 69 *n.*, 74.

[2] S. Uyehara, *op. cit.*, pp. 284–6.

[3] A. Andréadès, *op. cit.*, pp. 70, 73.

[4] H. G. Moulton, *op. cit.*, p. 588.

the successful prosecution of her policy Japan urgently needed foreign capital equipment. Furthermore, her supply of raw materials was scanty, and heavy imports were therefore necessary for her growing manufactures. To acquire these goods in the quantities necessitated by her rapid economic growth, a substantial export trade had to be developed; for the policy of foreign borrowing could be regarded only as a temporary expedient. Consequently, the Government did its utmost to foster exports. As early as 1880, a special bank, the Yokohama Specie Bank, had been established by the State to finance foreign trade, and this bank still handles about half of the exchange business of the country. It has always had very close connections with the Bank of Japan, from which it has borrowed extensively for its operations, and the Central Bank is authorized to advance loans up to a certain amount to the Exchange Bank at a specially low rate of interest.[1] Thus, the merchant or industrialist engaged in the export trade was encouraged at the expense of those dealing with the home market. Subsidies to shipping and foreign trading companies and the provision of low railway rates on goods destined for export, formed part of the Government's scheme; and there was indeed a very great increase in exports between 1900 and 1914. In spite of this, however, the problem of the balance of payments gave rise to anxiety just before the War.[2] By then, Japan's annual payments had become not only heavy, but also highly inelastic, partly because of the necessity for providing interest on her large foreign loans, partly on account of military and naval expenditure abroad, and partly because of the imports of equipment and materials required for industrial development. A reduction of these imports, of course, would have meant an abandonment of the political and economic objectives which the Government had set up. The export trade, on the other hand, was liable to extreme fluctuations. This trade was highly specialized. In 1913 raw silk, silk fabrics, and cotton goods accounted for 55 per cent. of the total. Moreover, the exports

[1] J. Inouye, *Problems of the Japanese Exchange*, pp. 185–6.
[2] *Ibid.*, pp. 1–2.

were concentrated on a few markets. Nearly all the raw silk, by far the largest export, went to the United States, and cotton goods and other manufactures were sent mainly to China. In 1913, 64 per cent. of the exports went to these countries.[1] This reliance on two markets was a vulnerable feature of the trade, especially as the demand for raw silk was particularly liable to be affected by alternations of prosperity and depression in America.[2] Thus, while the amount of Japan's annual payments was relatively fixed, her receipts were subject to wide fluctuations; and at times the resulting financial strain was very great, especially as the Central Bank was not in a position to attract short-term funds to Japan.

These exchange difficulties were mitigated by the large foreign balances which Japan had begun to accumulate shortly after her adoption of the gold standard in 1897.[3] A proportion of these funds was owned by the Bank of Japan and was counted as part of the gold reserve against its note-issue. But, as a result of the adverse balance of payments, this exchange fund was diminishing rapidly in the four or five years prior to the War,[4] and had this process continued Japan would have been obliged, either to deflate her note-issue, or to abandon the gold standard. The former policy would inevitably have led to a period of intense industrial depression; the latter would have enforced a curtailment of imports and a loss of credit. Either result must have slowed down the tempo of Japanese economic expansion and enforced a change of general policy. This may throw some light on the apparently meaningless statement of a former Minister of Finance: "Japan is inherently an excess importer."[5] He meant, presumably, that the debit balance

[1] Sources of statistical data, unless otherwise stated, are the *Financial and Economic Annual of Japan* and the *Statistical Year-Book of the Empire of Japan.* For the purpose of these comparisons China includes Hong Kong and Kwantung.

[2] The American crisis of 1907 resulted in a steep decline in the value of Japan's exports of raw silk. Cf. S. Uyehara, *op. cit.*, p. 102.

[3] Matsukata, *Report on the Post-Bellum Financial Administration in Japan*, pp. 224–5.

[4] G. Odate, *Japan's Financial Relations with the United States*, p. 29.

[5] J. Inouye, *op. cit.*, p. 156.

of Japan on income account was certain to continue as long as the existing policy was pursued. The apparently insoluble problem which presented itself was: how could Japan maintain equilibrium in her balance of payments and at the same time press on with her schemes of economic and political expansion?

The War temporarily obscured the issue; for it not only permitted the expansionist policy to be pursued still more vigorously, but it also solved for a time the exchange and currency problems associated with that policy. After the middle of 1915 an urgent demand for Japanese goods and shipping services arose both from the belligerent Powers and also from countries deprived of their normal means of supply of manufactured goods. Consequently, the rate of industrial advance was accelerated and exports of manufactured goods grew very quickly. As far as can be calculated, the quantum of commodity exports increased by nearly 40 per cent. between 1913 and 1918; in value they more than trebled; and a favourable trade balance of great dimensions resulted. As invisible exports, chiefly in the form of receipts from shipping services, also increased, Japan's surplus on her trading account during the four years of war was very large, and by 1919 she had been transformed from a debtor to a creditor country.

The huge export surplus would normally have led to a gold drain to Japan. But owing to the embargoes on gold exports during the War, the yen rose high above par. Consequently, the Yokohama Specie Bank could not transmit the proceeds of its export bills to Japan, and, therefore, it found difficulty in maintaining advances to exporters. The Bank of Japan and the Government, however, desirous of facilitating exports, purchased the exchange banks' balances which had accumulated in New York and so provided funds for additional advances. As a result of these transactions the note-issue rose rapidly, prices increased, and further industrial growth was stimulated. The end of the boom in 1920 found Japan far more industrialized than in 1914, a creditor instead of a debtor country, and with short-term balances abroad amounting to over 1,300 million yen. Her domestic gold reserves had also greatly increased.[1]

The course of the post-War depression of 1920–1 in Japan was at first similar to that in other countries. A few industries, especially shipping and mining, which had greatly extended their capacity during the War, suffered from a chronic slump; but on the whole, although the post-War decade is now regarded by Japanese business men as a time of great difficulty, progress, if irregular, was not seriously checked. The Mitsubishi Index of Industrial Production, though limited in scope, provides some indication of the trend. It rose from 110 in 1924 (base year=1921–5) to 124 in 1926 and to 159 in 1929.[2] The rise in the production of certain important commodities is shown in the table on page 123.

This growth is to be accounted for in some degree by the persistence of the pre-War expansionist policy on the part of the State; and subsequent financial troubles bear out this view. In the first place, it is clear that the post-War liquidation of unsound undertakings was not carried so far in Japan as in the United States

Year	Bank of Japan's Index Number of Wholesale Prices (yearly averages)	Note-Issue of Bank of Japan (in million yen at end of year)	Gold Reserves of Bank and Government (in million yen) at end of year: At Home	Abroad
1913	100	426	130	246
1919	236	1,555	702	1,343
1920	259	1,439	1,116	1,062

International Debt and Investment Position

	Indebtedness to Foreigners (in million yen)	Investments Abroad (in million yen)	Net Position
1913	2,070	846	—1,224
1919	1,822	3,221	+1,399

(H. G. Moulton, *op. cit.*, p. 274.)

[2] The movements in the Index compiled by the Nagoya Commercial College (base year=1905) show the same tendency.

Year	All Products	Manufactured Goods
1913	157	164
1920	232	289
1924	258	366
1926	285	435
1929	328	532

or even as in England. A comparison of the movements of the wholesale price index numbers of the Bank of Japan and of the United States Bureau of Labour shows a much wider divergence between them after the end of 1920 than can be accounted for by differences in their composition. The index numbers suggest that during the next three years the purchasing-power parity between the yen and the dollar was roughly about 20 per cent. lower than the par rate of exchange. Japan was much criticized both by foreigners and by Japanese economists for her delay in returning to the gold standard and in carrying deflation to the degree necessary to implement that return, even at the expense

Year	Cotton Yarn (million lb.)	Raw Silk (thousand metric tons)	Coal (million tons)	Pig Iron (thousand metric tons)
1913	607	14·1	21·3	240
1921	725	23·4	26·2	473
1926	1,043	34·3	31·5	809
1929	1,117	42·3	34·3	1,087

of a prolonged depression in the industries which had been so greatly extended under the influence of high prices. But drastic action of this kind was, of course, entirely out of accord with the Government's expansionist policy. Furthermore, it conflicted with the paternal traditions of the Japanese State. *Laisser-faire* and its implications have never won much support in Japan, and classes suffering from economic change have usually been able successfully to claim financial assistance from the Government.[1] These claims were not resisted in 1920. In that year, for example, the State supported a silk valorization scheme, and in the following year, under the Rice Control Act, it attempted to relieve

[1] It has been suggested that the close association between the banking and the industrial interests in Japan makes it difficult for the Government to secure the financial co-operation necessary to carry out a deliberate deflationary policy. For a fuller treatment of this subject, see "The Recent Currency and Exchange Policy of Japan," in the *Economic Journal*, March 1925, pp. 76–8.

agricultural distress by operations designed to stabilize the price of that cereal. Schemes such as these resulted in very heavy losses to the Government[1] and were partly responsible for a great increase in its expenditure, which rose from 1,172 million yen in 1919–20 to 1,430 in 1922–23. This additional expenditure was covered by borrowing,[2] and thus the post-War liquidation was arrested in an early stage.

Although the Government was unable or unwilling to bring Japanese prices into line with those of the gold standard countries, it did not wish to see a depreciation in the exchange value of the yen. Thus the pre-War problem reappeared. Could Japan maintain exchange parity and at the same time press forward with her expansionist policy? But the problem seemed of little urgency in the early post-War years because of the huge foreign balances which had been accumulated during the War. The Government now resold these balances to the exchange banks to enable them to meet their import bills, and the yen was maintained at within 3 per cent. of dollar parity. Thus, from 1921 until the end of 1923 the yen was over-valued on the exchanges. This helped to restore the import surplus and the foreign balances steadily diminished. This phase of Japanese financial history may be compared with events in Great Britain between 1925 and September 1931. This country, which was unable to bring its internal prices into line with those of the world, succeeded in maintaining the over-valued pound at par by attracting short funds to London, until the withdrawal of these funds during the financial crisis of 1931 drove the country off the gold standard. Similarly, Japan kept the exchange value of her currency at an artificially high level by drawing on her foreign balances until September 1923, when the Kwanto earthquake, which necessitated the purchase of huge quantities of reconstruction materials, so reduced these balances that further support of the exchange became impracticable. By April 1924 the exchange had fallen to under 40 dollars to the 100 yen (par being

[1] During the first seven years the cost to the Government of its operations under the Rice Control Act amounted to 221 million yen, excluding losses likely to be incurred in the disposal of rice still in stock. H. G. Moulton, *op. cit.*, p. 318.

[2] A. Andréadès, *op. cit.*, p. 90.

49·85), and until the end of 1925 the yen remained about 20 per cent. depreciated.

The earthquake led to a further period of inflationary finance. The rapid reconstruction of Tokyo and Yokohama was considered essential, and firms whose assets had been adversely affected by the disaster had to be assisted. Easy credit conditions necessarily accompanied this policy; and in order to relieve financial institutions whose assets had become frozen as a result of the earthquake, and to accelerate the work of reconstruction, the Bank of Japan was authorized to discount specified bills (Earthquake Bills) under a Government guarantee against loss up to the limit of 100 million yen. The increased Governmental expenditure resulting from the earthquake was borne partly by the disposal of most of its remaining foreign balances, but mainly by borrowing both at home and abroad. The national debt (excluding the special debts) was about 75 per cent. greater in 1926 than in 1918. At the same time, local and colonial government indebtedness greatly increased, and public utility companies all over Japan raised large sums at home and abroad for public works.[1] Prices rose sharply in 1924 and 1925 and there was a boom in most branches of industry. Thus, just as the Government's policy had served to check deflation after 1920, so, after 1923, it led to a further period of inflation.[2]

[1] H. G. Moulton, *op. cit.*, pp. 306 *et seq.*, 495.

[2]

Year.	Bank of Japan's Index Number of Wholesale Prices (1913 = 100).	Note-Issue of Bank (in million yen at end of year).
1921	200	1,547
1922	196	1,588
1923	199	1,704
1924	207	1,662
1925	202	1,632

	Gold Reserves of Government and Bank (in million yen at end of year). At Home	Abroad
1920	1,116	1,062
1921	1,225	855
1922	1,215	616
1923	1,208	445
1924	1,175	326
1925	1,155	258
1926	1,127	230

The situation was obviously unstable. A long series of unbalanced budgets and much reckless borrowing seemed to threaten the yen with the disasters that had engulfed so many other post-War currencies. In 1926 the Government, doubtless influenced by the British return to the gold standard in the previous year, attempted to restore financial stability. Economies were effected in administration, new taxes were imposed, and, as a preliminary to the removal of the gold embargo, the Government tried to secure the liquidation of the outstanding Earthquake Bills.[1] The first effect of this new policy was to give rise to speculation in the yen on the part of operators in Shanghai and New York, and from a low level of 41 dollars in November 1925 the exchange rose to just under par in the early months of 1927. This rise in the exchange disorganized the exporting industries, particularly the raw-silk producers, and a severe financial crisis followed in the spring of 1927. The crisis was the inevitable result of the attempt to check the boom. For several years Japan had been stimulated by inflationary finance, and a reversal of the policy was bound to have disturbing effects. Yet the alternative appeared to be a heavy depreciation in the currency.

The course of the crisis deserves a moment's attention. In April 1927 the Government proposed to compensate the Bank of Japan for losses incurred in discounting Earthquake Bills by delivery to it of Government bonds. Bonds were also to be lent to the ordinary banks for the same purpose. Parliamentary discussion of these proposals revealed the extent to which banking assets were frozen, and provided the occasion for the crisis. It developed into a panic. There was a run on the banks and they responded by attempting to call in loans. Ultimately thirty-six banks, including the Bank of Formosa, a semi-official bank which was deeply involved in the Suzuki sugar interests, and the Peers' Bank, suspended payment. A moratorium had to be proclaimed, and the

[1] Cf. T. Jones, "The Recent Banking Crisis and Industrial Conditions in Japan," in *Economic Journal*, March 1928; and J. Inouye, *op. cit.*, pp. 123 *et seq.*

State guaranteed advances by the Central Bank amounting to 700 million yen. The panic was arrested by these measures; but by this time the Government whose policy had produced the crisis had lost office,[1] and its attempt to restore the gold standard was abandoned by its successor. It is true that the crisis brought about a fall in prices and some liquidation of frozen credit conditions; but the State could not carry through the drastic measures necessary to implement a return to gold.

The crisis involved the extensive readjustment of industry to the new price conditions; but it does not appear to have given more than a temporary check to expansion. However, this proceeded at a slower rate than during the previous period. Although there was a rapid growth in certain new industries, some of the older staples, such as mining and cotton manufacture, grew very slowly, and there does not appear to have been any increase in industrial employment between 1927 and 1929. The fact that industrial development during this period, though real, was unevenly distributed is indicated by the widespread resort to output-restriction schemes on the part of many industries which had extended their plants during the post-earthquake boom. Meanwhile, the failure of the Government's deflationary policy of 1926–7 was followed by further budgetary deficits, and it was not until the summer of 1929, when the Minseito party came into office with a programme of deflation and economy, that a serious attempt to secure budgetary equilibrium was made.

Throughout the post-War period, in addition to the stimulus of cheap credit provided by the Government and its financial institutions, several important Japanese industries continued to receive official subsidies. Throughout this period, too, economic penetration in Asia was pushed forward. Too much space would be required to examine this penetration in detail, or to assess the net advantages that have accrued to Japan as a result of it. But this at least can be said. Although the development of continental resources led to a substantial interchange of raw materials and

[1] See Chapter V, p. 88.

manufactured goods between Japan and the regions in which she had acquired "special interests," yet there were grave disadvantages associated with her policy. State finances were burdened by many unremunerative loans made for the purpose of extending Japanese control. The iron-ore resources of Manchuria and China Proper, in the development of which much Japanese capital had been invested, proved insufficient for the needs of the iron and steel producers, and Japan was forced to look further afield for her ores, to the Malay Peninsula and to north-western Australia. Ironically enough, the development of the coal mines belonging to the South Manchuria Railway was retarded after 1926 by limitations imposed on coal imports into Japan for the benefit of domestic coal-owners. Later, attempts were made to restrict imports of Korean rice, the production of which the Government had been at great pains to encourage, so as to protect the Japanese peasants. Thus, a conflict arose between what were conceived to be the interests of the State and the interests of particular industrial groups. Most serious of all, the Chinese "rights recovery" campaign was threatening Japanese interests in Manchuria and, through the boycotts that were associated with it, was damaging the export trade in manufactured goods to China proper. It was thus becoming increasingly difficult for Japan to reconcile her two policies, political and economic penetration and the development of exports.

Before we deal with Japan's financial history in the period immediately after 1927, it is well to glance at the country's international trade during the post-War period. In 1919, according to the estimates of Professor Shibata, the volume of both exports and imports was about 30 per cent. higher than in 1913. After a fall in 1920 it rose steadily, except in 1923—the earthquake year—and by 1929 it was more than twice as great as in 1913.[1] Professor Shibata's figures, moreover, underestimate the actual increase that has taken place, for they do not cover the trade of Japan Proper with her colonies. The proportion of the exports taken by the colonies to

[1] For Shibata's Index see foot of next page.

[*Reproduced by the courtesy of the N.Y.K. Line*

AUTUMN IN THE COUNTRYSIDE

the total rose from 11·6 per cent. in 1913 to 17·5 per cent in 1929, and as Professor Shibata's Index stands at 233 for the latter year, we can conclude that Japan's total exports were about two and a half times as great in 1929 as they were in 1913. In spite of a rise in invisible receipts, the balance of payments on income account was adverse for every year between 1920 and 1928 (inclusive). From the figures given by Mr. H. G. Moulton and Mr. Juichi Ko, it would appear that the aggregate deficiency of the period 1920–28 amounted to 1,700 million yen.[1] As before the War, expansionist financial policy and an adverse balance of payments were inevitably associated. The rigidity of the Japanese demand for foreign currencies was, in one respect, even more pronounced than in pre-War days; for the home production of foodstuffs was becoming

Shibata's Index of Volume of Japan's Foreign Trade
(Excluding Trade with Colonies)

Year	Exports	Imports
1913	100·0	100·0
1920	105·1	119·2
1921	115·3	134·0
1922	144·5	170·0
1923	118·0	167·2
1924	154·8	185·1
1925	186·1	183·0
1926	191·5	206·2
1927	207·8	226·4
1928	212·0	216·1
1929	233·0	221·1
1930	195·3	189·4
1931	196·2	210·1
1932	219·5	216·5
1933	214·0	236·8
1934	240·1	245·6

(Tokyo Association for Liberty of Trading, *A Brief Analysis of Japan's Foreign Trade*, p. 23.)

[1] H. G. Moulton, *op. cit.*, pp. 517 *et seq.*

increasingly insufficient for requirements. Whereas before the War Japan imported only about 5 per cent. of her rice consumption, during the greater part of the last decade her annual imports amounted to between 15 and 20 per cent. of the consumption, although her own production of rice also greatly increased.[1] This change was associated with the growth in the population by about 15 per cent. in the post-War decade. In estimating the significance of the rise in production and foreign trade as a whole, this increase in the population must, of course, be taken into account.

Meanwhile, certain of the leading characteristics of the export trade were accentuated.[2] We have seen that before the War about 55 per cent. of the value of exports consisted of raw silk, silk tissues, cotton yarns and fabrics; by 1928–29 this proportion had risen to 66 per cent. Thus the export trade became even more specialized than formerly. The concentration of the trade on a few markets also increased. The United States and China, which took 64 per cent. of the exports before the War, in 1928-29 took 68 per cent. India then took about 10 per cent. of the total exports. Thus the economic advance of Japan, her ability to import the commodities necessary for her expansion, depended on her capacity for selling increasing quantities of silk to America and of cottons and other manufactures to China and India. The growth in the American market for silk was especially marked in the post-War period, and this accounts for the increase in the proportion of silk in the total export trade from 30 per cent. in 1913 to 37 per cent. in 1928–29. In a large measure, therefore, the growth in Japan's export trade, and, so, her capacity for economic expansion since the War, was bound up with "American prosperity." Apart from the danger arising from this degree of dependence upon a

[1] This loses some of its significance when it is found that most of Japan's imports of rice in this period came from her colonies, which are part of her monetary system.

[2] In this paragraph, as elsewhere in this chapter, by "export trade" is meant the trade of Japan Proper with countries outside her own Empire.

single commodity and a single market, there were features of the trade that made it especially vulnerable. Raw silk, as shown in Chapter VI, is produced by the peasantry. As this class was suffering from the diminishing returns to agriculture, it was devoting itself more and more to satisfying the American demand for silk. But partly because production in Japan grew even faster than the demand, and partly because of the competition of artificial silk and Chinese silk, the price of raw silk fell much more than general prices after 1923.[1] As the cost of production of raw silk was not considerably reduced, it is clear that the great expansion of the silk-export trade took place only because the peasants were willing to work harder without compensation in proportion to their efforts. Obviously this process could not continue indefinitely. The impoverishment of the peasants even before 1929 had already produced grave social problems, and any contraction of the American demand was bound to have serious reactions on their position.

At this point Japan's financial history may be resumed. The Minseito Government, which came into office in the summer of 1929, immediately put into operation its programme of reducing public expenditure and returning to gold. The moving spirit behind this policy was Mr. Inouye, Minister of Finance. He was a man of great experience and ability. He had for years been conducting a campaign in favour of deflation and a removal of the gold em-

1

Year	Bank of Japan's Index Number of General Wholesale Prices (1913 = 100)	Index Number of Silk Prices (1913 = 100)
1923	199	236
1924	207	203
1925	202	214
1926	179	175
1927	170	148
1928	171	142
1929	166	141

bargo, and by this time he had convinced the industrial interests that the fluctuations of the exchange were more harmful to them than would be the adjustments needed to restore the gold standard. His policy, known as the "No Loan" policy, was launched under what appeared to be favourable circumstances. Trade was improving in 1929; the continuance of "American prosperity" was causing an exceptionally rapid expansion in the demand for raw silk; the increased demand for Japanese cotton goods on the part of India was assisting the other great export; the general improvement in foreign commerce was raising receipts from the mercantile marine; and a series of remarkably good harvests was reducing rice imports to insignificant dimensions. In 1929 the balance of payments appears to have been favourable to Japan for the first time since 1919. Further, although the short-term balances held abroad had become very small, the ratio of the Bank of Japan's gold reserve to its note-issue was 65 per cent. and to its note-issue and deposits combined, 49 per cent. There seemed, therefore, ample security against speculative withdrawals of funds once the yen had reached par. The announcement of the new Government's policy led to a rise in the exchange from its low level of 43 dollars in June 1929, and the embargo was removed in January 1930.

No more unfortunate moment could have been chosen for the operation of this new policy. Even had the world boom continued, the rise in the exchange value of the yen and the fall in domestic prices would have placed a strain on the economic system, especially as financial relations had been for such a long period in a process of consolidation at a level of prices well above that of the world. But the steep decline in world prices which coincided with the return to the gold standard accentuated the difficulties of adjustment. Japan, having insulated herself against world price movements throughout the post-War decade, committed herself to following them at a moment of drastic decline. The Japanese wholesale price index fell between June 1929 and December 1930 by 46 points, or 27 per cent., a much greater decline than that of the indices of the United States or England.[1] Japanese financial authorities assumed that this fall in the price index, which was accompanied by steep declines in wages and in costs of production, was an indication that their country had adjusted itself to the new situation.[2] But this view was too optimistic. Japan was unable to maintain the balance of payments without large shipments of gold, and the Bank lost 260 million yen, about a quarter of its gold reserve, during the year.

The chief source of the country's difficulties was the collapse of "American prosperity" and, with it, of the demand for raw silk. In April 1929 the average monthly price of a standard grade of raw silk at Yokohama was 1,401 yen per 100 kin; in December 1929 it was 1,169 yen and a year later it had fallen to 625 yen.[3] Raw-silk exports (which represented over 36 per cent. of the entire export trade in 1929) amounted in 1930 to only 53 per cent. of their value in the previous year. The peasantry suffered terrible distress in consequence, and the Government was obliged to modify its financial policy. In the Spring of 1930 it launched a scheme for the valorization of silk that proved very expensive, and it was impelled to increase its expenditure on public works in rural areas and to give financial assistance to the distressed classes of producers. These additional expenses, together with the fall in receipts from taxation, forced the Government to abandon its "No Loan" policy. Although the collapse of the American market was the chief cause of the trouble, Japanese sales of manufactured

[1] The decline in the Bank of Japan's note-issue is also indicative of the severity of the deflation:

Year	Note-Issue (in million yen at end of year)
1928	1,678
1929	1,603
1930	1,426
1931	1,324

[2] Cf. Baron K. Iwasaki, "The Economic Outlook in Japan," in *A Picture of World Economic Conditions at the Beginning of 1932* (National Industrial Conference Board).

[3] *The Japan Silk Year-Book*, 1935–36, p. 229.

goods in Asia were also affected, though somewhat less seriously, by the world slump. Exports of cotton tissues declined by 34 per cent. in value and 12 per cent. in quantity. The value of the entire export trade in 1930 was 32 per cent. less than that of the previous year. This decline was far greater than that experienced by world trade as a whole.

In 1931 the situation quickly deteriorated. The Government was obliged to resort extensively to borrowing to meet its expenses, as resistance to deflation became stronger. The decline in raw silk at Yokohama continued, and the total value of raw-silk exports in that year amounted to only about 46 per cent. of that attained in 1929. Exports of textiles and other leading manufactures also dropped sharply. The following table shows how the export trade as a whole was affected.[1]

Year	Volume of Exports (1913 = 100)	Value of Exports (in million yen)
1929	233	2,149
1930	195	1,470
1931	196	1,147

As imports also fell steeply, the rise in the adverse balance of trade was relatively small—from 67 million yen in 1929 to 89 million yen in 1931—but the loss of confidence that the intense depression caused resulted in a flight from the yen, and there were further heavy losses of gold by the Central Bank.

Throughout the year the Government made determined efforts to preserve the yen; but these efforts aroused antagonism in powerful sections of the community. The Finance Minister, in order to reduce his budgetary deficit, pressed for a reduction in military

[1] This table does not cover trade between Japan Proper and her colonies. This inter-Empire trade declined substantially, though not to the same extent as Japan's foreign trade. Consequently, the proportion taken by the colonies of Japan's total exports rose from 18 per cent. in 1929 to 21 per cent. in 1930 and to 22 per cent. in 1931.

and naval expenditure. But this proposal enraged the military and naval cliques which were already incensed by the Government's conciliatory attitude towards China and by its policy at the London Naval Conference of 1930.[1] As already shown, the military and naval cliques had been losing their power during the post-War decade; but the depression, by discrediting the financial and industrial groups and the politicians who depended on them, caused a change in popular opinion. The collapse of "American prosperity," indeed, was indirectly responsible for undermining constitutional government in Japan and for throwing power into the hands of groups hostile to parliamentary methods. The course of political change during these years, however, will be traced elsewhere; and here only the final events in the financial sphere that brought this period in Japanese history to an end need be referred to.

A serious blow was given to the Government's deflationary policy by Great Britain's abandonment of the gold standard in September 1931. Immediately, exports of manufactures and the receipts of the mercantile marine began to suffer from British competition; while Japan's financial position was weakened by the depreciation of its funds in London.[2] At the same time, the Government, unable to restrain the military group from its Manchurian adventure, found its finances still more severely strained. The flight from the yen was accentuated, and the gold reserve dwindled until, towards the end of the year, it was less than half the amount at which it stood in January 1930.[3] In December, the Government fell, the embargo on gold was re-imposed, and the exchange value of the yen was allowed to slide downwards. Two months later, what were regarded as the economic consequences of Mr. Inouye provoked a "patriotic" association to murder him. Thus, the great

[1] *See* Chapter X, pp. 186 *et seq.*

[2] The Japanese banks are said to have held about 100 million yen in London in September 1931. See *The Financial Times, Japanese Supplement*, February 29, 1932, p. 15.

[3] *Ibid.*, p. 1; and *Statistical Year-Book of the League of Nations*, 1931–32, p. 263.

depression overwhelmed the peasantry, gave a serious check to industrial development, brought an end to "orthodox" financial policy and shattered the Government that had tried to pursue it. With that Government there disappeared, also, the more liberal influences in Japanese political life, and the forces of democracy and internationalism that had been making a tentative yet real advance in the post-War decade were thrown back in disaster and confusion.

CHAPTER VIII

INDUSTRIAL RECOVERY AND THE INVASION OF MARKETS

> "*Whether we may not, with common Industry, and common Honesty, under-sell any Nation in Europe?*"
>
> GEORGE BERKELEY

THE first post-War decade was regarded by the majority of contemporary English business men as a period of chronic depression; it was only when the world slump occurred in 1929 that they began to realize that they had been in error and that what they had taken for a depression was actually a period of growth and activity. In much the same way, the Japanese business man now thinks of the years from 1920 to 1931 as a time of stagnation in trade. Yet, except in the last two years of that period, industrial output and foreign trade advanced substantially, as was shown in the last chapter. The reasons for this misconception are the same in both countries. In Japan as in England, the period was one in which maladjustments caused by the Great War were in process of correction, and in which first one part and then another part of industry was subjected to severe pressure on account of violent changes in prices and exchange rates. Japanese manufacturing industry, especially the heavy trades, had been stimulated by the War and her price level had risen very high. In the early post-War years, therefore, she was compelled to effect a redistribution of labour among different industries; her heavy industries had to contract; and high-cost producers were weeded out as the price-level fell. This process, however, was not continuous. It was checked for a time by the earthquake of 1923 which was followed by another period of rising prices and great activity in the constructional trades—a period which came to an end in the financial crisis of 1927. From then until the beginning of the world slump, the process of adjustment and industrial reorganization was resumed. There was a weeding out of inefficient firms that only could exist in times of boom; and although production grew, yet industrial development was uneven. Business men whose anxieties are intensified in periods of quickly changing conditions of demand and price naturally overlook the progress that may then occur. For this reason the post-War decade lingers in the memory of the Japanese as a time of stagnation, although figures of trade and output provide weighty evidence to the contrary.

There can be no doubt, however, about the intense depression from which Japan suffered in 1930 and 1931, and the circumstances of this depression have been sufficiently described in the previous chapter. Nor can one question either the rapidity of the recovery that occurred in 1932 after Japan had left the gold standard or the remarkable industrial development in subsequent years. The magnitude of this growth in industry as a whole and in certain fields is shown by the following tables:[1]

Indices of Industrial Production

Year	Oriental Economist 1928 = 100	Mitsubishi 1927 = 100
1929	110	121
1930	109	114
1931	108	109
1932	124	117
1933	148	139
1934	166	154
1935	192	170
1936	212	179

[1] Only Japan Proper is covered by these tables.

Production of Certain Commodities

Year	Rayon Yarn (million lb.)	Cotton Yarn (million lb.)	Pig Iron (thousand metric tons)	Steel (thousand metric tons)	Woollen and Worsted Yarn (million lb.)
1929	29	1,117	1,087	2,034	64
1930	36	1,010	1,162	1,921	55
1931	47	1,027	917	1,663	78
1933	90	1,240	1,424	2,792	101
1935	201	1,424	1,907	4,028	113
1936	262	1,462	2,120	4,640	123

The remarkable growth in industrial production as a whole is not the only significant feature of this period. Before 1929, as we have seen, Japanese manufacturing industry, so far as it was engaged in the production of Western-style products, was highly specialized. The textile trades then provided about half of the total employment in manufacturing industry (excluding employment in workplaces with under five persons), and the cotton and silk industries were responsible for about 90 per cent. of employment in textile factories. Since then, although the textile trades have grown, other industries have grown faster, and the textile industries now provide only two-fifths of the total employment in manufacturing industry. Among the textiles themselves, the greatest progress has been made in newer branches of the industry like rayon-weaving, wool-spinning, wool-weaving, and hosiery—trades that were of little importance before 1929. But the industrial groups that have made the most spectacular growth have been the metallurgical and chemical. The output of steel and of engineering products, formerly very small, has now become very substantial, and in the production of rayon yarn Japan rivals the United States. It is not merely the large-scale trades that have expanded since recovery began in 1932. A host of minor small-scale industries have sprung up or have grown very quickly during the last five years—among them the trades producing metal smallwares, electric bulbs and cheap finished consumption goods in endless variety. So the Japanese industrial system, since its recovery from the depression, has been developing on new lines, and it is now far less specialized than it was a decade ago.

The extension in the scope of manufacturing enterprise is forcibly brought out by a glance at export figures. The value of exports, having fallen from 2,148 million yen in 1929 to 1,147 million yen in 1931, rose after that date and reached 2,693 million yen in 1936 and 3,175 million yen in 1937.[1] This growth was accompanied by a pronounced change in the composition of the trade. In 1928–29 nearly 38 per cent. of the total value of exports consisted of raw silk (including waste); while silk manufactures and cotton yarn and manufactures together accounted for about 28 per cent. In 1935-36 the proportion of raw silk exports (including waste silk) to the total had fallen to 15 per cent.; and silk manufactures and cotton yarn and manufactures stood at just under 25 per cent. In other words, these major textile goods, which made up nearly two-thirds of the total exports in 1928-29, accounted for only two-fifths in 1935–36. Even though exports of cotton tissues grew by over 50 per cent. in quantity and 17 per cent. in value between 1929 and 1936, their proportion to the total had fallen between those two dates. This change was associated with a rapid development in the exports of a multitude of minor exports, from canned goods, rayon and woollen textiles, to metals, machinery, toys, and miscellaneous consumption goods. There has been a change of equal importance in the markets to which the exports are sent. In 1928-29 the United States took 42·2 per cent. of the exports, China (including Manchuria, Hong Kong, and Kwantung Province), 26·1 per cent., and these two areas together with British India and the Dutch East Indies took four-fifths of the exports. By 1935–36 exports to America had fallen absolutely and the proportion was only 21·7 per cent.; China and Manchukuo took 25·9 per cent.; and the four areas mentioned above were responsible by then for only 63 per cent. of the exports.

[1] Excluding exports to Japanese colonies.

It is clear, then, that the tendency of the post-War decade, when the export trade was becoming more highly specialized both in markets and commodities, has been reversed. Japan's export trade now has a much broader basis than before the depression. These relative changes have become pronounced since recovery set in after 1931.

Having set out the facts, we must now consider how it is that Japan has been able to make such a great advance in production and exports in the last five years, and how it has been possible for her to diversify her production, trade, and markets so successfully. Several explanations have been put forward by European and American observers, and it will be well to consider each of them in turn.

It is often said that the main reason for the recovery has been the heavy depreciation in the exchange value of the currency. In terms of gold this fall, has, of course, been much heavier than that of sterling, and since the middle of 1933 the yen has stood at about 1s. 2d., compared with its par rate of about 2s. There can be no doubt that progress in foreign trade has been associated with the decline in the exchange; but it cannot be assumed that this decline was the result of manipulation by the Government or that the currency has been undervalued on the exchanges during the last few years. Deliberate undervaluation of the currency is, of course, the implication of writers who emphasize this aspect of Japan's recovery. Yet, if their views were correct, one would expect that Japan would have developed a large export surplus, or at any rate that she would have piled up foreign credits. For this there is no evidence whatever. Imports have risen even faster than exports since 1931; the adverse trade balance has increased; and there has been no accumulation of gold or short-term balances abroad. The fall in the yen may have been carried somewhat further than would otherwise have happened by the encouragement given by the State to heavy investment in Manchukuo; but this effect has been indirect, and the Government has done something to counteract it by exercising supervision over transfers of capital from Japan to other markets. During the last two years, indeed, the anxiety of the financial authorities has been to prevent a further depreciation of the yen rather than to encourage it, and since the beginning of 1937 import and foreign exchange dealings have been regulated by licence with that end in view. Japan, therefore, can easily refute the charge that she deliberately manipulated the yen in order to stimulate her export trade.

Japan's successful competition is attributed by some writers to the relatively low wages paid to her workers; but this, too, is an unsatisfactory explanation. The wages of other Asiatic workers compare even less favourably with Western European wages, and yet producers in those countries have not encroached on the established markets of Western manufacturers. Workers in the textile industry of Japan and of Britain receive higher wages than do similar types of workers in India or China; but this disparity does not preclude both Japan and Britain from having a market for their textile products in those countries. Wage differences alone cannot be a major cause of the development of Japanese exports and of the dwindling markets for certain Western manufactured goods in Japan; for, a few decades ago, when Japanese competition in these fields was unimportant, the differences were even greater. Some writers, however, go on to suggest that recent developments are to be explained by a fall in Japanese wages since the depression, and they imply that this fall has made competition between Japan and Western countries in some way "unfair" and that equity demands a greater uniformity. The wage problem as a whole will be considered in the next chapter, but we shall show in a moment how this implication is to be regarded.

Finally, many Japanese and some Westerners claim that Japan's success in manufacturing trades since 1931 is to be attributed to a rise in industrial efficiency. This explanation seems at first sight the least convincing; for great improvements in technique have been effected in Western industries in the last eight years, and it seems incredible that the Japanese rate of advance in this field can have been so much faster than that of her competitors as to make possible extensive inroads into their established markets. This point, too, will be dealt with presently.

Now, none of these explanations, taken alone, is satisfactory. The recent industrial progress has, it is true, been associated with the movements in exchange rates, wages, and efficiency; but the association is not so simple as is often suggested. No single movement can be said to be the *cause* of that progress, and, paradoxical as the statement may appear, the best approach to an understanding of the problem is by considering the fortunes of the single major industry which has not shared in the general increase in production and exports. The steep decline in the value of raw-silk exports after 1929 has already received comment. From 784 million yen in 1929 these exports fell to 375 million yen in 1931, and in subsequent years there was only a slight recovery, so that in 1936 they amounted to only 393 million yen, about half their pre-depression value.[1] In 1929 nearly two-fifths of Japan's exports consisted of this commodity, and the heavy fall in silk exports meant a substantial decline in the income which Japan could obtain from abroad. The yen probably became overvalued as soon as Japan's exchange reached par in the later months of 1929—even before the depths of the slump in silk had been reached—and it was impossible for her to sell other kinds of goods abroad to compensate for this fall in raw-silk income at the level of exchange that was maintained in 1930 and 1931. The deflation of that period was undertaken in order to bring down costs to a level at which these alternative exports would be possible; but it could not be carried far enough, in view of the conditions of international trade as a whole, to reach a successful issue. Consequently, the yen had to be allowed to fall until it reached a point at which the prices of Japanese manufactured goods in foreign markets were low enough to attract a demand for them sufficiently large to secure equilibrium in the balance of payments. Had the demand for silk been elastic, then the fall in the yen might have led to a recovery in that export. But the demand for that commodity proved highly inelastic, partly because of the competition of other textiles, especially rayon, and partly because the demand came almost entirely

[1] In 1937 these exports were valued at 407 million yen.

from a single country, the United States. Markets for manufactured goods were more diversified, and the demand for them more elastic, and so equilibrium was secured by this substitution of exports of manufactures for exports of raw silk. At its simplest, then, the rise in Japanese manufacturing industry and in exports of manufactured goods after 1931 can be attributed to a chain of causes that were set in operation by the heavy slump in silk, and the failure of silk prices to recover meant that this tendency was carried further in later years. The exchange depreciation was part of the process by which this substitution of one group of commodities for another group in the export trade, and the transference of resources from one kind of industry to another, were effected. There was no deep-laid scheme for ruining Western manufacturers; the Japanese Government did not plan this great advance in exports of manufactured goods. The explanation is to be sought in the working out of a set of economic forces with which every country at some time and in some degree has been familiar.

This process of substitution was associated with a downward movement in industrial wages; while the depreciation of the yen was arrested at an earlier stage than might otherwise have occurred because of the improvements in efficiency effected during the deflationary period. These movements deserve further consideration. The fall in silk prices meant a heavy reduction in the income of the rural community. The farmer's receipts from sales of his cocoons declined, and the volume of employment and the wages provided by the reeling mills to the female members of his family were lowered. At the same time merchants and landowners who previously furnished the capital for the industry found fewer opportunities for profitable investment in it. Thus, strong economic pressure was brought to bear on these producers causing them to transfer their activities elsewhere.[1] The male members of the

[1] The prices of other agricultural products also fell very steeply. The price of rice, the chief crop, fell from an average of 29·0 yen per koku in 1928 to 18·5 yen in 1931 (for a standard grade in the Tokyo market), and in 1933 it rose to only 21·5 yen, in spite of the efforts of the Government to raise the price by various devices. One koku=4·96 bushels.

[*Reproduced by the courtesy of the N.Y.K. Line*

WINNOWING THE RICE CROP

farming families flocked into the towns or sought employment in local manufacturing industries; while many of the girls tried to find work in the cotton, rayon, and woollen mills. This increased competition for industrial employment forced down the wages in manufacturing trades, especially those of female workers in the textile industries and of unskilled male labourers. Costs of manufacture were thus lowered and industrial employers assisted to acquire fresh markets, especially in foreign countries, and so to increase the volume of their output. This does not apply only to employers in the large-scale industries. The fall in wages was one of the factors which stimulated the growth of new units in a multitude of small-scale industries. These workshops were often established by skilled workmen formerly employed in the large factories, or even by farm households which previously had been engaged in some branch of manufacture as a by-employment and now, because of the agricultural depression, were impelled to devote more of their time to it. The continued influx of cheap labour from the land as the depression in raw silk became chronic, is one reason why money wages continued to fall in some industries (even in the rapidly-growing textile trades) after recovery began in 1932. The decline in money wages in manufacture had a less damaging effect on the *real* wages of urban workers than might be supposed because of the heavy fall in the price of rice (the staple food) during the years of depression, and this was one reason why it was accomplished without much resistance on the part of the wage-earners. The improvements effected in technique and organization in the large-scale industries, especially during the deflationary period 1930 to 1931, were another factor responsible for the wage-reductions; for these improvements meant that the demand for labour failed to increase in proportion to the rise in output. Had it not been for the decline in costs brought about by the fall in wages and the improvements in manufacturing efficiency, the degree of depreciation in the yen required to restore equilibrium would necessarily have been much greater.

Some indication of the extent and nature of these improvements in manufacturing efficiency must now be given, although it is not proposed to venture upon a long technical discussion. There can be little doubt that over a wide range of industry progress in technique and organization has been marked. Up to 1927 it was slow; but after that date, and especially under the stress of falling prices in 1930 and 1931, it was rapid and substantial. The experience of foreign technicians and business men residing in Japan fully bears out this contention. In the large factories, new and better types of machinery were introduced, economies were effected in the use of power, costs were saved through improved methods of internal transport, and more attention was paid to the effective use of operatives. Even in the small-scale industries progress was considerable. Units became more highly specialized, and mechanical methods tended to replace manual labour. In the industrial quarters of the towns an observer can see multitudes of very small workshops equipped with machine-tools driven by electric motors; and stores exhibiting for sale a wide variety of new and second-hand lathes, drilling machines, and presses, are common features of those quarters. In the early twenties workshops and stores of this kind were rare.

The extent of the improvements may be judged from statistical information available about certain industries. In the cotton-spinning industry output per operative, which had changed very little between 1914 and 1926, rose in the next decade from 5,700 lb. of yarn to 9,300 lb., largely through the almost universal adoption of high-draft spinning. In the weaving sheds belonging to the great combined spinning-weaving concerns output per operative increased by 122 per cent. in the same period chiefly because of the introduction of automatic looms. In the specialist weaving branch of the cotton trade, about three-eighths of the looms were handlooms in 1923, while narrow power looms were far in excess of wide power looms. Now, handlooms are few, and two-thirds of the equipment consists of wide power looms. In the woollen-weaving industry, well over half the looms were handlooms in the early part of the post-War decade; now, power looms are almost exclusively employed. The same tendency is pronounced in the silk-weaving and rayon-weaving trades. Indeed, during the Showa era a technical revolution has been accomplished in all branches of weaving.[1]

Perhaps the most remarkable progress of all has been achieved in the engineering industry. Ten or fifteen years ago foreign technicians employed in Japanese engineering works complained of inefficiency and over-staffing, and Japan relied upon foreign countries for most of the power-generating plant that she required. Now, both workers and staff have achieved a much higher level of skill, and Japan can produce her own generating plant, textile machinery, and the simpler kinds of machine tools. Both the quantity and the quality of Japanese steel have improved greatly, although in the primary branches of iron and steel industry she is still behind the leading Western nations, partly because of her lack of suitable ores and coking coal. The chemical industry has made great strides, and in the rayon trade, which was in a rudimentary condition in 1929, huge and highly efficient plants are now operating and costs are only one-third of those of the pre-depression year.[2]

These statements must not be taken to imply that Japanese manufacturing industry necessarily compares favourably with British or American industry in efficiency and organization. In some branches of textiles and in pottery, there is probably little to choose; but in the metallurgical and chemical trades she still lags behind. The significant fact, however, is that the disparity between Japanese and Western industries in these respects has narrowed in the last decade. During the twenties, as many of the instances given above show, Japan was industrially immature, and manufacturing efficiency was on a low level when judged from

[1] Information in this paragraph is based on the half-yearly reports of the Japan Cotton Spinners' Federation, statistical reports of the Ministry of Commerce and Industry, the Japan Silk Year-Book, reports on various industries prepared by the Japanese Council of the Institute of Pacific Relations and submitted to the Yosemite Conference in 1936, and on personal inquiries.

[2] Information provided by the *Oriental Economist*.

the standpoint of the West. Since then, however, many of these deficiencies have been removed, and technical equipment and methods of production over a wide field of industry have been raised much nearer to the level reached in Western Europe and the United States.

In the promotion of Japanese industries in recent years, as in earlier times, foreign technicians and merchants have played an important part. Foreign industrialists who reflect ruefully on the success of this apt pupil of the West should remember that assistance was not afforded out of kindness of heart; for those who have instructed the Japanese, or have opened markets for their goods, have reaped high returns for their efforts. English firms helped in the establishment of textile and paper mills, supplied the machinery (at a profit) and taught them to operate it (for adequate fees). English engineers have instructed them in the building of ships and the manufacture of aeroplanes. English companies have joined with Japanese companies in capitalizing firms for the production of rubber goods, steel, and engineering products. American technicians have been employed in the steel-rolling mills, and in the oil-refining, canning, and motor-car trades; and the great American trusts have taken a leading part in the development of the electric-power-generating and electrical-apparatus industries. Several large firms in these and other industries have been capitalized jointly by the Americans and Japanese; and the American firms have provided much technical advice and up-to-date machinery for the machine-tool, flour-milling, fertilizer, munitions, and cement trades.[1]

From early in the Meiji era foreign merchants have been active in the development of the Japanese export trade. For instance, for many years past American firms have owned and operated the chief factories in Shizuoka for the curing, sorting, blending, and

[1] In 1935 direct investments by American corporations in commercial and industrial properties in Japan were estimated at 60 million dollars (U.S.), and investments in Japanese securities held by financial institutions and individuals were estimated at 163 million dollars (United States' Department of Commerce).

packing of tea for foreign markets, and the bulk of the export trade has been handled by them. The first successful production of toothbrushes was by an American-owned and -managed factory in Osaka which shipped its entire output to the United States, where the goods were marketed under a nationally advertised trade-mark. Branches of British and Indian merchant firms have long been assisting in the promotion of the cotton trade, and indeed there are few exports which, at one time or another, have not been handled extensively by foreign houses established in Japan. That Japan owed much to the enterprise of Europeans and Americans in the early days of her Westernization is well known; but that the recent growth in exports has been greatly assisted by their efforts is less often recognized. A few well-established instances may be given. When the yen began its steep decline in 1932, buyers from European and American importing houses and chain stores flocked into Japan with samples which they induced the Japanese to copy at low prices, and the rise in the exports of miscellaneous manufactured goods during the last six years has owed much to the efforts of these buyers and of the foreign agents and export houses in Yokohama and Kobe. Most of these goods are produced by the small-scale industries, and the foreign merchants and buyers approached the Japanese merchants who financed these trades with requests for large quantities of the goods; some of them even got into touch with the small producers directly. As both the domestic merchants and the producers are engaged in highly competitive industries, the foreigners had little difficulty in inducing them to cut their prices.

A visitor to the small factories and workshops of the great cities is shown samples of foreign bicycles, gramophones, toys, and countless other articles that the manufacturers have been asked to copy. Considerable quantities of the Japanese goods sold in the cheap stores of the United States and other Western countries are produced in this way, and owe their presence in the stores to the enterprise of foreign traders. For example, an American agent for a number of department stores in the United States receives every year from his principals a selection of samples of "novelty" pottery and porcelain wares (such as lamp stands), and he contracts for a supply with a number of small Japanese producers. A Chicago department store has its own buying office in Japan through which it obtains quantities of porcelain wares made to its own designs. In 1932 an American chain store sent buyers to Japan and, in co-operation with some exporters in Kobe, bought up vast numbers of cotton canvas shoes, sent them to the United States where they were sold for 20 cents (about 10d.) a pair. Protests from American manufacturers of rubber shoes led to a rise in the tariff in 1933 and so reduced the trade. Then the buyers began to develop a large export of canvas "Oxford" shoes which were sold at 10 cents a pair, retail, in America. As these goods were produced at prices that left little profit for their producers, the Japanese Manufacturers' Association in this industry tried to curtail competition for orders by issuing lists of minimum prices; but the buyers found various means of evading this restriction.

For some years, cotton gloves have been produced in Japan for the home market; but exports were small. In 1934 American buyers approached Japanese manufacturers and obtained from them supplies of low-quality cotton gloves for export at about one-third of the price of the product sold in the home market. Several American chain-store buyers after 1932 brought samples of Czechoslovak glass bottles, atomizers, and table-ware to Japan, and encouraged the Japanese to produce them. Prices were driven down and quality was reduced far below the level of goods previously sold in the domestic market. A certain Yokohama manufacturer of lamp-shades had long been producing hand-made, high-quality articles of real silk for Japanese department stores. The wholesale price of these shades was from 2 to 10 yen each. An American buyer, through a Japanese exporter, induced this manufacturer to take orders for 10,000 dozen shades a season at prices ranging from 1·35 yen to 1·20 yen a dozen (that is, about 1½d. a dozen). Naturally, quality was cut; the frames were electrically welded and the covering consisted of very low-grade material. About the same time (1932) American importers began to place large orders in Japan for cheap pencils (with erasers) for sale in department stores. Whereas the wholesale price of pencils for the home market was from 2 to 3 yen a gross, the export price was forced down to 1 yen a gross. These goods had to be produced from the cheapest wood and graphite and were covered with inferior paint. They were, and are, manufactured by domestic workers under "sweated" conditions. Similar examples could be given of the hosiery, rug, rayon kimono, rubber goods, silk-necktie, and other trades; in all of these multitudes of small producers were encouraged by foreign buyers to turn their activities to the production of low-grade articles of American design for export. In Kobe there are several British merchant firms in the woollen and worsted piece-goods trade that were formerly concerned with the import of Yorkshire fabrics into Japan; since 1932 their main business has consisted of handling Japanese worsteds for export. Many Indian firms have established themselves in Kobe in the same period for the purpose of conducting an export trade in Japanese cotton piece-goods and other commodities to India and the East Indies. At the time of the boycott of Italian goods in 1935–36, an Italian merchant in Kobe procured from Italy samples of hats formerly sold in the United States, had them copied, and supplied the American market from that source.

These activities on the part of foreign merchants are, of course, perfectly legitimate. Had it not been for their enterprise, the cheap goods would not have been available in such quantities for the poorer consumers of other countries, and Japan would have found greater difficulty in adjusting her economy to the strain to which it was subjected by the fall in raw-silk prices. But it is amusing to reflect that, while Japan was being accused in Western countries of selling at ridiculously low prices, of ruining foreign industry, destroying the high standards of life of Western workers, and sweating her own people, the merchants of those very countries were playing a prominent part in bringing down Japan's export prices and in stimulating her foreign trade. Even when the Japanese Government, fearful of the rise of tariffs and export-restrictions, attempted to enforce control over quantities and prices through the development of associations among exporters and small manufacturers, means were found of evading the regulations. For instance, when an association placed a limit on the volume of exports to a particular market, it often happened that exporters consigned their goods to some other country whence they were shipped to the market to which the regulation applied. Of course, the responsibility of the foreigner must not be exaggerated. Japanese merchants, also, have been active in the development of trade in these miscellaneous goods, and they, too, have shown ingenuity in the evasion of the regulations. But, since foreigners have been very prominent in stimulating certain of the exports which have provoked the greatest hostility abroad, it is well to stress the irony of the contrast between the popular attitude in Western countries towards the Japanese trade expansion and the enterprise of the nationals of those countries in bringing it about.

Another factor which has exercised a powerful influence in promoting the boom in Japanese industry and has been largely responsible for the rise in importance of the capital-goods trades, is the financial policy of the State. When the Minseito Government was overthrown at the end of 1931, its deflationary policy fell with it, and succeeding Governments embarked upon a programme of reflation. By that time the business classes, except for a few conservative financiers, welcomed this change of policy; while the military and naval cliques, which had secured a greater measure of influence, strongly supported it, because it removed the chief obstacle to the realization of the programmes of expansion in armaments. In the next few years the expenditure of the Government was greatly increased, and much of this increase was financed by domestic bond issues. The tables opposite show the extent of this borrowing and the effect of it on the national debt.

The rise in Government expenditure, financed mainly by internal borrowing, checked the downward trend of prices after 1931 and

*Government Expenditure and Revenue**
(*In million yen*)

Financial Year (ending March 31st)	Revenue (excluding receipts from loans)	Expenditure	Expenditure on Army and Navy	Army and Navy Expenditure as percentage of total	Deficit
1930–31	1,559	1,558	442	28	—
1931–32	1,411	1,477	455	31	66
1932–33	1,586	1,950	686	35	364
1933–34	1,578	2,255	873	39	677
1934–35	1,504	2,163	942	44	659
1935–36	1,444†	2,225†	1,023†	46	781†
1936–37	1,602†	2,312†	1,060†	46	710†

* *Japan-Manchukuo Year-Book*, 1936–37, p. 303.
† Budget estimates.

Government Bond Issues and National Debt
(*In million yen*)

Financial year (ending March 31st)	New Issues	Year	National Debt Outstanding at End of Calendar Year*
1930–31	—	1930	6,029
1931–32	214	1931	6,003
1932–33	781	1932	6,549
1933–34	847	1933	7,821
1934–35	830	1934	8,651
1935–36	761	1935	9,581
1936–37	685	1936	10,395

* The external debt, which is included in these figures, has continued to be stated in the accounts at about 1,400 million yen throughout this period, although the depreciation of the yen since 1932 has, in fact, considerably increased the value in yen of debts payable in sterling and dollars.

soon caused them to move upwards. As rates of money wages, for reasons already given, were not increased between 1932 and 1936, a stimulus to industrial development was given, particularly to the trades producing capital goods. These trades, which normally expand during periods of rising prices, received a special stimulus from the direction of a large part of the Government's increased expenditure towards munitions and towards the encouragement of trades, such as shipping, considered necessary from the standpoint of national defence. The increase in the borrowings of local governments had the same effect, for much of the money raised was spent on public works and various kinds of industrial equipment. The amount of local bonds outstanding rose from 1,650 million yen at the end of 1931 to 2,511 million yen four years later. At the same time, Japanese financiers and industrialists were pressed by the Government and the Army to provide capital for the development of Manchukuo, chiefly through subscription to the issues of the South Manchuria Railway, which until recently was the chief organ for Japanese economic penetration in that area. It is estimated that Japanese investments in Manchukuo between 1931 and 1936 amounted to about 1,166 million yen;[1] and much of this money was expended on equipment produced in Japan Proper. All these circumstances were specially favourable to an expansion of the capital-goods industries.

Rates of interest have also fallen. The Bank of Japan's discount rate on commercial bills, for instance, fell from 6½ per cent. at the end of 1931 to 3¼ per cent. at the end of 1936, and this tendency has been followed by other short-money rates. Costs of trading and stock holding have thus been considerably diminished; but, what is more important, the long-term rates have also dropped. Japanese industrial and financial concerns have been accustomed to raise much of their capital by issuing debentures; and many of them, in 1931, were heavily indebted to the banks. They took advantage of the situation in the capital market after 1931 to arrange for conversions of these debentures on favourable terms, or to

[1] *Far Eastern Survey*, May 12th, 1937, p. 111.

issue new debentures at low rates to pay off their bank loans. The magnitude of these operations is shown in the table below; they were accompanied by a fall in the average rate of interest on outstanding debentures from 6 per cent. at the end of 1931 to well under 5 per cent. at the end of 1935.[1]

In these circumstances it is not difficult to understand how it is that the industrial boom has been particularly evident in the capital-goods industries, or why in the last eight years changes

(*In million yen*)

Year	Debenture Issues for Conversion*	New Debenture Issues*	Debentures Outstanding at end of half-yearly periods*	Bank Loans of 327 Leading Industrial Companies in Japan Proper at end of half-year
1931	180	25	2,570 (1st half)	949
1932	214	74	2,583 ,,	946
1933	847	78	2,584 ,,	899
1934	1,253	218	2,822 (2nd half)	725
1935	573	283	3,025 ,,	—

* Applies to companies (excluding financial concerns) domiciled in the Japanese Empire, Kwantung, and the South Manchuria Railway Zone. Foreign debenture issues are not included. Source: Bank of Japan.

in the composition of Japanese industry, which have greatly increased the importance of the metallurgical, engineering, and chemical trades, should have taken place. In view of the long series of unbalanced budgets, and the heavy borrowing of both central and local governments, it is more difficult to explain why the rise in prices up to 1936 was so moderate and why rates of interest have continued to fall. The Mitsubishi wholesale price index, it is true, shows a rise from 100 on December 10th, 1931, when Japan left the gold standard, to 153 in December 1935; but wholesale prices of goods for domestic consumption rose only from 100 to 125 during that period. The explanation seems to lie mainly in the partial scope of the boom. A very large section of

[1] K. Takahashi, *Factors in Japan's Recent Industrial Development*, p. 24.

the Japanese economy, namely, agriculture, including the raw-silk trade, remained chronically depressed. If agriculture had completely recovered after 1932, then resources could have been attracted to the munitions and export industries only if manufacturers in those industries had bid up the prices that they were prepared to pay for capital and labour. This would have raised costs, increased the expenses of the Government in carrying out its rearmament programme, and so led to a vicious spiral of inflation. As it was, however, capitalists who formerly invested their money in agriculture and in raw-silk production were seeking for new openings, and there was a vast amount of unemployed and under-employed rural labour. The Government's financial policy in the circumstances, therefore, did not have the inflationary effect that was anticipated, but merely assisted the transference of resources which the economic situation demanded.

The fall in the rate of interest must not be exaggerated; for there are several distinct markets for loans in Japan and all these did not share in the movements that have been described. It seems, for instance, that farmers and small producers have had to pay as much for their financial accommodation as previously. Nevertheless, it is true that the rate of interest on Government stock and industrial bonds fell substantially at a time when heavy Government borrowing and heavy investment in Manchukuo and Japan were taking place. The diversion of capital from agriculture and raw silk, no doubt, provides one explanation. But the main reason is probably that the sums disbursed so lavishly by the Government helped to increase the industrial profits, which were being favourably affected by other causes, and that a considerable proportion of these profits were used for reinvestment in the businesses or for repaying outstanding bank loans. These operations provided the banks with idle funds which they were able to employ in purchasing subsequent issues of Government bonds. The figures on page 157 seem to bear out this analysis, for they show that an absolute fall in bank loans was accompanied by a heavy increase in purchases of Government securities.

Between the end of 1931 and the end of 1935, these two classes of banks increased their holdings of Government bonds by 1,565

*Selected Assets of Ordinary Banks**
(In million yen)

End of Year	Central Government Bonds	Other Securities	Loans and Discounts	Call Loans	Total of (1) to (4)	Percentage of (1) to (5)	Percentage of (3) to (5)
	(1)	(2)	(3)	(4)	(5)		
1931	1,146	1,783	6,742	155	9,826	11·7	68·6
1932	1,210	1,731	6,440	320	9,701	—	—
1933	1,567	1,758	6,251	420	9,996	—	—
1934	2,017	1,878	6,133	369	10,397	—	—
1935	2,205	2,038	6,413	390	11,046	20·0	58·1
1936	2,561	2,235	6,660	—	(11,456)	(22·4)	(58·2)

*Selected Assets of Savings Banks**
(In million yen)

End of Year	Central Government Bonds	Other Securities	Loans	Total of (1) to (3)	Percentage of (1) to (4)	Percentage of (3) to (4)
	(1)	(2)	(3)	(4)		
1931	562	452	467	1,481	38·0	31·5
1932	696	460	406	1,562	—	—
1933	860	458	349	1,667	—	—
1934	934	457	335	1,726	—	—
1935	1,068	517	329	1,914	55·8	17·2
1936	1,016	508	239	1,763	57·6	13·5

* Provided by the Bank of Japan.

million yen, the special, or semi-official, banks and the Bank of Japan by about 600 million yen, while the Treasury Deposits Bureau and other Government financial organs raised their holdings by 1,052, and the trust and insurance companies by about 350 million yen.[1] Thus, these institutions together absorbed practically the whole of the Government bonds issued between 1931 and 1935, and they were able to do this without restricting credit to industry and without producing the symptoms of uncontrolled inflation.

[1] Cf. *Far Eastern Survey*, September 29th, 1937, p. 225.

CHAPTER IX

THE CONDITION OF THE WORKERS

> "*Whether it be not a good Rule whereby to judge of the Trade of any City, and its Usefulness, to observe whether there is a Circulation through the Extremities, and whether the People round about are Busy and Warm? . . . And whether the Labouring Ox should be muzzled?*"
>
> GEORGE BERKELEY

DISCUSSIONS of Japanese labour problems are frequently disfigured by *naïveté* or by a complete lack of historical perspective. Western writers are apt to concentrate their attention upon the low level of Japanese wages, the long hours of work, the weakness of trade unionism, official oppression of incipient labour organizations, the ineffectiveness of the Factory Acts, and the absence of advanced forms of social insurance. They deplore the workers' lack of liberty and they refer with contempt to the survival of "feudal" relationships in industry. Japanese apologists, on the other hand, assert that in their harmoniously constituted society the machinery for negotiation and for the protection of the workers that exists in the West has no function to perform. Militant trade unionism is an anachronism. The employer is said to regard his workers as a father regards his children, and conflicts of rival interests seldom arise. "The relationships between lord and vassal, master and servant, protector and protégé, are such as to make it impossible to conceive of one side resenting and the other abusing them."[1] Unemployment insurance is unnecessary in a community in which the family system provides effectively for the relief of persons in distress. Left-wing movements among workers are the result of delusions created by Western propaganda. In a word, conservative Japanese declare that industrial relations

[1] *Contemporary Japan*, March 1934, p. 639.

in their country have assumed a different form from those existing in the West, because of peculiarities in their social organization. Now these opposite judgments are clearly too extreme, and it is doubtful if the Western critic would be so ready to condemn or the Japanese "apologist" to affirm the nation's peculiarity, if either were to reflect upon the social history of other countries.

In the first place, common sense should suggest that the labour problem in a country which has only recently been industrialized cannot be discussed entirely in terms of categories and ideals associated with older industrial civilizations. It has been shown elsewhere that only a small proportion of the Japanese occupied population is engaged in large factories. Nearly half of that population is found in peasant agriculture and fishing; and in manufacturing industry the majority of the employees work in small shops. Many of the workers in large establishments come from country homes and return to them after a few years' service; while of the permanent labour force in great transport and manufacturing undertakings the major part comes from families which followed agricultural pursuits only a generation ago. Thus, the wage-earner employed in a great establishment is not yet the typical figure of Japanese industrial society, and even the representatives of this class who do exist bring with them traditions and an attitude of mind associated with more primitive forms of industrial organization.

These general statements must be supported by information derived from studies of conditions in typical industries. In the great textile mills nearly three-quarters of the workers consist of girls who are drawn mainly from rural families. They are engaged through the medium of mill agents who reside in the districts from which the labour supply is drawn and who arrange with the parents of the girls that they shall work in the mills for a given period. The operatives are housed in dormitories owned by the employers; they are given meals and clothing, and medical treatment and various kinds of recreation are usually provided for them. The labour turnover in these mills is very high—in the cotton industry

FISHING

PILGRIMS

it amounts to one-third of the total number of operatives—for the girls usually return to their homes on reaching marriageable age. The earning of these girls makes an important contribution to the incomes of their impoverished families. Professor Uyeda and Mr. Minoguchi have given an interesting example of how large a part of the peasant's money-income is obtained by this means. In the village of Ikazawa in Niigata prefecture, there are 773 peasant families, and from these families, at the date of the enquiry, 216 girls had gone to work in cotton-spinning mills, and 170 in silk-reeling mills. These girls earn on an average 150–160 yen a year, of which 50 yen is retained by the employer for lodging, board, and insurance; 40 to 50 yen is used as pocket-money; and 50 to 60 yen is sent home, either to help their families or to provide a dowry. Of the rice, which is the main product of agriculture in that village, very little is marketed, and the main cash income of the peasants is obtained from sales of cocoons and charcoal, and from the earnings of their daughters. The latter are estimated to make up one-fourth of the cash-income from all sources.[1]

In most of the large mills and in some of the small ones the accommodation and food are far better than the operatives could hope to receive at home, and their life is probably more interesting; and for these reasons girls are anxious to take service there. But in many of the small establishments the conditions are not good, though it is doubtful if they are often worse than those existing in their homes. The most objectionable feature attending this system from a Western standpoint is the lack of personal freedom; for the girls are under strict discipline and they can leave the mill-compounds only when permission is given to them. But it must be remembered that they are very young, that they could not be left to fend for themselves in a strange city, and that they would not enjoy much liberty if they remained at home. The system lends itself to abuse at the hands of unscrupulous, brutal, or indifferent managers; but to some extent this danger may be averted

[1] T. Uyeda and T. Minoguchi, *The Cotton Industry* (Japanese Council, Institute of Pacific Relations), pp. 32–3.

by the necessity that a mill should establish a good reputation in order to attract easily the large number of new recruits which it annually requires. Mills that enjoy such a reputation find that they have to spend very little money on recruiting-agents.

Just as the mill-girls receive a substantial part of their income in the form of bonuses and payments in kind, so the male workers in large factories are given bonuses to supplement their wages, and, if married, they are often provided with houses at low rents by their employers. The practice of making presents of money to workers on the occasion of family-bereavement or the birth of a child is common. Some firms, including, for instance, a certain department store, often give presents to mark some event in the family of the proprietor. The relationship is essentially "paternal." Wages are very seldom determined by collective bargaining; but, on the other hand, the employers are not free to discharge a man unless they give compensation. If the workers have little power of improving their conditions of work, their opinion cannot be ignored and employers are often prevented from imposing unwelcome conditions by mass-demonstration of disapproval. Thus, workers in a certain foundry insisted successfully upon being provided with separate bathing accommodation from that used by the machine-shop operatives on the ground that the latter were unpleasantly oily. Just as labourers often wear "happi" coats on which the style of the firm employing them is prominently printed, so many workers in modern factories are given caps or some other article of clothing adorned with the name of the firm or with a picture of its product. In a cycle-hub factory visited by the writer, each man wore a cotton cap on which a cycle-hub was printed. This was an obligation; but it was apparently not resented by the men.

Generalizations about conditions of work within the factories should be treated with caution; for a wide diversity is found. There are many large factories and some medium-sized ones in which conditions do not differ from those found in up-to-date workplaces in the West. They are clean and well lit and some have air-conditioning systems. On the other hand, in many of the small factories conditions are bad. Frequently, the machinery in such workplaces is crowded, and inadequate protection is provided for the workers who operate it. Many shops have bad flooring and are dark and dirty. The artificial lighting is often unsatisfactory. It is not uncommon to see a man working at a job that requires accuracy with a powerful naked electric bulb suspended a foot or two from his eyes. Very little effort is made to reduce fatigue. It is rare for seats to be provided for girls working at benches on assembly work. Of course, defects such as these are far from uncommon in Western countries. They are naturally more numerous in Japan because of her comparative immaturity as an industrial nation.

The greater part of Japan's industrial processes, as we have seen, is carried on in little workshops. Many of these take the form of sheds attached to farm-houses or urban dwelling-houses. Some are small dwelling-houses which have been converted into workshops. Others consist merely of the front rooms of dwelling-houses, open to the view of passers-by. In this type of workplaces there is naturally a wide diversity in conditions. Some are reasonably healthy; others, especially those in the slums of great cities, are dark and unpleasant, and where machinery is used, little care is taken to protect the workers from entanglement in the moving parts. The proprietors of many of these workplaces are usually financially dependent upon large factory proprietors or merchants; some of them are merely outworkers in receipt of piece wages. The staff of these workshops is made up of members of the family, together with a few apprentices and hired labourers. In the old days, the *detchi*, or apprentice, usually lived with his master during the period of his apprenticeship and often for some years afterwards, and received no wages except pocket-money; but his master was expected to set him up in business after an appropriate interval. Nowadays, however, the apprentice in many of these small-scale trades is not trained for a craft, but is merely a low-paid workman, who lives with his master and, in times of prosperity, may hope to receive a supplement to his scanty wages in the form of a bonus. The situation in the small-scale foundry trade of Kawaguchi may be given as an example. About 18 per cent. of the workers in this trade are apprentices, who live and board with their employers until they reach maturity. When the contract of apprenticeship (for a term of from 3 to 5 years) is made with a boy's parents, the latter receive a sum of from 30 to 80 yen. The boys are given clothes twice a year and a little pocket-money ranging from 50 sen to 1 yen a month at the beginning of their term to 3 yen at the end of it. After their apprenticeship is over, they frequently remain under much the same conditions as before, although their monthly wage rises to 5 or 6 yen. Usually part of the pocket-money is withheld from the apprentice for a time and paid to him in a lump sum when his term is over. Not infrequently the masters are unable to pay the amounts which they owe. Even when, because of the development of a trade, the workshop is transformed into a small factory, similar conditions persist. For instance, in the bicycle and enamelled-ironware trades the apprentices still live in dormitories and are boarded by their employers. In the latter trade, the apprentices' parents usually receive about 250 yen at the beginning of their three years' term. A few of these apprentices sooner or later set up workshops of their own; but many continue to work as low-paid journeymen in the shops of their masters. Some trades make much use of seasonal labour. The Arita pottery works, for example, are staffed by members of agricultural families who ride to the factories on bicycles during times when there is little to be done on the farms. They are engaged by contract for a period. There are other industries that are conducted entirely by agricultural families as by-employments without the use of hired labour.[1] In the cities, persons who work in factories during the day often carry on certain pro-

[1] Valuable information about working conditions in the small-scale industries is contained in articles published in *Shakai Seisaku Jiho* (*Social Reform*) for May 1934 and April 1935. The data in this paragraph are drawn mainly from this source.

cesses (such as the finishing of hosiery and garments) in their spare time within their homes to the orders of merchants.

It is evident that factory wage-earners form only a small proportion of Japan's working class, and conditions of economic life are such as to have prevented the growth, except in a limited proportion of the population, of the outlook associated with the proletariat of other great industrial nations. As might be expected, methods of wage-payment have been far less systematized in Japan than in the West. Only in the shipping industries and a few minor manufacturing trades has any form of collective bargaining been set up, and consequently there are no standard rates of pay. Wide disparities exist between the wages of similar workers in each industry. This is largely because several distinct markets for labour exist. There are, for example, the girls who are prepared to live in the dormitories of great factories, far from their homes, and there are other female workers who require intermittent employment close at hand. The large combined cotton spinning-weaving mills and the silk-reeling mills pay wages which are, on an average, 20 per cent. higher than those received by workers in the small weaving sheds and reeling mills. The latter are situated in rural areas and can draw on a local labour supply that is not available or suitable for prolonged and disciplined work in a great factory. Even among employers of the same type, wage-policy varies extensively. In some large cotton mills the operatives receive relatively low wages but are given generous bonuses, good food, and accommodation, and ample welfare facilities. In other mills of the same class, they receive higher wages, but allowances and welfare facilities are inferior. In nearly all the large Japanese factories, however, the "paternal" relationship which exists between workers and employers is demonstrated by the custom of paying semi-annual bonuses varying with the prosperity of the firm and the length of service of the worker. Payments in kind (in the form of food, accommodation, and recreation facilities) also make up an important part of the workers' total income. The practice differs so much from firm to firm and from trade to trade as to defeat any attempt to generalize about the proportion of bonuses and payments in kind to the worker's total income. In the more prosperous firms it is fairly common for the bonus paid to a workman with several years' service to be equivalent to from one to three months' wages. Besides this, employers are now compelled by law to give certain workers two weeks' wages when they are discharged, and much more than this is given by the leading concerns. For instance, in the cotton-spinning industry the discharge allowance is in many cases at the rate of two weeks' wages for every year of employment. Other bonuses are given for regular attendance. In the textile industry as a whole in 1931 allowances in kind and money were equivalent to a quarter of the operative's total income from his employer,[1] and since then this proportion has risen with the prosperity of the industry.

The system of giving bonuses on individual output has been extensively adopted in recent years in industries that pay time-wages, and in some of the great metal factories skilled workers have been able to earn twice their daily rates. Wages, though calculated according to the number of days worked or to the daily output, are usually paid twice a month. In trades that employ juveniles, however, the length of service and the wage-rates are fixed by contract between employer and parent, and frequently the former makes an advance which is refunded out of the worker's earnings. This practice of making advances by the employer often results in the workers becoming heavily indebted to them and has been criticized as in effect depriving them of their liberty. A system of annual hiring is still followed in some trades, and in the mines a gang or subcontracting method is in force. The head of the gang, or subcontractor, agrees with the employer to provide a certain output at a fixed price per unit, and the proceeds are afterwards shared among the members of the gang or the underhands working for the subcontractor.[2] This will recall to students

[1] K. Akamatsu and Y. Koide, *Industrial and Labour Conditions in Japan*, p. 32.

[2] Cf. *Industrial Labour in Japan* (I.L.O.), p. 199.

of economic history the conditions that existed in many British industries in the middle of the nineteenth century.

Another important characteristic of the Japanese system is that wages vary widely according to seniority, and this applies even to piece-wages. Thus, it often happens that men working side by side at the same kind of job and with equal efficiency receive very different wages. This is an encouragement to employers to engage young workers, and when technical changes make it possible for an industry to use juveniles without loss of efficiency (as has happened in cotton spinning during the last ten years), then wage-costs may be considerably reduced. The older workers are, however, protected to some extent against the danger of replacement by young people by the obstacles which public opinion places in the way of employers who seek to discharge their employees. In the cotton industry, of course, the girls are only prepared to offer themselves for employment for a few years, and so the replacement of older by younger girls can easily be carried out. As already indicated, in the very small workplaces a wage-contract scarcely exists; for in many of them the hired workers receive board and lodging, a small sum as pocket-money, and occasional bonuses.

Hours of work are longer than in British manufacturing industries. The hours of work of women and young persons under the age of sixteen engaged in factories with ten or more employees, and in certain dangerous trades, are limited to eleven, including a break of one hour. This limitation has since 1931 applied to all textile factories which employ power, irrespective of the number of employees. The Factory Act also prohibits the employment of women and young persons from 10 p.m. to 5 a.m., although with the permission of the authorities such persons can be, and frequently are, employed up to 11 p.m. No legislative restriction is placed, however, on the length of the working week. In practice, a great diversity is found. The large cotton spinning-weaving mills run with two shifts, from 5 a.m. to 2 p.m., and from 2 p.m. to 11 p.m., with a break of half an hour in each shift, and this is characteristic of other large textile mills. In the more up-to-date factories in several other trades, hours are eight or nine per day; but in the metallurgical and chemical trades they are much longer. The labour statistics for 1934 showed that actual working hours in factories with over ten employees amounted to just over nine per day; but since then longer hours have been worked owing to the prosperity of certain industries, and in most of the engineering, chemical, and metal works actual working hours are usually at least ten per day. Several of the medium-sized plants in the engineering trade visited by the writer in 1936 were working eleven or twelve hours a day. Nevertheless, during the last fifteen years there has been progress. Since 1922 actual working hours have been reduced from eleven to eight and a half in the cotton spinning and weaving trade, and a fall of 10 per cent. has probably occurred in factory industry as a whole.

It is not in the length of the working day but in the absence of a weekly rest-day that Japan is in sharpest contrast with most Western countries. Women and young persons, under the Factory Act, have to be granted two days' holiday a month, and in a large number of industries this is, in fact, all that they and the male workers receive. Usually, it is only in the most up-to-date factories, or in industries in which a trade association has sought to curtail output by enforcing a suspension of work, that the operatives are able to enjoy a weekly rest-day. In addition, the workers are usually granted holidays at the New Year and at the time of *O-Bon*, and sometimes the factories close for certain national holidays; but, taking these into account, it is doubtful if factory workers have enjoyed on an average as many as four rest-days a month in recent years.[1]

In the workshops not covered by the Factory Act hours of work are often very long indeed. Twelve to fourteen hours are not uncommon, although, of course, the length of the working day fluctuates widely according to the activity of business. Naturally, the people whose labour is so prolonged do not work as

[1] The Bureau of Statistics gives an average of twenty-seven working days a month for all factories in 1934.—*Japan-Manchukuo Year-Book*, p. 234.

intensively as disciplined factory-operatives; but the labour in many of these small industries is so exhausting as to have alarmed the authorities, who are fearful of a deterioration in national physique. Consequently, the Bureau of Social Affairs (a sub-department of the Home Office) and prefectural authorities have brought pressure to bear on associations of small manufacturers not covered by the Factory Act, with the object of inducing them to shorten hours of work for juveniles and women. For instance, in a branch of the woollen industry in Shizuoka prefecture eighty-three members of the manufacturers' association, on the initiative of the local authorities, drew up a formal agreement according to which the maximum length of the working day was fixed at twelve hours, financial penalties were to be imposed on those who infringed the rule, and co-operation with the police was promised in its enforcement. The authorities have also intervened in some of the purely domestic industries. For instance, the fan-making trade of Marugame in Kagawa prefecture is carried on mainly by workers in their homes with the assistance of their wives and children, and formerly the hours of work ranged from thirteen to sixteen a day. The Mayor of Marugame asked the Bureau of Social Affairs to investigate the conditions and to suggest a remedy, and in February 1934 the Bureau, together with the local authorities and the Chief of Police, induced the employers' association to sign an agreement by which actual working hours were to be limited to eleven hours a day, night work was to be abolished, a definite time was to be allowed for meals and rest, and the first and the fifteenth day of each month were to be granted as holidays.[1]

These and other attempts by the authorities to improve working conditions in industries which from their nature could not be brought within the scope of the Factory Acts were sufficiently successful to lead the Minister of Home Affairs to instruct the prefectural police to bend their energies not merely to seeing that legislative provisions concerning hours were properly carried out,

[1] J. Kitaoka, "A Reform Measure for Japanese Small-scale Industries," in *Shakai Seisaku Jiho* (*Social Reform*), April 1935, pp. 166-80.

but also to securing reductions in the length of the working day in small-scale trades. The peculiar position occupied by the police in Japan gives them great influence in matters of this kind, even if no legislative authority is conferred on them, and during the last few years employers' associations in a considerable number of small-scale trades have been induced to draw up and to observe agreements similar to those just described. Of course, only a small part of industry has been covered by these agreements; but still it is evident that the authorities are not indifferent to the conditions of the workers in these "sweated" industries, and a beginning has been made in removing the more obvious evils. The Home Office has now drawn up a Bill which provides that when an association has made an agreement about the reduction of hours the authorities can, on request, enforce it over non-members as well as members, can inspect the workplaces and impose fines for infringement. So far as can be learned, this Bill has not yet been presented to the Diet.[1]

We must now consider briefly the exceedingly complicated problem of wage-rates and earnings. Because of the absence of standard rates, generalizations in this field are very difficult, and as published figures of wages do not include the semi-annual bonuses and payments in kind, they are apt to be misleading. Even if these extra payments are taken into account, there can be no doubt that, compared with the earnings in the West for similar types of work, the Japanese standard is low. The average daily wages of female factory operatives, according to official figures, amounted in 1934 to about 75 sen, that is, about 10½d. a day at the current rate of exchange; while the average daily wages of male factory hands was about 2 yen 50 sen, that is, about 2s. 11d. If we take account of the semi-annual bonuses, retirement allowances, and payments in kind, however, a considerable addition must be made before we can arrive at the true income of the workers.

[1] Since 1927 a national scheme of Health Insurance for factory workers has been in existence, and about two million workers are now covered by it. Very small undertakings are not included within the scope of this scheme.

Thus, according to F. Maurette, male workers in cotton-spinning mills who get an average cash daily wage of 1·44 yen receive as much as 2·29 yen, if payments of all kinds are included; while female workers in cotton-spinning mills whose average daily wage is 62 sen actually receive 1·20 yen.[1] These substantial additions to wages, however, apply only to the large and prosperous companies, and over the greater part of factory industry they are much less. Further, the average figures for all factory employees given above cover medium-sized and large factories; wages in small workplaces are usually much lower. The normal wages received by workers of various grades of skill and in different types of workplace are given in the table on page 172, which is based partly on official statistics and partly on personal inquiries made by the author in 1936.

Although these wage figures are liable to error, they are fairly representative of the situation in Japanese industry as a whole, and they exhibit certain striking features which are confirmed by common-sense observation. Among these features is the wide disparity between the wages received by skilled workers in different industries and between the wages in the same industries in different parts of the country. Further, it is evident that the gap between the wages of skilled workers and those of labourers is much greater than is the case in this country. And finally, the figures for the bicycle trade bring out the extent to which wages vary according to seniority. This last fact is of great importance when we are making international comparisons or are considering movements of average wages over a period of years; for a very large proportion of the Japanese industrial labour force is in the younger age groups, and the rapid growth of industry, together with the great increase in population in recent years, has increased that proportion.

These features are not difficult to explain if we take account of the economic situation as a whole. The relatively high wages paid to skilled workers in the metal and engineering industries

[1] F. Maurette, *Social Aspects of Industrial Development in Japan* (I.L.O.), p. 31.

Industry or Kind of Worker	Sex	Average Daily Wage (in yen)	Year	Remarks*
Silk Reeling	F	0·65	1934	13 large cities
Silk Reeling	F	0·74	Nov. 1935	Tokyo
Silk Reeling	F	0·41	1935	Nagoya
Operative in large cotton spinning-weaving concerns	F	0·82	1930	16–17 years of age. Whole country (large mills)
Operative in specialist cotton weaving mills	F	0·66	1930	16–17 years of age. Whole country (medium mills)
Rayon weaving	F	0·40 to 0·60	1933	Fukui Prefecture (small and medium mills)
Hosiery	F	0·62	1935	Nagoya (small and medium mills)
Hosiery	F	0·73	1934	13 large cities
Hosiery	M	1·44	1935	13 large cities
Hosiery	M	1·56	1934	13 large cities
Enamelled Ironware Trade	M	3·50	1933	Highly skilled workers in large factories
Enamelled Ironware Trade	M	0·80 to 1·30	1933	Unskilled labourers in large factories
Rubber Goods	M	1·32	1933	Osaka factories
Rubber Goods	F	0·70	1933	Osaka factories
Electric Lamp	M	1·30 to 1·50	1933	Medium factories
Type Compositor	M	3·00	Nov. 1935	Tokyo
Type Compositor	M	2·30	1935	Nagoya
Geta Maker	M	1·12	Nov. 1935	Tokyo } small workshops
Geta Maker	M	1·10	1935	Nagoya } small workshops
Lathe Machinist	M	5·00	Nov. 1935	Tokyo
Pattern Maker	M	4·47	Nov. 1935	Tokyo foundries
Blacksmith	M	2·90	Nov. 1935	Nagoya
Blacksmith	M	4·76	Nov. 1935	Tokyo
Cement Maker	M	2·54	Nov. 1935	Tokyo
Cement Maker	M	2·11	1935	Nagoya
Day Labourer	M	1·44	Nov. 1935	Tokyo
Day Labourer	F	0·78	Nov. 1935	Tokyo
Day Labourer	M	1·10	1935	Nagoya
Day Labourer	F	0·60	1935	Nagoya
Bicycle Trade	M	1·87	1930 †	Workers in large factories aged 20 to 29
Bicycle Trade	M	3·94	1930	Workers in large factories, aged 30 to 39
Bicycle Trade	M	4·12	1930	Workers in large factories, aged 40 to 49

* Tokyo is a high-wage centre; Nagoya, though a large city, is typical of low-wage urban centres. The figures include an estimate of the value of payments in kind but not apparently the semi-annual bonuses.

† Between 1930 and 1933, wages in this industry fell by about 15 per cent.

can be attributed to the scarcity of this type of labour. Until recently these trades were not highly developed in Japan, but since 1931 they have grown very rapidly and the demand for workers with the appropriate skill and experience has advanced correspondingly. The relatively low wages of unskilled workers, especially of the day labourers, are a reflection of the depressed condition of agriculture and of the overpopulation of the countryside. A vast number of unskilled workers who can find no employment on the farms have been forced into the industrial labour market, and the high birth-rate of the rural population accentuates the problem. Another important factor in producing a relatively low level of wages for unskilled workers is the immigration of Koreans into Japan. From about 40,000 in 1920 their numbers have increased to about half a million at the present time. Most of them come from the land, and in Japan they engage in some of the heaviest, dirtiest, and worst-paid jobs, such as road-making, mining, and unskilled work in the rubber and match trades. They are especially numerous in Western Japan, and it is estimated that 67 per cent. of the Koreans in Kobe earn a monthly income of less than 40 yen (£2 7s.).[1] We have seen that women textile workers come mainly from rural families and that their supply, also, has been augmented by the increased difficulty of finding work in their own locality; this accounts largely for the low level of wages in the textile trades. Geographical differences can be explained chiefly by the barriers to migration that distance places in the way of a poor community.

These disparities in wages bring out another important difference between the Japanese and the Western economic systems. In Great Britain the activities of nationally organized trade unions, and the public regulation of wages through trade boards and other types of official wage-bargaining machinery, have tended to promote uniformity of wages in the same trade, and to raise the level of wages in industries formerly regarded as "sweated," and among unskilled workers. Such machinery is of little importance in Japan,

[1] *Far Eastern Survey*, June 23rd, 1937, p. 151.

and changes in economic conditions in different parts of the industrial field are easily communicated to wages.[1] This has serious disadvantages; for when pools of low-paid workers are created in a prolonged depression, the quality of the workers deteriorates and their earning capacity may be permanently affected. On the other hand, the controls set up in England, buttressed as they have been by Unemployment Insurance, have increased the rigidity of the economic system as a whole, and have been responsible in some degree for the heavy chronic unemployment from which the country has suffered since the War. Japan, however, still retains much of the resilience in adapting herself to changing economic conditions and the capacity for redistributing her labour supply quickly as demands change, that were formerly possessed by Western countries. She has, therefore, avoided the serious difficulties associated with heavy chronic unemployment, although, as we shall see presently, she has her own problem of labour transference which has not yet been solved. That problem, however, is much simpler in a country in which the population is rapidly increasing than in European countries which are approaching a condition of stationary numbers. The rise of some industries and the decay of others through changes in relative costs and in the nature of demand occur in all countries. But decaying industries are likely to decline less rapidly in a country whose numbers are still increasing than in a country whose numbers are stationary.[2] Further, since the adjustments of numbers engaged in different industries are brought about mainly by a change in the direction of recruitment, they can be effected quickly when a large part of the population is in the younger age-groups which supply the

[1] In the small-scale industries, of course, changes in economic prosperity lead to a decline or improvement in the living conditions of the small manufacturers and the workers who board with them; while in large factories where the bonus makes up an important part of the workers' income, the employees share with the employers the financial burden of depression and the advantages of good times.

[2] Because the rise in the total number of consumers helps to offset the disadvantages to old industries of the shift of demand to new kinds of products.

new recruits. This condition is naturally found in a country where the population is rapidly growing. In such a country not merely are resilience and adaptability likely to be far greater than in a country with a stationary or falling population, but also the difficulty of establishing controls over prices and wages which might reduce that resilience is more formidable; for the pressure on the industrial labour market exerted by the huge stream of new recruits is likely to be irresistible. In Japan during recent years, as we have seen, this pressure has been particularly strong because of agricultural depression. Thus, here, as in other phases of her economic activity, Japan bears a much closer resemblance to England during her period of expanding population and transformation from a predominantly agricultural country than to England to-day.

The economic resilience of a country where wage-rates are plastic must not be exaggerated. If Japan has no large body of permanently unemployed, she has a great mass of persons who are under-employed. In the retail shops and in most of the trades providing personal services, this phenomenon is evident to a casual observer at the present time, and brings home to him the partial nature of Japan's boom. During the years of depression, 1930–31, some of the young workers who could not find the customary openings in industry, or whose employers had gone bankrupt, remained with or returned to the peasant households to which they belonged, and in view of the agricultural depression, their help on the farms was of little value.[1] In earlier times when the industrial population was relatively small, this ebb and flow between town and country did much to ease the strain of depression; but now that the urban population has become large, and as agriculture has become chronically depressed, the capacity of

[1] This statement is not, of course, inconsistent with the earlier statement that agricultural depression forced workers off the land or out of the rural industries into urban employment. The point is that the agricultural depression was so severe as to leave agriculture over-staffed in spite of a large drift of workers to the towns. Industry was not able to absorb new workers until the industrial depression lifted after 1932. In the depths of the slump in 1931 the demand for labour everywhere was low.

agriculture to take the strain of an industrial slump has declined. Certain areas of Japan, especially the agricultural districts of the north of the main island, have come to resemble the "special" areas of Great Britain. It is true that there is no mass of permanently unemployed workers in those regions; but the returns to farming labour have become so small as to give rise to famine conditions. The Government is taking steps to improve the lot of the inhabitants by encouraging the development of small-scale industries in these regions, and the Army and Navy try to distribute orders for materials so as to benefit them. So far, however, these measures have been inadequate to alleviate the terrible conditions that exist there.

It is sometimes suggested that international comparisons of money wages fail to do justice to Japan; her peculiar and cheap standard of living enables persons to lead a satisfactory life on an income which would be quite insufficient for a Westerner who must gratify numerous conventional wants before he is satisfied with his lot. This is a very difficult argument to handle because it is concerned with differences in subjective satisfactions that are not susceptible to measurement. There is, of course, some truth in it. A Japanese family can maintain a civilized and refined life in a house which is very small by Western standards and almost devoid of furniture; its food is less elaborate, and its pleasures simpler than those demanded by persons of a roughly equivalent social grade in England. In other words, squalor and wretchedness can be avoided in Japan with a much lower income than is needed in England, provided one does not value material comfort highly and has Japanese tastes. A good deal of the expenditure of the middle class and even of the well-paid artisans in England falls into the category of what Veblen called "conspicuous waste"; a man owes it to his position to maintain a certain living standard; some of his expenditure is necessary to satisfy a class convention. In Japan the calls of convention can be obeyed less expensively.[1]

[1] Some writers have tried to support a favourable view of the Japanese standard of living by showing that even poor households spend at least as

The incomes of Japanese officials and professional people compare just as unfavourably with corresponding incomes in England as do those of the workers. A Governor of a prefecture receives only about 5,000 yen a year (£335); the Director of the Bureau of Social Affairs receives 5,800 yen (£390); a university professor from £200 to £250 a year; a primary school teacher about £5 10s. a month, and the maximum salary of a policeman is about £5 5s. a month.

These considerations are important, but propagandists have, of course, tried to prove too much from them. There are certain objective standards of well-being, and these are attained by a much smaller proportion of the Japanese population than of the English population. Dieticians are agreed about the inadequacy of the food eaten by the greater part of the peasants, wage-earners, and small producers, and in consequence the Japanese are less healthy than Western peoples and their physique inferior. Sanitary conditions are bad, and housing and working conditions are below the standards reached in this country. Both the workers and the directing and professional classes present the appearance of being subject to a greater nervous strain which comes from prolonged labour and feverishly pursued ambitions than is evident in most Western countries, where the ordinary demands of living can be satisfied more easily. Some of the pathos which to the foreigner seems characteristic of Japanese life can perhaps be attributed to this association of ambitious effort and scanty reward.

The problem of the standard of living at present reached by the people is scarcely as important as the problem of whether that standard is improving or declining. Some general indications have been given elsewhere to show that in the towns and the rural areas not far distant from the main centres of population, standards during the present century have risen substantially, although this

high a proportion of their income on "amenities" as do households of a similar type in most Western countries. In qualification of this argument and of the views set out above, it must be remembered that Japanese convention enforces a relatively heavy expenditure on presents.

probably does not apply to the more remote rural areas. It has been estimated, for instance, that by 1929 real wages in the cities were 60 or 70 per cent. above those of pre-War days.[1] Movements in the last eight years, however, are more difficult to interpret. Money wages fell very heavily during 1930 and 1931; but as the cost of living declined even more, those wage-earners who retained their jobs were probably better off except in so far as a reduction in bonuses offset the rise in real wages. But in these years there was an increase in unemployment and in under-employment; and the incomes of small producers, shopkeepers, and especially of the peasants dropped very steeply. So, on balance, there can be little doubt that the living standards of the poorer members of the community were lowered. After 1931 the different sections of the population were variously affected. The cost of living rose, although by the end of 1936 it was still short of the level of 1929. General money wages and actual earnings did not rise significantly until 1937, and the index shows that they were then much lower than they had been in 1929. But the movements differed from industry to industry. In the metallurgical and engineering industries, especially among the skilled workers, money wages rose far more than the cost of living in this period (1931–36); whereas in the cotton industry money wages continued to fall. In the larger mills this fall has probably been offset by a rise in bonuses, which, of course, has been substantial in all large-scale trades. In most of the small textile mills and in many of the little workshops, so numerous in Japanese manufacturing industry, it seems probable that real wages have definitely fallen since 1931, and that they are below the level attained in 1929. This applies also to the condition of the unskilled day-labourers. On the other hand, unemployment and under-employment have been reduced.

It has seemed extraordinary to some Westerners that wages, even money wages, should have fallen in certain Japanese industries during a period of boom. The chronic depression in agriculture, as shown previously, affords an explanation. We may,

[1] *Far Eastern Survey*, July 15th, 1936, p. 156.

perhaps, be allowed to repeat the arguments that have been used. The price of rice recovered after 1931, though until 1935 it was well below the 1929 level; but cocoon prices have remained very low. Members of farming families, especially the girls who previously found employment in the silk mills, have been obliged to enter the industrial labour market, with depressing effects there upon the wages of female textile workers and of unskilled labourers. The technical improvements, especially in textiles, which have enabled increase of output to take place without a proportionate addition to the labour force, have also kept down wages in trades in which these improvements have been prominent.

These changes are such as might be expected in a period in which the country has been transferring her resources from one group of industries to another on a very large scale, and in which the composition of the industrial labour force has been greatly altered. The movements may be summed up without excessive simplification by saying that, compared with the situation in the pre-depression years, skilled industrial workers in the large-scale trades are now better off, but that in agriculture and in a great part of small-scale industry and commerce and especially in those trades in which the labour supply has been most markedly augmented by the agricultural depression, real earnings have certainly not improved, and in many cases have deteriorated. This tentative conclusion may seem to be at variance with the figures which show the great rise in industrial output since 1929. More goods are being produced than before, and yet a large part of the population has not improved its standards; what, then, has happened to this increased output? The following answer may be given. First, the population of Japan Proper rose from 64 millions in 1930 to 69 millions in 1935. There are more consumers among whom the goods have to be distributed. Secondly, the rise in output has been substantial only in the capital-goods trades; that is to say, Japan has been bending her energies to building up equipment for future production of consumable goods rather than for greatly increasing the immediate supply of those goods. Some part of this production, of course, has been in the capital goods destined for Manchukuo, and this investment may or may not bring in a satisfactory return. Another part has consisted of additions to the Navy and the supply of munitions, and from this no future return can be expected. Finally, Japan's terms of trade with the rest of the world have worsened since 1931. In the last few years she has been obliged to send a larger and larger quantity of manufactured exports in order to obtain a given amount of imports of industrial raw materials. For this unfavourable movement the restrictions placed by foreign Governments on Japanese exports are in part responsible. The problem of a deterioration in the terms of trade is one of the most serious which Japan has to face. For many years to come she will have to import increasing quantities of raw materials for her rapidly growing population. To obtain these imports she must export manufactured goods. If exports to the chief foreign markets are restricted she will have to seek other markets for their disposal and she will have to sell them on worse terms than before. This prospect is ominous; if present tendencies in international trade persist she will find great difficulty in raising the standard of living of her people.

The economic structure of Japan, the system of industrial relations that exists there, and the paramount political influences, are all hostile to the development of strong labour organization. About 45 per cent. of the factory workers consist of women whose industrial experience is short and who cannot therefore be effectively organized.[1] In many of the large-scale industries where trade unionism might be expected to become an active force, the prevalence of the bonus system and other devices associated with "paternalism," or what socialists call "welfare capitalism," is unfavourable to attempts to organize the workers on a craft, occupational, or industrial basis. A large part of the railway system and important undertakings in the heavy industries are in the hands of the Government or of semi-official bodies, and here the difficulties encountered by trade unionism are even greater. In the

[1] "Factory workers" are those in workplaces with five or more workers.

great mass of small-scale trades the intimate personal relationships between employers and workers delay the growth among the latter of a consciousness of a common interest distinct from that of their

Wages Indices

1926 = 100

Year	(*a*) Bank of Japan's Index of Actual Earnings	(*b*) Bank of Japan's Index of Wage-Rates	(*c*) Bank of Japan's Retail Price Index	Index of Real Earnings $= \frac{a}{c}$ *
1929	103·9	98·6	91	114
1930	98·7	96·2	78	127
1931	90·7	91·3	68	137
1932	88·1	88·1	69	128
1933	89·2	85·1	73	122
1934	91·2	82·9	75	121
1935	91·1	81·3	76	120
1936	91·8	80·7	80	115

*Real Earnings in Various Industries**

1926 = 100

Year	Cotton Spinning	Silk Reeling	Machine Manufacturing	Metal Manufacturing	Cement, Pottery & Glass	Woodworking, Furniture
1929	103·6	101·3	110·0	111·5	106·2	102·5
1931	99·4	90·5	119·3	125·1	113·0	118·0
1933	80·6	79·5	129·7	124·1	107·8	107·4
1935	72·0	75·4	111·0	116·8	97·8	86·1

* No account is taken here of semi-annual bonuses, which were low in the depression years and high afterwards. Thus, while the index shows the varying trend in different industries, it under-estimates considerably the growth in the real income of workers since 1931 in the more prosperous industries. In those industries, moreover, the proportion of younger and, consequently, lower-paid workers to the total has greatly increased since 1931, and this is responsible for reducing the average real earnings in them, so that the average figure is misleading as a guide to movements in the wages of adult skilled men. Small workshops are not covered by these wage indices.

employers. The absence of any form of public regulation of wages, the development of which in Great Britain has encouraged trade unionism, must also be noted. The existence of powerful unions is, moreover, dependent in some degree on the possibility of their securing a monopoly of the labour supply in particular trades. In Japan the throng of new recruits which annually crowds into the industrial labour market for reasons already described, places insuperable obstacles in the way of any policy designed to create such a monopoly, and one of the chief motives behind trade-union development in other countries is perforce of little account.

The total membership of Japanese trade unions is about 380,000, and the only industries in which the workers are powerfully organized are the transport industries, especially the mercantile marine. It is only in the latter field that the principle of collective bargaining has been recognized. About four-fifths of the members are covered by a Trade Union Congress, formed in 1932, of which the largest constituent is the General Federation of Japanese Labour. This group favours an essentially moderate and "constitutional" policy. It is largely concerned with obtaining improvements in hours, working conditions, measures for the relief of unemployment, and the legal recognition of collective bargaining through legislation. A Trade Union Bill, sponsored by the Federation, passed the Lower House of the Diet in 1931, but was rejected by the Peers, and this measure has now little prospect of reaching the Statute Book in view of the present political tendencies in Japan. Since the adoption of universal manhood suffrage in 1926, the trade unions have tried to build up political parties representing the workers; but they are divided in aim and they have achieved little success in this venture. The poverty of the Japanese masses has prevented the unions from amassing large funds for strike-pay or for the granting of friendly society benefits, and so one of the chief means for retaining the loyalty of members in times of difficulty is lacking.

Although the labour movement is in a very early stage of development, workers, both those who are members of trade unions and those who are not so organized, are not incapable of bringing pressure on employers, and strikes for higher wages, adequate dismissal allowances, and the prevention of victimization are far from uncommon. They are, indeed, more successful than might be supposed from the apparent weakness of the trade unions; for employers, like all in authority in Japan, have a real fear of the public opinion of their subordinates. In recent years these strikes have been especially numerous in the smaller factories in which both employers and workers have reaped fewer benefits from the industrial boom than have their counterparts in the large enterprises. These strikes are, however, usually confined to single works or enterprises, and widespread national movements for improvements in wages are difficult to organize because of the arbitrary interference of the police. The employers, on the other hand, in many industries have agreements with one another which are intended to restrict competition for labour in times of good trade. The Japan Cotton Spinners' Association, which covers nearly all the spinners, was originally formed mainly for this purpose, and such agreements are found even in small-scale trades. For example, the manufacturers in the wool textile industry of the Nagoya neighbourhood hold what is known as a *Kotatsu* meeting from time to time, in a local restaurant, for the purpose of fixing their employees' wages.[1] Only in the shipping industry and a very few others has machinery for conciliation been set up, or a recognized procedure to be followed in cases of disputes been agreed upon by workers and employers.

The vast majority of the trade unions "accept" the capitalist system and are conservative in their general social policy; but there are a few organizations which have embraced Marxism. In the early part of the post-War decade this and other left-wing doctrines had an important influence on the minds of certain groups of workers and of the intelligentsia, especially university students;

[1] Here we have an example of Japanese punning. The *Kotatsu* is a simple heating device. Burning charcoal is placed in a container covered by a *futon*, or quilt, under which the guest sits. But *Kotatsu*, written with different characters, also means an announcement, or verbal notification.

so much so that the authorities became alarmed and dissolved the left-wing unions in 1928. For some years afterwards, however, especially during the depression, Marxism increased the number of its adherents, and societies for propagating communist doctrines continued to flourish both among workers and students, although it is doubtful if they ever possessed any real political significance. Since 1931 communist and left-wing organizations of all kinds have been suppressed; and hundreds of their adherents have been arrested and forced to recant by the police. It is impossible to estimate whether these movements still continue to exercise any considerable influence, or whether they have been stamped out. The fact that the police still find it necessary to make periodical mass-arrests of so-called communists has led some people to think that Marxism leads a vigorous underground existence. This inference may, however, be unjustified. Illiberal Governments which fear any kind of criticism are apt to apply the term "communist" to any group of persons who venture to give expression to "dangerous thoughts," with the object of gaining support from timid conservatives or the politically indifferent mass. In the judgment of the writer, the likelihood of a powerful revolutionary movement from the left is negligible. The most serious political movement among the poorer members of Japan's society has arisen not from among the industrial workers but from the poorer tenant farmers. Disputes between landlords and associations of the impoverished peasants over questions of rent have been very frequent in recent years, and a strong feeling of dissatisfaction towards the present social order has grown up among the rural population. But on the whole, as we shall see later, the poor farmers look, for the amelioration of their lot, towards a revolution from the right rather than from the left.

CHAPTER X

JAPAN INTO NIPPON

"I had thought there was a pushing to and fro
At times like this, that overset the scale
And trampled measure down."

W. B. YEATS

DURING the era when the tide of democracy was flowing strongly and when nations without representative political systems were regarded as poor and disreputable relations by the rest of the world, Japan strove to cast her institutions in a form which bore at any rate a superficial resemblance to those of the great Western Powers. These new institutions were not, however, securely based upon popular sentiment, and political democracy was scarcely in accord with her traditions. Still, in the more generous and impressionable minds, liberalism found a ready response, and during the first post-War decade it seemed probable that industrial development would strengthen forces hostile to the older governing cliques and that Japan would ultimately come to possess a kind of government comparable to that found among the Western democracies. There was reason for hoping, also, that with the decline in the power of the military cliques, she might come to adopt wholeheartedly a more pacific foreign policy and might be counted on as a loyal adherent of the League of Nations. But in the general return to primitive methods of government and to international anarchy during the last eight years, Japan has led the way. She has cast off completely the garments of liberalism which she was just beginning to wear without discomfort, and she has assumed, almost with relief, her native armour, adorned though it may be with a plume borrowed from the Western dictators. Since 1931, fanaticism has steadily grown in strength, and, as elsewhere, rational humanitarianism has been forced into an ever-narrowing circle within her national life.

The economic causes which helped to bring about this change in political trends have already been examined. The Great Depression, by discrediting the business cliques and the party Governments that largely depended on them, prepared the way for a reversion of power to other groups. The distress of the peasantry, accentuated by the return of unemployed industrial workers to their rural families, gave rise to a formidable torrent of discontent directed mainly against the great capitalists and politicians. This discontent was shared by multitudes of urban workers and small shop-keepers, traders, and manufacturers, who still had close family links with the farmers, and who were suffering severely from the rationalization of industry and from the increasing concentration of economic power in the hands of the *Zaibatsu*. It was communicated, also, to the Army; for the soldiers were drawn chiefly from the land and many of the young officers, since the military reforms of 1925 had come from the small landlords, themselves the victims of agricultural depression. The general dissatisfaction was used by the military and naval cliques as a lever for overthrowing the Government and for reverting to a policy that was in accordance with their own ambitions. For this opportunity they had been waiting for several years. The foreign policy of the Minseito Ministry had outraged their own sense of Japan's lofty destiny, and the tendency for power to shift to the civil authorities, if continued, must have led to a subordination of the fighting services to the Cabinet. In this connection, the internal conflict that arose over the London Naval Treaty of 1930 had far-reaching implications and deserves a more than perfunctory discussion.

When Japan consented to participate in the London Conference for the limitation of naval armaments, her delegates were instructed to insist upon certain claims deemed essential by the Admiralty. These included a demand for 70 per cent. of the United States' strength in 10,000-ton 8-inch-gun cruisers, and a similar ratio in all auxiliary craft. The delegates to the Conference included

R. Wakatsuki, a politician and former Minseito Prime Minister, T. Matsudaira, a member of the family of Court Nobles and the Ambassador at London, and Admiral Takarabe, a son-in-law of Admiral Yamamoto, head of the Satsuma naval clique. It soon became evident that the aims of the Navy and the Cabinet were in conflict one with the other. The Cabinet, especially the Prime Minister, the Foreign Minister, and the Finance Minister, were anxious to effect an agreement in the interests of international relations and of budgetary stability. The Navy, however, was determined to insist upon a 70 per cent. ratio, and since the United States' proposal was for a 60 per cent. ratio, the Navy's policy meant a breakdown of the Conference. Takarabe and his technical advisers were, however, out-manœuvred, and he was led to give his consent to a compromise drawn up by Senator Reed, an American delegate, and Matsudaira. But Takarabe could not carry the naval chiefs with him. His leadership was disputed by Admirals Kato, Okada, and others, who insisted that the original demands should be maintained. Hamaguchi, the Prime Minister, strengthened by a great party victory at the elections of February 1930, decided to overrule the naval cliques, and instructed the delegates to sign the Reed–Matsudaira compromise.

The Government immediately came under fire. Both during the Conference and afterwards the naval cliques, through various societies which they controlled, tried to win public support by widespread propaganda in favour of their policy. In the House of Representatives the Seiyukai bitterly attacked their rivals on the ground that national security had been jeopardized. From the standpoint of the future of parliamentary government this attempt to oust the Minseito from office was ill-advised; for the essential conflict was not so much over the terms of the Treaty as over the right of the Cabinet to assume responsibility for national defence. In the House of Peers it was urged by many opponents of the Government that questions affecting the Army and Navy should be decided by the general staffs and not by civilian politicians. The Government, however, evaded this fundamental issue and declared that the Treaty had been signed by the Minister of the Navy (Takarabe) and after consultation with the naval experts. Indeed, had the Prime Minister definitely claimed Cabinet responsibility for naval affairs, then the resignation of the Service Ministers would have followed, and the Government would have been forced to resign. Outside Parliament, however, this issue was widely discussed. Professor Minobe, the great jurist, explicitly stated that the power to decide on the military and naval strength of the State rested, not with the general staffs, but with the Throne, to whom the Cabinet alone could give responsible advice; and he added that this principle applied to the making of treaties. The liberal Press and the greater part of the informed public supported these views. Nor was the Navy united in opposition. Apart from Takarabe, Admiral Saito, Governor-General of Korea, favoured the ratification of the Treaty, and declared that the ultimate decision in these affairs rested with the Cabinet. What was even more important was the support given to the Ministry by the personal advisers of the Emperor, Prince Saionji (the *Genro*), Count Makino (Lord Privy Seal), the Minister of the Imperial Household, and other Court officials. With this powerful backing, the Government felt strong enough to advise the Emperor to displace Admiral Kato, its leading opponent, from his position of chief of the naval general staff, and, although the Supreme War Council had reported unfavourably on the Treaty, to petition the Emperor to refer the matter to the Privy Council. There were powerful opponents in this Council; but with the *Genro*, the Court officials, the Cabinet, the Lower House, and the Press in favour of ratification, and in view of divergence of opinion in naval circles, the Council could not reject the Treaty, and so advised its acceptance. It seemed that constitutional government (in the Western sense) had won a striking victory over the forces of reaction; but its triumph was short-lived. The powerful naval clique was alienated; both the Services became alarmed at the threatened destruction of their political influence; and when the tide of popular approval for the Government's policy began to ebb with the deepening of the depression, the cliques were ready to seize their opportunity.

In February 1931 Baron Shidehara, the Foreign Minister, committed a serious blunder by stating in Parliament that the Emperor's ratification of the London Treaty was evidence that national security was not endangered by its provisions. As we have seen, an attempt to consolidate a political victory by use of the Emperor's name is abhorrent to the Japanese political system, and the Government lost credit on this, as on previous occasions. The crisis came, however, with the outbreak of the trouble in Manchuria in 1931. In this affair the Cabinet came into conflict with the Army and, weakened by its struggle with the Navy in the previous year, it succumbed to this more powerful attack. The Manchurian "affair" in its international aspects will be dealt with in the next chapter; here it will be considered only in so far as it affected, and was affected by, the Japanese internal political situation.

All Japanese Governments in the post-War period, whatever their "complexion," insisted upon the "special position" of their country in Manchuria and regarded any interference in that region by other Powers as an infringement of that position. There were, however, marked differences of opinion about the methods by which that "special position" could best be maintained. Shidehara and the Minseito Government followed a policy of conciliation and friendship towards China, believing that the political interests of Japan could best be promoted by fostering good relations with the State so intimately concerned with her Manchurian claims. This attitude was supported by the financial and industrial interests. The Seiyukai under Tanaka, the Choshu General, were in favour of an aggressive foreign policy with regard to China, and in this they were backed by the Army cliques. The Navy cliques were, on the whole, supporters of the Minseito policy; for they held that Japan's destiny pointed to the South Seas, and they feared that the resources necessary to carry out a programme of naval expansion might be dissipated by large-scale military adventures on the Continent.

The failure of Tanaka's "positive policy" in China had been one reason which carried the Minseito into office in 1929, and for a time the growing liberalization of public opinion provided a foundation on which Shidehara could build. But by the early months of 1931 there had been a shifting of forces which was threatening to undermine the Government and to overthrow its foreign policy. China's efforts to ruin the South Manchuria Railway and the boycotts of Japanese goods that accompanied the "rights recovery" campaign alarmed the financial and industrial interests and gave rise to doubts in those circles about the effectiveness of conciliation. The Navy, as a result of the London Naval Treaty, had been converted into a bitter enemy of the Government, and the Army, though not without *schadenfreude* at the discomfiture of the rival Service, felt that its own political power might next be challenged by the Cabinet. This challenge seemed to be imminent in the first part of 1931; for the Finance Minister, Inouye, was known to be contemplating reductions in military expenditure in the interests of sound finance, and proposals for disarmament were warmly greeted in the Press. When the military cliques in May 1931 declared that no reduction in military expenditure was possible, the liberal Press denounced them and began to criticize vigorously the system which conferred on the Army a political power independent of the Cabinet. Dissension between the civil and military Ministers over this major constitutional issue as well as over Manchurian policy grew steadily in the summer of that year. Meanwhile, the worsening of the agricultural depression had convinced a section of the rural classes that a complete change in the political and economic system was a necessary condition of the amelioration of their lot, and this view was strongly held by the rank and file of the Army and the younger officers, who were drawn mainly from the land. "Patriotic" societies formed by fanatical nationalists both inside and outside the Army began to demand radical changes in methods of government, and Manchuria occupied a prominent place in this turmoil; for territorial expansion seemed to offer to the farmers and landlords a means of alleviating their poverty, and it was over Manchurian policy that the divergent aims of the civil and military members of the Government were most clearly revealed. Finally, the development of communism and other left-wing movements among workers and the intelligentsia had been accelerated by the circumstances of the world depression, and this had the effect both of alarming conservative Japanese into favouring a stern reactionary policy and of weakening parliamentary government by reducing the number of its adherents in those very classes on which it might expect to count for most whole-hearted support.

The result was that when the Army began to make elaborate preparations for war in Manchuria, and when the War Office assumed the initiative in the conduct of Sino-Japanese affairs, the Cabinet was powerless. After the outbreak of the "war" on September 18th, the civil Ministers continued to urge caution and restraint; but the Army commanders on the spot ignored their orders, and the Government had no choice but to acquiesce in military operations which were beyond their control. The actions of the military cliques did not pass without criticism from liberal Japanese in the autumn of 1931; but these dissenting voices became subdued as the war proceeded. The Government was violently attacked in the House of Representatives by the opposition party, and there were defections from the Ministerial ranks. In December it resigned, and Inukai and his Seiyukai party formed a new Cabinet. In February there were elections which gave him a large majority.

The Seiyukai, in the previous two years, had allied itself with the military and naval cliques, in order to oust its rival; but, as events were to prove, in doing so it had helped to dig the grave for representative government as a whole. By the time Inukai came into office, the public enthusiasm for Parliament had waned, and among the young officers of the Army its destruction was vigorously advocated. The opposition of the Foreign Office to the Army's actions in Manchuria, and later, at Shanghai; the failure of the Government to relieve rural distress; the alleged corruption of the politicians and their subservience to the demands of the *Zaibatsu*, were all denounced as a condemnation of parliamentary government. The *Zaibatsu* themselves were attacked. They were said to have pursued selfish commercial interests and to have acted contrary to the ideals of the State. They had attempted to monopolize the more profitable industries, and in doing so they had ruined small traders and manufacturers. Mitsui's Trading Company,[1] in particular, was a target, because this enterprising concern had entered successfully many lines of business which had previously been in the hands of small country merchants. It had been active in obtaining financial control over numerous small manufacturers; and whenever a new export market was opened up by traders and showed signs of being profitable, Mitsui stepped in and captured that trade for itself. It was said that Mitsui had made great profits out of exchange dealings in anticipation of the fall of the yen at the end of 1931, and had supplied the barbed wire which held up the Japanese advance at Shanghai in the spring of 1932. Nor was this hostility on the part of extreme nationalist groups limited to the politicians and the *Zaibatsu*; certain "privileged" groups which in the previous decade had shown themselves to be favourably disposed to parliamentary institutions and to the newer political forces were also the object of attack. These included the *Genro* and the Court officials. The military hierarchy found this antagonism to rival governmental cliques useful in consolidating its power. General Araki, Minister of War in the Inukai Government, said in Parliament that "the soldiers might be moved to action unless the social maladjustments were rectified so that they could devote all their thought and endeavours to military affairs."[2]

The first violent expression of this internal conflict came with the assassination of the Minister of Finance in the Minseito Government, Mr. J. Inouye, in February 1932, and of Baron Takuma Dan, the managing director of Mitsui Gomei Company, in March. These political murders were followed on May 15th by the shooting of the Prime Minister, Inukai, at the hands of a "patriotic" society known as the *Ketsumeidan*, or Blood League, which was composed

[1] Mitsui Bussan Kaisha, known among foreign business men as M. B. K.
[2] T. Takeuchi, *op. cit.*, p. 381.

PLATE X

A STREET VENDOR

of military and naval officers, farmers, and others. At the same time, bombs were thrown at the headquarters of the Seiyukai, the home of Count Makino (Lord Privy Seal), the Metropolitan Police Board, the Bank of Japan, the Mitsubishi Bank, and the power stations in Tokyo. The Blood League was shown later to have drawn up a "death-list" which was nicely representative of all the "privileged" classes outside the Service cliques; for it included the names of three Seiyukai and three Minseito statesmen, three Mitsui *banto* (officials), two Mitsubishi *banto*, Prince Saionji (*Genro*), Count Makino (Lord Privy Seal), Count Ito (Court Chamberlain), Prince Tokugawa (President of the House of Peers), and one *banto* from each of the following *Zaibatsu*, Yasuda, Okura, and Sumitomo. These high personages escaped, however, some to be attacked another day.

The aims of the groups responsible for these outrages require some discussion. A desire to wreak vengeance on those responsible for the London Naval Treaty and the encroachment of the civil authorities on the political privileges of the Services was certainly one important motive. But the Blood League had other and more ambitious aims. It wished dramatically to demonstrate the hostility of the young officers and the peasants towards capitalism and its allies among the privileged classes, and to prepare the way for a Showa Restoration—that is to say, for a form of government which would make the military and naval authorities the sole effective advisers of the Emperor. The group had been inspired by several fanatics. Among them was K. Tachibana, a propagandist who tried to convert farming communities to a belief that the existing political and economic systems were hostile to the interests of the farmers and so to those of the State. Reform could come only by concerted efforts of farmers and soldiers, who should sweep away by violence all who opposed their aims. A Buddhist priest, A. Inouye, who held "fascist" views, exercised a profound influence on the minds of young officers and was himself directly responsible for the murders of J. Inouye and Takuma Dan. Dr. S. Okawa, another nationalist zealot, gained many adherents from military circles and from among the masses for his policy of direct action, and he it was who actually supplied ammunition and funds to the perpetrators of the outrages on May 15th. These funds were stated in evidence at the trial to have been provided by a great business house which desired to overthrow Mitsui and Mitsubishi from their dominant position. Some Japanese, moreover, had an uneasy suspicion that these officers acted at the instigation of their superiors; but, although the latter profited by their action, this suspicion was probably ill-founded. Undoubtedly, what the murderers hoped to do was to throw the populace into such a panic as to require the imposition of martial law. From martial law to a military dictatorship (under the Emperor) was but a step.

These plans, however, were not successful. There was no panic, and martial law was not declared. But though the chief purpose was not achieved, these acts of violence had, as always in Japan, a result very different from what might have been anticipated. In most countries the brutal murder of a statesman by his political opponents would be certain to win public sympathy for the party to which the victim belonged. In Japan it is otherwise. The murderee is held to bear the major part of the responsibility for the murder, on the ground, apparently, that he is guilty of provoking his assassins. The murderers were arrested and charged; but a large section of public opinion regarded them as patriots, and the greater part of the Press, which only a year before had been critical of the military cliques, now denounced the politicians. In the end, the murderers received comparatively light sentences. Mitsui gave the unfortunate Dan's post in the firm to a person who believed in a less aggressive commercial policy, and "this appointment was generally interpreted as a recognition on the part of the Mitsui interests of their moral responsibility for the occurrence of the May 15th affair."[1] At the same time, Mitsui announced the cessation of their expansionist policy so far as small-scale trade was concerned; those responsible for that policy were relegated to positions of obscurity in the firm; certain companies were thrown open to public investment

[1] *Contemporary Japan*, December 1933, p. 505.

so as to meet the charge of monopolization; and the House made large donations to the social services. The Army and Navy were also affected. The regulations of the Naval General Staff were revised so as to place its power over naval affairs in relation to that of the Cabinet beyond any doubt, and the prior claims of military over other kinds of expenditure, which were in debate before the murders, were admitted easily afterwards. In other words, the admirals and generals, though they might deplore the events of May 15th, got what they wanted as a result of them.

In another respect, too, power shifted back to the older cliques. When the question of a new Government arose, Prince Saionji originally proposed Dr. Suzuki, the President of the Seiyukai, for the premiership. But the Army refused to countenance any party Cabinet, and so Saionji had to be content with a Government of the old bureaucratic-military type. The advance towards representative government had thus sustained a definite set-back. If the military and naval cliques were willing to gain political profit from the popular disapproval of politicians and from the activities of the "young officers" and their peasant associates, yet they could not contemplate a Government drawn from the ranks of "fascist" demagogues. They could view with equanimity the downfall of the parties, the weakening of the liberally minded *Genro* and Court officials and the check to the *Zaibatsu*; but this did not mean that they were prepared to see power pass from the "privileged" groups to peasant idealogues and "young officers." They were happy to be able to use the popular outburst against capitalism and economic liberalism for their own ends; but they did not wish to see upstarts and demagogues in the saddle. So a Government of compromise came into being, a Government which, since it was mainly in the hands of the military and naval cliques, was likely to prove acceptable to the discontented peasants and young officers, and which, at the same time, would have little sympathy with any nonsense like a Showa Restoration. The older military leaders knew full well that they could not dispense with the experienced administrators whom the *Zaibatsu* and the civil service could supply, nor indeed without the wealth and productive resources of the *Zaibatsu*. The "young officers" might say, as they did, that Manchukuo was won with the blood of the Army, and must not, therefore, be a field for capitalist exploitation. But if the capitalists were to be excluded or harassed, where was the money coming from to exploit it at all?

Attempts were made to persuade Prince Saionji to recommend Baron Hiranuma, Vice-President of the Privy Council, as Prime Minister; for Hiranuma was known to have "fascist" sympathies. But he chose, instead, Admiral Saito. Saito had long experience of Korean administration, and unlike the dominant members of the naval clique in the past, he was not a Satsuma man, and so he could be regarded as aloof from partisan rivalries. In other words, he was a conservative administrator who had little sympathy with the Japanese brand of "fascism." Although bureaucrats and militarists received many portfolios in the new Cabinet, the parties were not excluded, for the Seiyukai held three Ministries and the Minseito two. The new Government was, therefore, a "national" Government, not a "fascist" or military dictatorship. It represented a new grouping of the rival cliques, with the business interests and parties subordinate, but not excluded. It had to do something to assist the depressed farmers; it had to placate the extremists in the Army by raising expenditure on armaments and by giving the Army predominance in the administration of Manchukuo; but it was not prepared to nationalize all the industries in order to create a war-time economy nor to carry out the fantastic schemes of economic reorganization that the extreme nationalists wanted.

The new Government proceeded to "recognize" the new State of Manchukuo, to secede from the League of Nations, and to adopt a reflationary financial policy. In this connection a greatly increased expenditure on the Services and on farm relief was authorized and was financed by internal borrowing. "Fascist" societies were put down; Dr. S. Okawa, the most prominent leader of the nationalist movement, was arrested; and the War Minister abjured the officers to cease from their political activities. At the same time there was a round-up of communists and others suspected of "dangerous" thoughts. The Government's position, however, was far from secure. The Seiyukai, which possessed a majority in the Lower House, believed that they ought to have been allowed to remain in office after Inukai's assassination, and factions within their ranks attacked the Saito Cabinet. At the same time the Army and Navy were dissatisfied with their appropriations, and Takahashi, the Finance Minister, who wished to keep reflation under control, had bitter quarrels with his military and naval colleagues.

The Saito Cabinet, in spite of several changes in personnel, survived these attacks until July 1934, when one of its members was implicated in the notorious scandal about the Imperial Rayon Company. Since all the accused connected with this case have lately been acquitted, it would seem that the whole affair was engineered by the Government's political opponents, partly with the object of bringing it down. Its resignation, however, did little to change the complexion of the Cabinet. The retiring Prime Minister, contrary to the usual procedure in such circumstances, was asked by the *Genro* to name his successor. He did so, and as the Lord Privy Seal, the President of the Privy Council, and other elder statesmen concurred in his choice, the *Genro* recommended Admiral Okada for the premiership. Several of the more important among the Ministers in the preceding Cabinet continued in office, and Okada also succeeded in securing the support of the Minseito party, which provided two Ministers. The Seiyukai, however, refused to co-operate, and expelled from the party the three of its members who accepted portfolios. This refusal was based on the view that Suzuki, their leader, should have been asked to head a national Government; and the party was indignant with Okada for having filled the chief Ministries before extending his invitation for co-operation.

The Okada Government, like its predecessor, was thus a "compromise" Government, composed of conservative bureaucrats and militarists with an admixture of politicians, representing the business cliques, although the latter had a smaller place in this Government than in the last. The compromise, however, was unstable. Takahashi, the Finance Minister, had to fight hard against the demands of the Services for greatly increased appropriations. The Army anticipated war with Russia, and a long period of "national emergency;" and they pressed hard for an enlarged military expenditure. Takahashi, however, though the initiator of a reflationary policy, was determined steadily to reduce the budgetary deficit, so as to prevent any danger of uncontrolled inflation. To a large extent he had his way, but only by keeping the expenditure on farm relief and public works far below what was demanded by the Seiyukai and the spokesmen of the rural communities. That he was able to pursue his policy for several years was largely attributable to the support of the Navy and the bureaucratic and business cliques represented in the Cabinet. It was no accident that the Prime Ministers in both of these compromise Governments were naval men. The Navy is, on the whole, more "respectable" than the Army; less infected with radical ideas about a Showa Restoration. It was anxious to check the ambitious plans of conquest in Asia held by the left groups of the Army; for it considered that Japan's destiny lay to the South and that heavy commitments in Manchukuo, Mongolia, and North China would dissipate financial resources that could best be employed in extending naval armaments. The rise in Japan's export trade after 1932 gave weight to the Navy's claim that the protection of this trade was of paramount importance; while the great business houses were anxious to defeat the Army's schemes for State control over industry. Thus, in these compromise Governments, the Navy and big business were in alliance for the purpose of putting a brake on the Army's extremists, and there were among the older and conservative Army leaders many who disliked the political activities and grandiose plans of the "young officer" groups. It is significant that General Araki, who in 1932 as War Minister had been the darling of the young officers, the spokesman of extreme nationalistic views, and the critic of capitalists and politicians, was replaced in 1934 by General Hayashi, a conservative general whose interests were mainly professional, and who had little sympathy with young-officer politics. In the following year Hayashi began to weed out the extremists from positions of influence in the Army and dismissed, among others, General Mazaki, Director of Military Education, who had strong sympathies with the plan for a Showa Restoration. But these attempts to curb the extremists did not pass unchallenged. In August 1935, as a protest against Mazaki's dismissal and the unfavourable attitude shown towards "fascist" officers, Lieutenant-Colonel Aizawa murdered Hayashi's chief assistant, Major-General Nagata. This forced Hayashi's resignation, since, according to the Japanese political tradition, those in power must accept responsibility for any violent expression of disapproval of their administration or policy.

Although power seemed to be in the hands of the moderates, and important sections of public opinion were again veering round to the view that parliamentary government might soon be restored, later events show the existence of strong forces, during the years 1932–36, which at all times threatened to overturn the precarious balance that had been established. The "fascist" groups were indignant because the destruction of parliamentary government had meant, not the downfall of the privileged classes (the elder statesmen, court officials, conservative Army and Navy cliques and the *Zaibatsu*), but merely a redistribution of power among those classes. The concessions made by the *Zaibatsu* to placate public hostility were regarded as mere camouflage, and it was said that the throwing open of great companies to public investment did not in the least disturb those who remained in control; while, of course, greater military expenditure brought yet more substantial profits to the *Zaibatsu* who owned the munition plants. The industrial and export boom had raised the incomes of great capitalists and of some classes of factory workers; but the rise in retail prices had offset the advantages of increased employment for the majority. In other words, small producers and many classes of wage-earners were working harder without receiving any substantially greater return, and this gave rise to resentment. Although the position of agriculture had improved slightly through the recovery of rice prices, the farmers in the silk-raising areas still remain depressed, and little had been done to alleviate their condition by public expenditure. Irrational and mystical political doctrines increased the number of their adherents. There was a growing insistence on the peculiar righteousness of the Japanese race and its political constitution, and on the magnificence of its origin and destiny. Aizawa had expressed the views of many extremists when he declared at his trial that the world was in distress because of capitalism, communism, anarchism, and atheism, and other doctrines imported into Japan from the West, and that it was the duty of Japanese to establish a form of society in accordance with the Emperor's wishes. Young men and women of the towns flocked to the modern dance-halls, cafés, and cinemas, and embraced the depraved customs of the West, indifferent to the crisis through which Japan was passing and to the claims of the Imperial Way of Life. "Dangerous thoughts" continued to emanate from the universities, and liberalism still flourished in intellectual circles. The "patriots" demanded that this careless assumption of Western habits and thoughts should be abandoned, and that the stern virtues of loyalty should be more firmly inculcated.

It was in the early months of 1935 that Professor Minobe was obliged to resign from the House of Peers, ostensibly because of his Emperor-Organ theory, but actually because of his views about the subordination of the fighting services to Cabinet control. This resignation was brought about, not by the wishes of the Government, but by pressure from extremists. Furthermore, the Kwantung Army, which constituted the *de facto* government of Manchukuo, had met with little success in its efforts to provide for the economic exploitation of that region. Banditry continued and made life and property unsafe. Investors were reluctant to provide funds for the semi-official enterprises of that country, for the prospects of securing a return on their money were not favourable in view of the strict control exercised over economic affairs by military authorities hostile to the *Zaibatsu*. This situation did not contribute to good relationships between business and the Army extremists. The liberal forces were weakened in consequence of the growth of restrictions imposed by foreign Governments on Japanese exports; for these restrictions provoked widespread indignation in business circles and strengthened the support for the extremists' plan to create an economic bloc consisting of the Japanese Empire, Manchukuo, and North China, as an alternative to the development of a great foreign trade with the outside world. Throughout 1935, moreover, the Ex-Service Men's Association was used as a medium for "fascist" agitations, and it began to press for "a clarification of national polity." This meant an assertion by the Government that it believed in the mystical views about the Emperor and State common to the Japanese brand of "fascism." The failure of the Government to make such a declaration gave rise to indignation in extremist military circles. Finally, Takahashi's policy of working slowly towards a balanced budget seemed to checkmate military ambitions which could not be realized without greater armaments. His declaration, in one of his periodical struggles with the military, to the effect that it was not to intrigues of foreign Powers but to the extravagance of the Army that Japan's critical situation could be attributed, sealed his fate.

It was symptomatic of the growing spirit of nationalism that a movement began at this time for changing the official name of the country, for foreign use, to Nippon. It was held to be derogatory for the country to be known abroad by a name derived from Jih-Peng, the Chinese pronunciation of the characters in which the Japanese write the name of their country, and introduced into Europe by Marco Polo as Zapangu. Nippon, which approximates to the Japanese pronunciation of the characters, was held to be more appropriate.[1] So in recent years numerous journals and books written by Japanese in the English language have adopted the term Nippon to indicate their country. Of course, sensible and intelli-

[1] Cf. *Contemporary Japan*, June 1934, p. 132.

gent Japanese—and there are many—regard this change of name as childish, as they do most of the absurdities of fanatical nationalists. But the influence of the latter has grown.

In February 1936 there were general elections, and the Minseito, which had gone to the country with a slogan of "Parliamentary Government or Fascism," returned with a majority; while the Shakai Taishuto (Social Democratic Party) was also surprisingly successful. The latter apparently received its main support from the lower middle class in Tokyo and Osaka and from workers in smaller industrial towns. The Seiyukai, which, in its efforts to bring down the Government, had flirted with the Ex-Service Men's Association and other "fascist" bodies, did very badly. The result of the elections seemed to indicate that the country had declared against fascism and that the more liberal forces were again reviving. Almost immediately afterwards (although it is doubtful if the election results were in any way responsible) the explosion occurred, and a phase in Japanese political history had come to an end.

On February 26th, 1936, some 1,500 soldiers, acting on the orders of their officers, mutinied. They murdered the former Prime Minister Admiral Saito (then Lord Privy Seal), Mr. K. Takahashi (Finance Minister), and General Watanabe (Director of Military Education), who had replaced General Mazaki in the purge of extremists two years before. Admiral Suzuki (the Grand Chamberlain), Prince Saionji, Count Makino (former Lord Privy Seal), and Admiral Okada (the Prime Minister), had narrow escapes. Many others who were held to stand in the way of a Showa Restoration were marked down as subsequent victims. The mutineers occupied the Diet, the War Office, the Police Headquarters, and many other buildings in the heart of Tokyo's administrative and chief residential quarter. The Navy was incensed at this pruning of its most distinguished leaders, and warships steamed into Tokyo Bay with guns trained on the buildings occupied by the mutineers. The area occupied was surrounded by loyal troops.

The masses of the people were, on the surface, little disturbed. In fact, however, they were shocked; for whereas they could view with equanimity the assassination of a few politicians and business men by individual "patriots," the revolt of a large body of soldiers and the imminent danger of an armed conflict between them and other sections of the forces were indicative of the fact that the boasted unity of the Japanese under a godlike Emperor was an obvious fiction. As an old workman said to a friend of mine: "We are fools, we Japanese; we fight against one another." It was not that the political murders excited horror; for individuals, however distinguished, are merely individuals. But for the Army to divide itself into factions ready to spring at each other's throats—that struck at the roots of national life. Yet this mutiny could never have occurred at all in a country in which acts of violence directed against unpopular persons were frowned upon by public opinion. The officers responsible for the murders of May 15th (1932) had been regarded as patriots and had been leniently treated. This more serious revolt was fostered by the sympathetic atmosphere that had hitherto surrounded such actions. Where the law does not protect individuals from arbitrary attacks on the part of their political enemies, there can be no decent public life. Yet the Chinese scholar who, in the hearing of the writer, drew the conclusion that the Japanese State was rushing towards destruction was in error. He argued that in China a revolt of this sort would be of little importance, because in Chinese civilization the Army had a subordinate rôle. On the other hand, the Japanese State, he said, was based upon military discipline, and when that broke down no unifying force remained. But the truth is that in Japan there is little military discipline of the Western kind. The Japanese Army, and, indeed, the whole nation, is held together not in a series of rigidly defined relationships between superiors and inferiors, but by strong sentiments of loyalty to the Emperor. Violent conflicts between groups, or between superiors and subordinates, can occur, while leaving that common sentiment unimpaired. Thus, while the mutiny was serious enough, the inference that the Army was so divided as to destroy its unity of action against the outside world, or even its efficiency, was not correct.

After a few days the mutineers laid down their arms. The leader disembowelled himself, and more surprising still, a large number of officers and civilians implicated in the affair were court-martialled and shot. This action was considered necessary to vindicate the honour of the Army. Many leading generals and admirals, including both those who were sympathetic towards the "young officers," and those conservatives whose administrative reforms could be regarded as having contributed to the revolt, were placed on the retired list. Mr. Hirota, a career-diplomat and a protégé of Toyama, the leader of the famous Black Dragon Society, was called to form a new Government; and with General Count Terauchi, a conservative member of the aristocratic military clique, at the War Office, the Government made determined efforts to stamp out "fascist" tendencies among the young officers and to restore unity to the Army. The War Minister's words, uttered shortly after he came into office, are significant: "As War Minister, I am convinced that I have the threefold duty of reforming national administration drastically, replenishing national defence, and establishing strict discipline in the Army. Only through the War Minister is the Army allowed to express its views on politics. I consider that any political activities of individual officers are not only contrary to their duties but alien to their aspirations."[1]

The suppression of the extremist factions in the Army did not, however, imply a reversion to parliamentary government and a liberal policy. Although the Minseito now had a majority in the Lower House, and although a few portfolios were held by party men as before, the new Government was essentially of the old bureaucratic type. While the Navy clique had definitely lost ground, the Army had certainly gained, and it was clear that Terauchi was the real force in the Government. Indeed, as other writers have suggested, and as events show, the governing groups seem, after February 26th, to have struck a bargain by which the

[1] Quoted in *Contemporary Japan*, June 1936, p. 7.

Army agreed to weed out its extremists; while the business and other privileged cliques promised to support the Army's claims for greater expenditure on rearmament and on development in Manchukuo, for national control of industries necessary for purposes of defence, and for the "reform" of political parties so as to remove the liberal tendencies which they exhibited. The *Zaibatsu* made a further strategic retreat. Several of them announced the institution of a retiring age for *banto* (officials), and the effect of this was to prepare the way for the removal of the older and more powerful *banto* whose policy had provoked criticism. Members of the Mitsui family gave up their directorships in the subsidiary companies controlled by the House, and measures were taken to prevent references to the *Zaibatsu* and their interests from appearing in the Press.[1] These concerns also became more active in investing resources in undertakings of national importance both in Japan and in Manchukuo. The Government prepared plans for the nationalization of electricity generation—a measure for which the Army was pressing and which could be regarded as the precursor of a wider movement for the State control of industry. The Broadcasting Corporation, a Government-operated concern, gave itself over to more vigorous nationalist propaganda, and the Education Department organized lecture schemes for combating "dangerous thoughts" among the workers and for instilling patriotism. The shift to the right was indicated by the retirement of the President of the Privy Council to make room for Baron Hiranuma, a nationalist who had been passed over for this appointment three years before.

The political situation throughout 1936, however, remained

[1] When the head of Yasuda *Zaibatsu* (the fourth greatest business house in Japan) died, his obituary notices and the Press accounts of his funeral were deliberately limited to a few lines. Mitsui prefers many of its gifts to charitable institutions to be administered anonymously, and it prevents its name from appearing, as far as possible, in the title of the companies which it controls. The *Zaibatsu* apparently think that the "fascist" hostility is less likely to be provoked if a decent veil is allowed to obscure their manifold activities.

exceedingly disturbed, as was evident even to foreign visitors to the country. Men in positions of authority in all branches of business and public life were alarmed for their safety. When I presented myself to the manager of a certain important business house at Osaka with a letter of introduction provided from an unimpeachable source, and with a request for information about industrial conditions, his embarrassment was extreme. "The Army is everything in Osaka," he said. "We will tell you all you want to know if you get its consent, but we dare not do anything for you until we know that it agrees." Actually, the matter was arranged without difficulty; but the manager's immediate reaction to this inquiry had been very significant. Yet the essential conflict was not so much between the Army and big business, as between the younger extremists in the Services, the civil service and big business on one side, and the older conservative or liberally minded leaders on the other. The latter feared that their turn for elimination in the process of "clarifying national polity" might come at any moment. From time to time the Press recorded that the police had arrested a fanatic who had come from some remote place for the purpose of bombing or shooting a Cabinet Minister, and spy mania became as prominent as it had been in England during the Great War. A leading member of a great business house informed me that the purge of February 26th had been of advantage to the country; for not only had it removed unpatriotic personages, but it had also turned the thoughts of business men away from the sordid pursuit of profits to a devotion to patriotic duties! But this was not the usual attitude in those circles. The wiser members of the business community and the civil service believed that the reorganization of industries under State control would reduce efficiency and would damage Japan's prospects of extending her export trade; while they doubted, too, whether Finance Minister Baba would be able to stand up to the Army's demands for extravagant expenditure as successfully as his fearless predecessor, K. Takahashi, had done. At the same time, the Government was criticized by the extremists for proceeding too slowly with projects of political and economic reform. Thus, a proposal brought forward by the Army for drastically reducing the size of the Cabinet and so destroying the last vestige of parliamentary control was not carried through, to the disgust of the "fascists" and to the relief of the moderates. Throughout the year the Government's policy remained vacillating and inconsistent. A well-informed Japanese said to me: "This Government dare not pursue any policy of its own. The Ministers for War and Foreign Affairs do what the Army and Navy tell them to do. The Minister of Commerce and Industry carries out the orders of big business. All members of the Government are under the control of some group outside the Cabinet. If they had not been amenable to these influences, they would not have remained in office, and some of them would be dead by now."

At the end of 1936 a crisis was rapidly approaching. The Finance Minister had agreed to increased expenditure on the Services and had decided to raise part of this new money by increasing taxes, especially those falling on the business classes. At the same time, determined efforts were being made to push through the electricity supply nationalization scheme. Big business, through the political parties, was determined to fight, and in the parliamentary session which began in January 1937 the Government was vigorously assailed. Mr. Hamada, a Seiyukai member, accused the Army of attempting to introduce a form of dictatorship through its virtual control of the Cabinet, and of forcing on the country a budget out of proportion to the country's financial capacity. He declared also, that the deadlock that had been reached in Sino-Japanese relationships was to be attributed to "military" diplomacy, and he denounced the unpopular Anti-Comintern Pact which Japan and Germany had signed two months earlier. This speech by Mr. Hamada was the culmination of a growing volume of criticism both within the Diet and in the Press, and the Government resigned.

Prince Saionji recommended General Ugaki, a former Governor-General of Korea, as best fitted to form a new Government.

In previous conflicts between the military and civil authorities, the choice of a moderate general with experience of civil administration had proved a useful way of reaching a compromise. Ugaki was acceptable to the political parties and the House of Peers, and thus could have formed a Government which would have had the confidence of the Diet; but he was disliked by the dominant military clique led by Terauchi and consequently no Minister of War could be found to serve under him. The main reason for this veto was that Ugaki had connections with the parties and business circles, and was likely to co-operate with them, whereas the Army wanted a Cabinet from which politicians were excluded. Ugaki, moreover, had been War Minister at a time when economies were effected in military expenditure, and so was regarded by the jingoist military cliques in 1937 as having endangered the unity and power of the Army. The Press was critical of the Army's attitude to Ugaki; but, in the end, he had to give up his attempt to form a Cabinet; although support for him was forthcoming from every quarter except the Army. The whole circumstances of Ugaki's abortive attempt to form a Government show how great the political influence of the military clique had grown. As the *Japan Chronicle* stated at the time:[1] "It is no new thing for the military to force the resignation of a Cabinet by withdrawing the War Minister, or to hinder the formation of a Cabinet when the policy of the new Premier has been clearly at variance with Army requirements. But never before have the military obstructed the efforts of a Premier-elect almost within minutes of the Imperial command that he shall attempt the formation of a Cabinet."

Ultimately, General Hayashi, Minister of War in the Okada Cabinet, formed a Ministry composed almost entirely of bureaucrats and military and naval chiefs. Indeed, although the Prime Minister offered portfolios to politicians, he made the condition that they must sever connections with their parties, and this meant that no leader of the dominant parties accepted office. He and the Army clique were, however, prepared to make some concessions

[1] January 27th, 1937.

PLATE XI

REPAIRING "TATAMI"—A HOME INDUSTRY

to public opinion and to big business by agreeing to reductions in budgetary expenditure. But the Diet was not placated, and Mr. Y. Ozaki, the old liberal politician, challenged the Army view that a crisis existed in the Far East which called for large military appropriations. These and other criticisms led Hayashi to dissolve the Diet very soon after he had taken office, and in the ensuing elections the Government and the Army brought pressure on the electorate and the candidates with the object of securing the return of an amenable House. Both of the major parties, however, together with the Shakai Taishuto (Social Democrats) fought the election with the slogan "Overthrow the Hayashi Cabinet," and only a few seats went to parties favourably disposed to the Government. The most significant result of the election was to double the number of votes secured by the Shakai Taishuto. Nationalist groups outside Parliament rallied to the support of the Premier; but in the end the Army threw him over and he resigned on May 31st. His successor was Prince Konoye, President of the House of Peers, and a member of a family of Court Nobles. He included the leaders of the Minseito and Seiyukai parties in his Cabinet, and succeeded in arranging a compromise among the rival cliques, although divergences of view were not wholly reconciled, as was seen in the disputes that arose between E. Baba, the Home Minister, a protégé of the Army, and other Ministers who represented business and financial circles. But Konoye had not been long in office before the outbreak of the war with China quelled any internal conflict and silenced the legislators.[1]

To a Western observer of the political changes of the last seven years it is particularly interesting that, although the overthrow of party government and the eclipse of Parliament have been brought about largely by an uprising similar to that which established national socialism in Germany, there has been no tendency

[1] In the 1938 session of the Diet the parties returned to the attack. The Government drew up a Bill which was intended to provide it with almost unlimited powers of control over industry, and this measure was bitterly assailed in the Lower House. Nevertheless, it became law.

towards the establishment of a personal dictatorship. Power has undoubtedly tended to shift steadily to the Army and the more chauvinistic elements in Japanese society, and each of the series of political assassinations has marked a stage in this development. The "fascist" groups have certainly exercised an important influence on policy. But each crisis has been settled by a compromise among the rival groups—a compromise increasingly favourable to the Army clique, but still a compromise which has left some place in government for all the different sections of Japan's governing classes. Men like General Araki, Mr. Takahashi, or General Hayashi during these years have each for a time appeared to gain a position of great personal authority, but they have all been swept away without difficulty when circumstances have changed and when the groups of which they were spokesmen have been forced into the background. If free and outspoken criticism in the Press and on the platform of men in high office is permitted even in illiberal periods such as the present, this is because the Japanese know that individuals count for little in their national life. The significant factors are groups; the individuals who come and go are merely impermanent instruments for the expression of group-interests and policies.[1]

The changes in the seat of political authority are well reflected in the development of economic policy since 1929. During the period in which the Minseito Government held office, economic policy was such as might be expected from a party which represented the interests of the *Zaibatsu* and the liberal financiers. The Government was committed to the maintenance of the gold value of the yen, and this involved a drastic policy of deflation. To implement the deflation an ambitious scheme of industrial reorganization was drawn up which had for its ostensible purpose the lowering of costs. A Bureau of Industrial Rationalization was set up as part

[1] Cf. Lafcadio Hearn, *Kokoro*, chap. ii: "Nothing is fixed except the Throne. Perpetual change is identical with State policy. Ministers, governors, superintendents, inspectors, all high civil and military officials, are shifted at irregular and surprisingly short intervals."

of the Ministry of Commerce and Industry, and its various committees tried to promote measures for the improvement of efficiency. Under the Major Industries Control Law, passed at this time, the large-scale industries were authorized to form cartels and associations which were supposed to carry out schemes for rationalization. The Government took compulsory powers for securing the adherence of reluctant manufacturers to these associations, but the powers were sparingly used and, in fact, the Law involved very little interference by the State in industrial enterprise. There was certainly a great improvement in industrial efficiency in the years of depression; but this advance occurred on the initiative of the manufacturers themselves, faced as they were with falling prices, and it owed little to Government intervention. There was, also, a considerable growth in the number of cartels which exercised functions of price-, output-, and market-control; but the conditions of the period were the main cause of this development rather than the provisions of the Control Law. Amendments to existing laws for the encouragement of associations among small-scale manufacturers and exporters with the object of improving their efficiency were passed in these years, but were not then of great significance. Thus, although the Government's schemes for raising silk and rice prices were important, its intervention in manufacturing industry cannot be considered to have had any greater influence than is likely to be exercised in any country by liberal Governments reluctant to use compulsory powers for the control of private enterprise.

With the fall of the Minseito and the institution of bureaucratic Governments, policy changed. The Major Industries Control Law came to be used not so much for the purpose of strengthening associations of manufacturers in the interests of cost-reduction or price-maintenance, but rather to prevent the unpopular business classes from gaining high profits in the boom conditions that came into being. The Exporters' Associations, instead of being regarded as a means for encouraging exports, came to be regarded as part of the State's machinery for restricting exports in order to carry out trade agreements with other countries or to forestall discrimination against Japanese goods abroad. The associations of small manufacturers received additional support; for they were held to be important organs for freeing the small producers from the control of the great financiers and merchants. In other words, the measures originally passed to raise the industrial efficiency of the country were now employed for the attainment of political and social aims that seemed desirable to the groups in power. New legislation was introduced with the same end in view. The Government gave great financial encouragement to rural co-operative societies, and the peasants who formed the majority of their members were thus able to free themselves in some degree from dependence on merchants and local moneylenders. Co-operative reeling mills, run by associations of silk-raising farmers, were also encouraged, to the detriment of the larger commercial filatures. Restrictions were placed on the growth of departmental stores in order to protect small shopkeepers who were suffering from their competition. The Army and Navy, whose political influence partly rested on the support of the country population, followed a policy of distributing orders for certain munitions and supplies in such a way as to promote small-scale rural enterprises.

Demands on the part of the Army, and especially of the extremists, for the control of private capitalism and for the institution of a war-time economy became more insistent as time went on. The Government brought about the amalgamation of several large private iron and steel firms with the State's own Yawata Iron Works, and a new semi-official company was formed to operate this enterprise which is now responsible for nearly all the pig-iron output and for the greater part of the crude steel production of Japan. A law was passed providing for official control over the mineral-oil industry and for the institution of the compulsory storage of oil by the operating companies. The fertilizer trade was subjected to control in the peasants' interests, and large subsidies were provided for the development of enterprises of military importance, such as shipping and the hydrogenation process. Efforts were made to encourage the use of home-produced substitutes for imported materials; for instance, there was a campaign for the increased use of staple fibre in the textile trades. Many other examples might be given; but the general trend was obvious. State control over industry was being steadily extended in order to develop industries of military importance and to strengthen those classes of producers who were believed for social and political reasons to deserve support against the *Zaibatsu* and large business interests. The trend was naturally opposed by the great industrialists and financiers, and the more far-sighted members of the bureaucracy realized that this type of intervention might endanger the growth of Japan's export trade, which is of vital importance for her future. This opposition delayed, though it could not check, the spread of State control. The extremists, however, were not satisfied with the rate of the advance in this direction; and events played into their hands in the early months of 1937, just when the business interests were fighting hard in the Diet for the preservation of their independence. The deterioration in Japan's financial position as a result of the long series of unbalanced budgets brought with it a marked tendency for the yen to fall towards the end of 1936. In January 1937 the Government was obliged to impose restrictions over exchange dealings and to subject imports to a licensing scheme. As the year went on these controls had to be tightened in an effort to defend the yen. The Government was thus compelled to intervene in yet another important sphere of economic activity; and then, in May, a Control Board was set up to exercise general supervision of the economic life of the country. So, even before hostilities began in China, the country was moving rapidly towards a war-time economy such as the extremist groups in the Army desired.

CHAPTER XI

MANIFEST DESTINY

"Hic, ait, hic pacem temerataque jura relinquo;
Te, Fortuna, sequor. Procul hinc jam fœdera sunto.
Credidimus fatis. Utendum est judice bello."

LUCAN

"*. . . whether . . . it would not be delightful to live in a Country swarming, like* China, *with busy People?*"

GEORGE BERKELEY

WHEN the Western European Powers in the days of their arrogant imperialism forced open the doors of the ancient Empires of China and Japan, they had little thought for the monstrous dangers to their supremacy in the East that they were thereby creating. To-day, when great possessions have made them ready to abandon imperialistic ambitions and to subscribe to a system of international justice, their statesmen may perhaps appreciate the tragic irony of a situation in which one of the victims of their predatory past has succeeded in shattering the most noble achievement of their benevolent present. For, whatever views one may hold about Japan's activities in Asia, this, at least, is clear: the downfall of the League of Nations and, with it, the destruction of hopes for a peaceful world, began with the conquest of Manchuria in 1931. From then onwards the Western democracies have seen, with horror and alarm, a faithful rendering of policies which they had pursued vigorously in their unregenerate past, but which, they hoped, had been made impossible in the enlightened post-War world. Just as Great Britain in South Africa and India had used breaches of treaties, signed under duress by the other parties, as excuses for extending the areas under her control, so Japan was seen to be following the familiar imperialistic course. Just as Great Britain buttressed her Empire by securing control over nominally independent Governments, so Japan, her apt pupil, has set up puppet States, and in this way has been able to gather the spoils of military victory while posing as a champion of oppressed peoples and a bestower of peace on a disordered land. And just as Great Britain invested her ambition for Empire with a high moral purpose, so Japan has discovered, also, that she has been selected by the gods for lordship of other nations and, in particular, that her destiny is to give peace to the East and to free it from the tyranny of Western Powers. The "white man's burden" has its parallel in Japan's mystical charge to overthrow communism, to bring discipline and unity to Asia, and to create a world ordered according to the divine Emperor's wishes. It is not agreeable for the Western democracies to be confronted with the same fanaticisms, excesses, and romantic follies that stained their own youth, just when they were prepared for a temperate and peaceful manhood.

Japan's policy in China certainly cannot be satisfactorily explained, as some have attempted to do, wholly by reference to her internal economic and political conditions. The pressure of a rapidly growing population upon resources in a country ill-furnished with agricultural land and raw materials has, no doubt, exercised a powerful influence on the attitude of the Japanese people towards empire; and the internal political stresses of recent years have certainly contributed to the breakdown of peaceful relations in the international sphere. But to offer these phenomena as a complete explanation of the drive towards territorial aggrandizement is to over-simplify an exceedingly complicated situation. This situation, indeed, has its roots in the past and can be understood only by considering the whole story of international rivalries in the Far East over a century. An attempt will be made here to bring out the nature of those rivalries in so far as they have led up to the present catastrophe.

The weakness of both China and Japan in the first half of the nineteenth century marked them out as fields for imperialistic domination by the Western Powers. As they were vulnerable to attack only from the sea, the menace to their independence first came, naturally, from the countries with great sea-power. France seized from China the territory now known as French Indo-China; Great Britain acquired Burma, which was, nominally at any rate, under Chinese suzerainty, and Hong Kong. Concessions and treaty ports were secured, and so the famous International Settlement and the French Concession at Shanghai were created. Japan afforded fewer prospects of exploitation; but the Powers nevertheless forced that country to sign treaties which infringed her sovereignty (for instance, Japan's right of levying import-duties was restricted), and in certain of the ports foreigners obtained extra-territorial privileges. Even before the Restoration (1868), Western countries intrigued in Japanese internal affairs in order to promote their own interests. Thus, France supported the Shogunate Government, while Great Britain assisted the Emperor's party. Both Japan and China resented this foreign interference and aggression; but their weakness forced them into acquiescence for a time.

The ultimate reactions of the two countries to the danger from abroad were, however, very different. China tried to protect herself by playing off one antagonist against another, and failed to effect any reorganization of her Army and administration that would have enabled her to deal with her aggressors on equal terms. But Japan, having learnt by painful experience the answer to the question

> What do the great and powerful care for rights
> That have no armies,

soon proceeded to reconstruct her administration on Western lines and to build up a strong military organization. The reasons for these very different responses to pressure from the West cannot here be discussed; they were bound up with the diverse social, political, and geographical conditions of the two countries.

In the first half of the nineteenth century, as we have seen, the Western invaders came from the sea; in the second half of the century, Russia, a great land-power, began her drive to the East, and so Japan and China were faced with a menace from another quarter. By the Treaty of Peking, signed in 1860, Russia obtained from China the Primorsk Province, and soon afterwards constructed Vladivostok. In 1885 she planned the Trans-Siberian Railway. Japan's apprehensions were aroused. The danger to her integrity from this third imperialistic Power seemed to approach by way of Korea. Korea, as has often been pointed out, has played the same part in Japanese foreign policy that Belgium has in British foreign policy. It was regarded as "a pistol pointed at the heart of Japan." While Korea remained in a position of nominal vassalage to a weak and disunited China, Japan was not alarmed. But if the pistol should become charged with powder and shot supplied by Russia, or by a strong China intent upon exercising a real suzerainty, then the menace would become immediate. In the seventies the circumstances were, for the first time, realized. Chinese, Russians, and Japanese manœuvred against one another for influence over the Korean Government, and in 1876 Japan sent an expedition to Korea and obtained three "open" ports and an acknowledgment of the independence of Korea. The Satsuma clique at this time wished to go further and to proceed to the conquest of the country, and the refusal of the Government to follow this policy was one cause of the abortive Satsuma Rebellion in 1877. In the next decade, China and Japan supported rival factions at the Korean Court, and there were frequent "incidents" which brought the countries to the verge of war on several occasions. Finally, when China, encouraged by the apparent disunity in Japanese political circles, asserted her ancient right of suzerainty over Korea, Japan declared war. As always, violent internal conflict among Japan's governing cliques proved consistent with perfect national unity against the outside world, and China was easily defeated. By the Treaty of Shimonoseki (1895) China recognized Korean independence, ceded Formosa, the Pescadores Islands, and the Liaotung Peninsula to Japan, and agreed to pay an indemnity. On the initiative of Russia, however, Germany and

France combined with that country in demanding the retrocession of the Liaotung Peninsula to China, and Japan had to give way.

Victory over China, far from freeing Japan from the threat of foreign aggression, merely raised a swarm of fresh dangers. Encouraged by the demonstration of China's weakness, the Powers began their "scramble" for China. Leases, concessions, and "spheres of influence" were granted in abundance by that unfortunate country, and in this "scramble" Russia led the way. She obtained the right of constructing a railway line across Manchuria; and in 1898 she acquired a lease of the southern part of the Liaotung Peninsula, including Port Arthur and Dairen, and the right to build a railway from these two ports to Harbin. After the Boxer Rebellion of 1900 Russia occupied the whole of South Manchuria and demanded that China should recognize Manchuria as a Russian "sphere of influence." Although two years later Russia promised China to withdraw her troops from Manchuria, she failed to do so, and Japan felt that her security was again being menaced. At this time Prince Ito was strongly in favour of reaching an agreement with Russia, and on several occasions Japan proposed that Korea and Manchuria should be recognized as Japanese and Russian spheres of interest respectively. Russia would not contemplate this proposal and, reluctantly, Prince Ito agreed to the proposed alliance with Great Britain to which the public, still smarting from the three-Power (Dreibund) intervention, and certain members of the governing cliques, were strongly inclined. When Russia continued to respond unfavourably to Japan's proposals about Manchuria, and when she actually began to encroach upon Korean territory, Japan decided upon war, although not without misgivings on the part of Ito and Inouye, two of the most powerful *Genro*, and of Admiral Yamamoto, an important member of the naval (Satsuma) clique. Victory in this war led to the recognition of Japan's special interests in Korea, the transference to her of South Saghalien, the lease of the Kwantung Peninsula, and the southern part of the Chinese Eastern Railway (which Russia had built in Manchuria), together with the surrounding zone. The South

Manchuria Railway Company, an official concern, was created in 1906 to manage this railway, and in 1910 Korea was formally annexed. At the close of the Russo-Japanese War China signed an important secret treaty with Japan by which she agreed not "to construct . . . any main line in the neighbourhood of or parallel to the (South Manchuria Railway) or any branch line which might be prejudicial to the interest of the above-mentioned railway."[1]

The United States at this time was using its influence for the purpose of maintaining the "open door" in China and the preservation of China's sovereignty. Japan had favoured this policy in the years before 1905, and in the Treaty of Portsmouth signed after the Russian War she and Russia both guaranteed to respect China's territorial integrity and to preserve an "open door" in Manchuria. In fact, however, these engagements were never kept. Japan proceeded to extend her railway zone and vetoed all efforts by other Powers to develop Manchuria, and when Mr. Knox, the American Secretary of State, proposed his scheme for the "internationalization" of all the Manchurian railways, she joined with Russia in rejecting it (1910). She also concluded with Russia a secret treaty by which the Western half of Inner Mongolia was added to the Russian "sphere of influence," while the Eastern half was added to the Japanese. After the Chinese Revolution of 1911 relations between Japan and China became strained. Japan was bent upon increasing her "sphere of influence"; while Chinese hostility was naturally directed mainly against the Power which was now proving to be the greatest menace to her integrity.[2] There

[1] Millard, *America and the Far Eastern Question*, pp. 541–2.

[2] Count Hayashi states in his *Secret Memoirs* (p. 257): "The Chinese will eventually try to limit our sphere of influence as much as possible, whilst we, on our part, must try to reserve as much room for our expansion in that country as possible. Consequently . . . it is impossible to avoid ill-feeling and a conflict of interest." Again, he says that it is impossible for Japan to try to extend her interests and at the same time to gain the confidence of the Chinese, who were not impressed by the argument that Japan had done them a service by driving the Russians out of Manchuria. "It is for our own preservation that we are holding Manchuria. We have not acted in the least from humanitarian considerations" (quoted Hershey, *Modern Japan*, pp. 291–2).

were frequent "incidents" between Japanese and Chinese railway guards in Manchuria, and Japan's refusal to permit a revision of the Chinese Customs Duties, to which other Powers had consented, aroused bitter feelings in China.

When the Great War broke out, Japan was not reluctant to seize her opportunity of avenging herself on Germany, a member of the Dreibund which had thwarted her after the Sino-Japanese War, and the Anglo-Japanese Alliance afforded her the excuse of participation in the struggle. Count Okuma, then Prime Minister, informed the American people that Japan had "no desire to secure more territory," and "no thought of depriving China or other peoples of anything which they now possess."[1] Count Kato, the Foreign Minister, explained to the United States that her motive in wresting Kiao-chou from Germany was to "ensure an abiding peace in Eastern Asia," to which that military base was a menace.[2] Yet in this campaign, Japanese troops violated China's neutrality, seized the whole of the Shantung Railway, and sent troops as far inland as Tsinan, some 260 miles from the coast. Then, when the Chinese President, Yuan Shih-Kai, announced the restoration of Kiao-chou to China, Japan presented her notorious "Twenty-One Demands" (January 1915). These had been prepared for some months previously. Japan was anxious to extend the period of her lease of the Kwantung Peninsula and the South Manchuria Railway Zone, and her wishes had been communicated to Sir Edward Grey, who offered no objection.[3] Japan, however, had further ambitions, and the Twenty-One Demands, had they been accepted in their entirety, would have reduced China to the position of a Japanese protectorate; while other Powers would

[1] Message to New York *Independent*, August 24th, 1914.

[2] Count Okuma stated at this time: "Japan's object is to eliminate from the Continent of China the root of German influence which forms a constant menace to the peace of the Far East. . . . She harbours no design for territorial aggrandizement, and entertains no desire to promote any other selfish end" (quoted T. Takeuchi, *op. cit.*, p. 173). Substitute "communist" for "German," and one finds a close identity to recent official statements about Japan's present aims.

[3] T. Takeuchi, *op. cit.*, pp. 184–5.

have been excluded from further leases and concessions. Largely through American protests, though also because several of the *Genro* viewed the policy with disfavour, the Demands were modified. Group V, which provided *inter alia* for the employment of Japanese advisers on political, financial, and military affairs, and in the Chinese police force, was not embodied in the subsequent treaties; but Japan was, nevertheless, able to tighten her grip on South Manchuria and Shantung and to extend her interests in the Yangtse valley and in Eastern Mongolia.[1] By secret treaties signed early in 1917 she obtained from the Allies assurances of support for her claims to Shantung and to the German islands in the Pacific.

This policy of downright imperialism was initiated not by a Government dominated mainly by the military and bureaucratic cliques, but by a Government headed by Count Okuma, and supported by the Kenseikai political party. Indeed, Count Kato, the Foreign Minister, tried at this time to prevent the *Genro* from exercising their customary influence in foreign affairs. He ignored a memorandum, submitted by Prince Yamagata, on Chinese Affairs, and he rejected the advice that a *Genro* should be sent to China to conduct negotiations. It seems that the influence of Prince Yamagata, generally regarded as the arch-militarist, as well as that of Matsukata and Inouye (other powerful *Genro*), was used to moderate Japan's demands; for these elder statesmen feared the effect of this ruthless policy upon world opinion.[2] Kato brought himself into such disfavour with these three *Genro* as a result of his policy that he was never recommended for the premiership, an office which he might reasonably have expected to hold, as long as they were alive. Ultimately the *Genro* secured his resignation, and when General Terauchi, a member of the Choshu military clique and a protégé of Yamagata, became Prime Minister

[1] The lease of Port Arthur and Dairen and of the railway zones in Manchuria was extended for 99 years. China also agreed not to employ foreign advisers, nor to grant railway concessions to foreign firms, nor to raise foreign loans for the development of Manchuria.

[2] The Seiyukai party was also critical of Kato's diplomacy on the ground that it had produced widespread boycotts of Japanese goods by the Chinese.

in 1916, Japan's policy towards China became more conciliatory. However, after the fall of Yuan Shih-Kai and the outbreak of civil war in China among the rival military governors, Japan tried to gain further advantages by financing the Anfu group of war-lords in Peking. Large sums, known as the "Nishihara loans," were advanced by Japanese bankers to that group.[1]

It was during the Great War that Japan's claim to a "special position" in Eastern Asia was formulated, or, at any rate, received considerable prominence. Okuma and others declared that their country had a "mission" to harmonize East and West and to bring peace to the Orient, and a kind of Monroe Doctrine for Eastern Asia was enunciated. The Ishii–Lansing Agreement of 1917, while it affirmed the adherence of Japan and the United States to the "open door" principle and declared that neither Government had any intention of infringing the territorial integrity of China, contained a clause by which the United States recognized that Japan had special interests in China. This seemed to the Japanese to accord her the peculiar right of intervening in China's affairs; but the Americans repudiated this interpretation and the Agreement was abrogated in 1923. But, said Viscount Ishii, the Japanese representative, this abrogation did not affect the actual position of Japan; her special interest was based not upon the Agreement, but "upon concrete realities of history and geography." Thus, during the Great War, Japan was moving towards the view, recently made explicit, that she was entitled to regard the exploitation of China's weakness as her peculiar privilege.

The Russian Revolution opened up opportunities for Japanese imperialism in a new direction. When the United States proposed a joint expedition to Siberia to rescue the Czechoslovak troops, Japan eagerly accepted, and, besides the forces which were sent to co-operate with the Americans, it was proposed, also, that she

[1] These loans were granted to the Anfu faction which was supreme in Peking from 1917 to 1920 before it was overthrown by a combination led by Wu Pei-fu and Chang Tso-lin. So Japan, in effect, backed the wrong party and lost her money.

should despatch a large independent expedition to "defend her own interests." Prince Yamagata and his powerful military clique were the sponsors of this policy. The plan was not carried out completely because of parliamentary opposition; but a large army was, in fact, sent to Siberia, and the Maritime Province and North Saghalien came under Japanese domination. The Americans withdrew their forces when the evacuation of the Czechoslovak troops was completed; but Japan remained in possession. The expedition, however, had been very unpopular among the liberals in Japan, and Viscount Kato, now leader of the Kenseikai, attacked the Government and charged the *Genro* and military cliques (to which he was ill-disposed on account of their opposition to his China policy in 1915) with having engineered a costly and useless expedition. America viewed the affair with great disfavour, and in 1922 the troops were withdrawn. So this abortive adventure discredited both the policy of opportunist imperialism and the military clique that had fostered it. The stage was set for a more liberal foreign policy.

The Japanese responded generously to the appeal of post-War idealism. The people were tired of war, and, ever eager to contemplate new ideas for ordering affairs, the educated classes welcomed the principles for which the League of Nations was intended to stand. Imperialism had brought little material profit to their country during the Great War and had, indeed, given it an evil reputation. So they were prepared to try new paths. The triumph of the Allies seemed to represent a triumph for democracy and international justice, and with the Russian danger removed and with the fear of Western aggression finally dissipated, there was less likelihood that the militarists would be able to rouse the people to support their policy of encroachment upon China's sovereignty by appealing to the claims of "self-defence." The students and the intelligentsia were influenced strongly by the development of communism and of left-wing movements abroad, and they became concerned with problems of social justice rather than with national ambitions. In this atmosphere Japan signed the Treaty of Versailles and became a member of the League of Nations, receiving as war gains mandates over German islands in the North Pacific and rights in Shantung.

In 1922 she became party to the Washington Treaties. By the Nine-Power Treaty she pledged herself to respect China's sovereignty and to use her influence to maintain the "open door" in that country. By the Five-Power Naval Treaty she accepted the 5:5:3 ratio between Great Britain, the United States, and herself, although the Cabinet had previously decided to insist upon a 70 per cent. ratio; and in return she was guaranteed against the construction of naval bases at Hong Kong and in the Philippines. On the whole, the Treaty was not unfavourable to her, for although she had to restrict her building, the regulations concerning naval bases gave her absolute supremacy in the Western Pacific and guaranteed her communications with China. She lost, however, the support of the Anglo-Japanese Alliance, which Great Britain was not prepared to continue because of the opposition of the United States and some of the Dominions. The collapse of Russia had removed a danger to British (and American) interests in China, and so, one of the chief reasons for the continuance of the Alliance. From the standpoint of Western Powers, Japan had now become the chief threat to those interests, and the Washington Treaties could be expected to maintain the *status quo*. In the same year, Japan restored Kiao-chou and the Shantung Railway in return for an undertaking by China to pay 40 million yen for the railway over a period of fifteen years.[1]

For the greater part of the next ten years, Japan pursued a policy of conciliation. The business groups which were in the ascendant at this time believed that friendship with China would be to the advantage of Japan's foreign trade, while aggression would produce only boycotts and heavier Government expenditure. Peace in the Pacific now seemed to be assured, and China was given an opportunity of establishing law and order from the internal chaos which had reigned since her Revolution. That these

[1] About £4,000,000 at par.

hopes were frustrated was due mainly to the intrusion of two new factors into the situation, the rise of Chinese nationalism and the recovery of Russia.

After Yuan Shih-Kai's fall in 1916, the real authority in China rested in the hands of the various military governors of the provinces who maintained private armies financed from the provincial revenues. They intrigued and fought with one another for the control of the Central Government at Peking; but none of them had any policy other than that designed to promote his own self-interest. At Canton, however, there was the Kuomintang, or Nationalist Party, which was held together by a political principle from which organizing ideas could spring. This principle was the creation of a united China with a reformed administrative system, and it was supported not only by students and intellectuals, but by merchants and bankers who were being ruined by the rapacity of the war-lords. In 1923 Sun Yat-sen, the leader of this Party, allied himself with the Communist International, and secured the help of Russian agents and military instructors. This step gained the support of the masses, and the Kuomintang set out on its task of overthrowing the war-lords and establishing a real national Government. Its advance was rapid, especially after 1925, when Chiang Kai-shek became its leader; and by March 1927 it had overrun the whole country south of the Yangtse and had established itself at Shanghai and Nanking. Chinese Nationalism based much of its appeal upon the "rights-recovery campaign" associated with it. China was protected against further aggression by the Nine-Power Treaty; she could bend her efforts, therefore, to re-establishing her sovereignty over territories which had been wrested from her by foreign aggression in the past. In 1927 the full force of this campaign was directed against the Western Powers (especially Great Britain) which were predominant in the Yangtse Valley. Foreigners were attacked at Nanking and were saved only by shell-fire from foreign warships; while an outbreak at Shanghai was only checked by the despatch of large bodies of troops, mainly British, to garrison the Settlement. Chiang Kai-shek, realizing the danger of embroilment with Western Powers, broke with his communist supporters, who had engineered these attacks on foreigners, and he dismissed his Russian advisers. Britain assisted him in his policy by showing willingness to give up certain rights secured by treaty, including the surrender of the Concession at Hankow. Although large areas of China remained under the domination of communist armies, Chiang Kai-shek consolidated his rule at Nanking, and, having come to terms with the Western Powers, he now proceeded to the subjugation of the northern war-lords.

Unfortunately, just at this time there were political changes in Japan. The Government of which Shidehara was Foreign Secretary gave place to a Government led by General Tanaka, a member of the Choshu military clique and the advocate of a "strong hand" in China. It was not, of course, by accident that he came into office just then. The advance of the Kuomintang had alarmed the imperialists and the conservative forces in Japan, and they seized upon a pretext for overthrowing the "liberal" Government and for putting into power at this juncture a Prime Minister who was likely to carry out their wishes. Japan had lent support to Chang Tso-lin who, since 1921, had been the chief power in Manchuria, and the destruction of his régime by the nationalist forces would inevitably lead to conflict over Japan's rights in that country. So, ostensibly in order to protect Japanese nationals in Shantung, the military clique, apparently without consulting their civilian colleagues in the Cabinet, decided to send troops to that area in order to check the Kuomintang's new move. There were clashes between Chinese and Japanese troops at Tsinan in May 1928, and large-scale operations seemed likely to develop. But Tanaka's policy was vigorously assailed in Parliament and was exceedingly unpopular among liberals and in certain business circles outside. When Chang Tso-lin was murdered shortly afterwards, apparently at the instigation of Japanese officials who wished to prevent a possible *rapprochement* between Chang and the Kuomintang, decent Japanese opinion was shocked, and Tanaka lost the confidence of the elder statesmen and had to resign. That this Government should have been in office during such a critical period was an unmitigated disaster for Sino-Japanese relationships and for the future of world peace. Its actions destroyed the continuity of the policy of conciliation which might have led to the peaceful settlement of disputes, and exacerbated Chinese feelings. Tanaka, indeed, played the same disastrous part in Sino-Japanese affairs as Poincaré in the post-War efforts to bring about Franco-German appeasement.

After Chang Tso-lin's murder, his son hastened to come to terms with the Kuomintang, and so the unification of China and Manchuria was achieved. Nationalist China thus came face to face with Japan and Russia in an area where both those countries possessed extensive interests. At this point we must pause to consider the revival of Russian power in the Far East. Although the Soviet in 1919 declared that it was prepared to restore to China the Chinese Eastern Railway, built in Tsarist times, in 1924 it signed a treaty with the Peking Government by which it acquired the rights formerly enjoyed by pre-War Russia in the railway and the contiguous territory.[1] The Peking Government hoped to use the Russians to hinder any further Japanese penetration in Manchuria and also to immobilize Chang Tso-lin, who was antagonistic both to the Russians and to the Peking Government, then dominated by the Chihli war-lords. Chang was not strong enough to oppose this move; but he strengthened his position in Manchuria by insisting that the Soviet should sign a separate treaty with him about the railway. Russia did this and the step was significant; for her admission that Manchuria was an autonomous State established a dangerous precedent and "paved the way for the proclamation of the independence of Manchukuo in 1932."[2] The immediate effect, however, was to bring back Russia into

[1] The southern section of the original Chinese Eastern Railway, it should be remembered, passed into the hands of the Japanese after 1905 and became the nucleus of the South Manchuria Railway. This treaty, of course, applied only to that part of the original Chinese Eastern Railway which had remained in Russia's possession after her defeat by Japan.

[2] G. F. Hudson, *The Far East in World Politics*, p. 211.

Manchuria as Japan's rival, and so to awaken again in Japanese minds the fears that the Revolution of 1917 had banished. Furthermore, early in the post-War decade Russia had secured a hold upon Outer Mongolia and later she extended her influence to Sinkiang (Chinese Turkestan). The building of the Turk-Sib Railway contributed to her power in this last-named area. At the same time she tried to extend her influence in China Proper, first, by assisting the Kuomintang and, later, by supporting the communist armies which were in opposition to Chang Kai-shek. The Revolution, then, broke only temporarily the continuity of Russia's Eastern policy.

After the unification of China and Manchuria in 1928, the Kuomintang (now synonymous with the Nanking Government) turned the full force of its "rights-recovery campaign" against Japan and Russia. These two countries exercised, in connection with the South Manchuria Railway and the Chinese Eastern Railway, large powers of political and economic control over a region that was regarded as an integral part of China. Russia was hated because she was helping the "red" armies in rebellion against the Kuomintang, and Japan because of her aggression in the past and the more recent examples of it in Shantung. To begin with, the Chinese attempted to harass the Chinese Eastern Railway Administration; but the Russians sent troops into Manchuria, inflicted serious defeats on the Chinese, and rejected overtures for settlement made by other Powers. China soon gave up the struggle (1929).

The next stage in the "rights-recovery campaign" involved an attack on Japanese interests. China felt that the South Manchuria Railway should have been returned to her in 1923 when the original agreements expired, and she held that the extension of the lease by the treaties of 1915 had been granted under duress, and was invalid. She began to build railway lines in competition with the South Manchuria Railway, and she financed this construction out of money which should have been paid to the Japanese as interest on capital previously borrowed from them for the purpose of constructing Chinese "feeder" lines for the South Manchuria

Railway. The Chinese also challenged other Japanese rights in Manchuria acquired under the 1915 treaties, and disputes among Japanese and Chinese authorities in the railway zone were frequent. China felt that she could act with impunity partly because of the protection afforded to her by the Nine-Power Treaty, and partly because she thought that Shidehara was not likely to be provoked into abandoning his conciliatory policy. But the Chinese, on this as on other occasions, misjudged the Japanese political situation. Shidehara did not abandon his policy, but, as we have already seen, Japan abandoned Shidehara, and the military cliques again took control of policy towards China. The circumstances of the Manchurian conflict itself with the attendant fighting at Shanghai have been frequently recounted. It is sufficient to say here that by the end of 1932 the whole of Manchuria was occupied by the Japanese, and early in the next year after another "incident," Jehol, too, was overrun. The puppet State of Manchukuo was set up, and Japan gave notice of her withdrawal from the League of Nations. Hostilities came to an end with the Tangku Truce of May 1933, which provided for the demilitarization of a wide zone south of the Great Wall. Japan had thus driven a wedge between Russia and North China, and had at last acquired effective control of a huge region long in dispute. Russia finally withdrew from North Manchuria by agreeing in 1935 to the sale of the Chinese Eastern Railway.

Japan defended herself against the League's stern criticism of her action in this dispute by several lines of argument. She pointed to the deliberate attempts of the Chinese to render her position in Manchuria untenable. China had built railways parallel to the South Manchuria Railway system, in spite of treaty provisions, and had refused to repay loans granted to her for various purposes. Diplomatic action had failed to bring redress for these violations of agreements and for attacks upon Japanese nationals and property in areas in which they had been granted special privileges by treaty. The development of the resources of Manchuria and the influx of vast numbers of immigrants from China

Proper had been made possible by Japan's administration of the Railway zone. Was Japan, therefore, to surrender to China's attack without a blow? The frequent boycotts of Japanese goods were unfriendly acts; Japan's only reply to them was military action. Secondly, Japan was fearful of the extension of Russian interests in the outlying parts of China's dominions and of communist influence in China Proper. Finally, as the Lytton Report clearly brought out, Japan held that her claim to a "special position" in Manchuria was based not merely upon treaties with China and other States but upon historical associations "which are the heritage of the Russo-Japanese War" and upon "pride in the achievements of Japanese enterprise in Manchuria in the last quarter-century." Manchuria was spoken of as Japan's "life-line." It was vitally important from a strategic and military standpoint and some believed that expansion in that area was forced upon Japan by her economic difficulties.[1] It was argued that Manchuria was necessary to give Japan access to raw materials and markets and an outlet for her increasing population. This argument has been received with more sympathy in the West than the others. Yet it is the least plausible. Experience has shown that Japanese are not likely to settle in Manchuria in great numbers; emigrants to that country from Japan have been, and are likely to be, officials and railway workers, rather than peasants, who are the chief sufferers from the alleged over-population of Japan Proper. Furthermore, Japan can obtain minerals and most other raw materials from the outside world more cheaply than she can obtain them from Manchuria, and that country is not likely for many years to provide her with a considerable market for manufactured goods, except those which are the direct consequence of her exports of capital. What is generally regarded as an economic argument is really a strategic one. Manchuria is useful

[1] Prince Konoye, the present Prime Minister, stated recently: "The Manchurian Incident was unmistakably an irrepressible outburst of Japan's instinct for self-existence." (*Contemporary Manchuria*, July 1937, p. 1.) This point of view was stressed by Japanese journalists and business men in many conversations which I had with them in 1936. "We were obliged to act as we did in Manchuria in order to live," said one of them.

to Japan, not because exploitation of the area will bring her economic gains, but because possession of it means that she can have access, in time of war, to certain raw materials essential to her military power.

China was able to reply to Japan's arguments by declaring that Manchuria was an integral part of China and that Japan's "rights" there had been secured by unjust treaties signed under threats. The conflict, however, was not merely between Japan and China, but between Japan on the one side, and the League and the signatories to the Nine-Power Treaty and the Kellogg Pact on the other. Japan had agreed with the Powers concerned to submit to the judgment of third parties in international disputes, to refrain from resorting to war for the promotion of national policy, and to maintain the territorial integrity of China. While it was true enough that Japan was following a course for which she could find many precedents in the history of Western Imperialism, her action was the more indefensible because, along with other nations, she had agreed after the Great War to renounce war as an instrument of policy and subject herself in cases of dispute to the judgment of a concert of nations. Many liberal Japanese, at the beginning of the Manchurian "incident," asserted that the League was justified in its intervention and that Japan was acting contrary to her treaty obligations.[1] But the opposite view, which steadily gained ground, was that the relationship between Japan and Manchuria was so peculiar as to place it outside the jurisdiction of the League and that intervention by third parties could not be entertained. Later, the argument was commonly advanced that Japan was forced to take the action she did by her own necessities, and as the machinery of the League was too imperfect to provide remedies for her grievances, Japan was justified in seeking her own solution.[2] No

[1] T. Takeuchi, *op. cit.*, pp. 362 *et seq.* (including notes).

[2] Prince Konoye has lately argued (*loc. cit.*) that the Western Powers should support Japan's policy in China. "Supposing she had to turn away her attention from the Continent of Asia, the consequence would be at least her enforced expansion towards the regions already considered by the Western Powers as their spheres of influence or their colonial possessions."

one can deny that the failure of the League, or rather, of the Great Powers that dominated it, to take measures for redressing the grievances of the dissatisfied nations has been a cause of its downfall, and that part of the blame for this, as for later catastrophes, can be laid at the door of the "satisfied" Powers who persisted in a short-sighted and selfish policy. Yet no system of international order can be established unless aggrieved Powers are willing to accept the decisions of third parties, even if they believe these decisions to be unjust.

The whole situation was greatly complicated by the defects in the systems of government existing both in China and Japan. In China, control over the provincial governments by the central administration was weak, and there was no guarantee that an agreement between the Nanking Government and another Power would be faithfully carried out if adherence to that agreement depended upon the action of provincial governors. In Japan, the dual system of government had an equally mischievous effect. A decision of the Cabinet on questions of foreign policy, especially in regard to China, could not be carried out unless it had the approval of the Army, which, indeed, was able to take the initiative without obtaining the consent of the civil administration. The Army has long had its own political agents in China, who are quite independent of the Foreign Office, and clashes between diplomatic and Army representatives over China policy have been frequent. In the handling of the Manchurian affair, the Cabinet was ignored by the Army which had assumed the initiative in foreign policy even before the outbreak. It was, indeed, a tragedy that when the first real test of the League came the parties to the dispute were both countries with an imperfectly developed system of central government.

Between 1933, when the Tangku Truce had been signed, and the end of 1936, Japan was engaged in establishing the new régime in Manchukuo and attempting to provide for its defence. From being a buffer State between Russia and Korea, Manchuria (now Manchukuo) had now become virtually part of the Japanese

Empire, and this extension of her frontier led Japan to take "defence" measures in contiguous areas. The increase of Russian power in Sinkiang and Outer Mongolia, and the creation of a great Far Eastern army by the Soviet as a counterpoise to the Japanese advance, made these increases the more necessary. Japan strengthened her influence in Inner Mongolia and, as a result of "incidents" in the summer of 1935, Chinese troops were forced to withdraw from Chahar. In the zone which had been demilitarized by the Tangku Truce, clashes between Japanese and Chinese were frequent, and a damaging boycott of Japanese goods persisted throughout the country. The Japanese military authorities made a series of fresh demands, ostensibly designed to carry out the terms of the Truce, and though the Chinese Central Government complied, in fact it did not always take effective measures to satisfy the Japanese.[1] This pressure from Japan ended in the attempt by the military to set up a government in North China independent of Nanking and working in co-operation with the Army. This policy was not carried through with complete success; but autonomous governments were, in fact, set up in Hopei and Chahar, and parts of East Chahar were occupied before the end of 1935 by Japanese troops. At the same time proposals were put forward for the establishment of a Japan–Manchukuo–North China economic *bloc*, and various associations and business groups were formed among Chinese and Japanese in North China to prepare plans for the industrial exploitation of that region. As a reply to the Chinese boycotts, and to the raising of Chinese tariffs, Japanese traders, with the connivance of the authorities, began organized smuggling into China, and among the goods so introduced opium had an important place. The Chinese declare that this was the result of a deliberate policy intended to break the stamina of the people.

By this time the doctrine, tentatively enunciated in earlier years, to the effect that Japan would not tolerate any interference by foreign Powers in Chinese affairs had been unambiguously set

[1] Royal Institute of International Affairs, *China and Japan*, p. 61.

forth. In the famous Amau Statement of April 1934, Japan declared that she would object to any measures on the part of other Powers likely to disturb the peace, such as the provision of loans, war materials, or military instructors to the Chinese Government. The maintenance of peace in East Asia was Japan's special responsibility. Thus, after the establishment of Manchukuo, Japan took a major step forward. Before then, her particular interests and responsibilities were held to cover the area north of the Great Wall; with the setting up of Manchukuo they were deemed to extend to the whole of China.

Early in 1936 the Japanese Foreign Minister enunciated the main demands made by his country upon China. They were: the cessation of boycotts and acts unfriendly to Japan; the recognition of Manchukuo; and the suppression of communist activities throughout the Chinese dominion, including Mongolia. The first and last of these demands were beyond the power of Nanking to satisfy, if it had had the will, and China in subsequent negotiations put forward a claim for the return to her of the rights of which she had been recently deprived in Hopei and Chahar. No settlement was reached between the parties, and meanwhile anti-Japanese sentiment was growing throughout China. In the course of 1936 there were several serious incidents which resulted in the deaths of Japanese nationals in China and the destruction of Japanese property. In October a Mongolian force, supported by the Japanese, attacked Suiyuan, and Chiang Kai-shek then broke off negotiations. This attack seems to have been engineered by the Japanese Army without authorization from Tokyo, and thus, again, the slender chances of a peaceful settlement were wrecked by the lack in Japan of a really strong centralized administration. This and other incidents in which the local military authorities acted independently of or contrary to the wishes of the Government at home recall similar events in the building up of the British power in India, Egypt, and South Africa.

In the first months of 1937 hopes of a peaceful settlement revived. Liberal criticism of the Government was growing, and it was explicitly stated in one influential journal that Japan had not acted in such a way as to promote peaceful co-operation with China. As we have seen, moreover, the heavy expenditure on the Army was leading to increased taxation, and so to misgivings in business quarters. There was a possibility that financial difficulties and the fears of inflation felt by the business circles might curb the militarists. Indeed, Mr. Sato, Foreign Minister in the Hayashi Government, in describing his proposed policy, gave some indication of a less aggressive attitude. Nevertheless, in this year the circles that were well disposed towards China were far smaller than they were in 1931. To some extent the discredit that had fallen on the League, and the resurgence of Germany and Italy under their ruthless dictators, had destroyed the faith of even liberal Japanese in the effectiveness of conciliation in international dealings. More important than this, however, was the intense resentment felt by Japanese business men who had previously advised caution in foreign policy, at the restrictions imposed by Powers with great empires on Japan's exports. Japan, they urged, could only maintain her national standard of life in the face of her increasing numbers, if she could export. Yet the doors were being slammed against her by those very countries which preached so loudly about respect for international treaties and a peaceful settlement of international disputes. It is true that the restrictions had not yet checked the growth of Japanese trade, though they must have necessitated the sale of her goods on worse terms than before. But these Japanese feared for the future in a world given over to economic nationalism. Therefore, they were more willing to listen to the imperialists who declared that to the closed empires of Western nations Japan must oppose her own empire in which she could enjoy monopolistic privileges, and that the extension of her control over wider areas of the Continent was the only solution available to her. The cooler heads might realize that Japan cannot dispense with a large trade with the outside world, and that to concentrate her activities upon the development of a self-sufficient Empire, including Manchukuo and North China, would be fatal to any hope of an advance in standards of living. But for the average Japanese business man, smarting under what he considered to be the unjust discrimination practised by Western Powers, these considerations had little weight. He was, therefore, prepared to view without his former antagonism the activities of the Army on the Continent. The effects of the Ottawa Agreements and the discriminatory duties and quotas on Japanese trade may have been exaggerated in popular discussion; but these restrictions were taken as an earnest of what was to come. It was not their immediate consequence but the trend of policy of which they were deemed to be the first expression, that alarmed Japan's traders and shattered the hopes of her liberals.

The Army, of course, was not satisfied at the prospect of leaving important matters of dispute unsettled. Chiang Kai-shek's power was increasing; China was busy increasing her armaments and reorganizing her army under German and Italian instructors, and there were prospects of large loans from England and America which might be used to increase China's strength. At the same time, the moment seemed appropriate for stern measures. England was immobilized by the continuance of the Spanish Civil War, and Russia, the real and most dangerous enemy, was being weakened by her purge of Army officers. The occasion was provided by a skirmish between Chinese and Japanese soldiers at Lukouchiao in North China, and by the end of July 1937 Japan was launched upon a war of which the ultimate results for her and the whole of the Far East are at present as obscure as they are likely to be momentous.

Japan has stated that she wishes merely to overthrow a Chinese Government that is hostile to her, and to strike a blow at communist activities in the Far East with which that Government proved unable or unwilling to deal. She has, she declares, no designs upon China's territory and no intention to interfere with the rights of other Powers. There can be little doubt, however, that in the likely event of her victory, the consequences will clearly resemble those which have followed her other "wars of defence."

Japan fought in 1894 to preserve the independence of Korea. Sixteen years later she annexed Korea. In 1904–5 she fought to protect herself from the Russian menace; she gained the Kwantung Peninsula and a firm footing in South Manchuria. In 1931 she fought to defend her interests in Manchuria; the result was the extension of her hegemony over the whole of that vast country. Victory in the present war, fought to consolidate her earlier gains, and not, as she affirms, with aggressive intentions, is likely to bring North China at least under her sway. The Japanese Government is not necessarily to be accused of disingenuousness or duplicity. That there are ambitious imperialists who have long desired a vast extension of the Japanese Empire is perfectly true. But the actual course of events has scarcely been determined by them so much as by the whole complex of political rivalries in the Far East at different points of time during the last half-century.

The circumstances are very similar to those that have attended the great conquests of the past. A vast country, with its outlying dominions always loosely held, has been passing through a period of chaos and reconstruction that invited encroachments from without. These encroachments are viewed as a menace by a powerful contiguous State whose geographical position gives her a peculiar interest in the fortunes of her neighbour. That State, to end the alleged menace, wars successfully against the most dangerous aggressor and becomes heir to its aggression. Once she has herself embarked on this course, there is no turning back. The "rights" which she has acquired in the territory of the ultimate victim of these rivalries provoke the hostility of its nationals, and this leads inevitably to disputes and "incidents" in the areas where the "rights" are enjoyed. So, further encroachment is necessary to protect those "rights." As the "interests" and "rights" become more widely extended, the danger from rivals intent on profiting from the victim's weakness is increased. So the powerful neighbour manœuvres for positions of strategic advantage in the struggle, and this, again, often leads to further inroads into the victim's territory. The anger of the victim at this repeated aggression increases; there are "incidents" on the fringes of the new dominion; and these can be "liquidated" only by another step forward. Thus, once imperialistic expansion has begun, it cannot easily be checked; for the aggressor's bounds must be set "wider still and wider," partly to check the angry reprisals of the victim and partly to meet the danger to existing interests from rival aggressors.

CHAPTER XII

CONCLUSION

"O, that so many pitchers of rough clay
Should prosper and the porcelain break in two!"
W. B. YEATS

INDIANS who visit England often find a strange contrast between the geniality of the people whom they encounter here and the arrogance of the ruling nation of which they have had experience in their own country. In the same way, Japan, viewed from a distance, in her rôle of aggressive imperialism is an unattractive figure, and yet the Japanese people are known by foreigners who have lived among them to be, on the whole, kindly, unassuming, and generous. It would be unfortunate, therefore, if the last impression of the reader of this book should be of the Japanese in their capacity as empire-builders, for in that capacity they reveal their worst qualities. This is true of most peoples. It is a platitude that as narrow "patriots" (in the Johnsonian sense) men are everywhere ready to perform actions which as private persons they abhor. So the lawless acts of Japan as a sovereign State and the prevalence of violence and fanaticism in her internal politics are not to be regarded as symptomatic of the character of the people in their ordinary life. The Japanese differ only in degree from other nations in this association of private virtue and political unscrupulousness.

The lover of things Japanese who at the same time finds the politics deplorable is in a dilemma when he tries to evaluate the tendencies of to-day, for sometimes the weeds and the flowers seem to be growing from the same root. For instance, much of the peculiar flavour of Japanese life must pass as the nation becomes urbanized, and as the peasant and the country families lose their place at the foundation of society. Yet, can one pray for the preservation of a way of life which, though picturesque and steeped in ancient traditions, involves incessant and unpleasant labour and a bare subsistence for the majority? Can one deplore its passing when one reflects that from the land has come in the past few years the main support for the reactionary forces that have turned Japan towards imperialism? "If honour sinks where commerce long prevails," yet commercial and industrial development alone can give the mass of the people better health and a higher standard of living than they now enjoy. Beauty is found chiefly in association with the old ways of life and with the occupations and trades that have come down from the past. But it is in the great businesses of the modern type that one finds the people who have the most rational outlook on the world and have freed themselves most successfully from narrow prejudice. Good manners and grace are found especially among the old-fashioned Japanese, but a liberal and enlightened outlook among those who have cut adrift from old conventions. The festivals and observances associated with *Shinto* add much to the colour and warmth of the Japanese scene; but *Shinto*, on one side, is closely linked with an aggressively nationalistic spirit and policy. The *geisha* is a delightful product of the Japanese past; but she could not exist in a society in which women have greater opportunities for self-expression than they have in Japan. If she disappears because of the freeing of women from the narrow bonds of convention in which they have hitherto been held, ought this to be regretted? One may sympathize with the conservative Japanese who wishes to discourage the adoption of the more fatuous Western habits and amusements, who bewails the popularity of jazz and American films and scorns the ungainly "*mobo*" and the ungraceful "*moga*."[1] But only too frequently this conservative Japanese also wishes to put down spontaneity and freedom of thought by force, and upholds all the cruder manifestations of the "Japanese spirit."

There are, of course, some Japanese who can wear the foreign garb with discrimination and their own without arrogance. Yet

[1] Japanese abbreviations for "modern boy" and "modern girl."

PLATE XII

TOKYO ROOF-TOPS

NEW DIET BUILDING—DISTANT VIEW

they, too, are faced with the most perplexing problem of values in their attempts to reconcile the old and the new. A working compromise between the Western and the Japanese way of life is generally recognized to be necessary; but the form of the compromise is violently disputed. This cultural conflict is one with the political and economic conflicts already discussed, and the ultimate solution will depend on many streams of influence. The kind of compromise to which Japan will move is not a matter of indifference to the West. In some measure, it will be determined by the foreign policies of other nations and by the course of international trade; at the same time the cultural compromise that is effected must profoundly influence all other branches of the nation's activities and so its relations with the outside world.

Westerners would be able to sympathize with the difficulties of the Japanese in their efforts to reach a working compromise between old and new, if they remembered that their own history provides parallels to many of the institutions and the political and economic situations that exist in Japan to-day. At the same time, the Japanese might approach their own problems in a more constructive frame of mind if they were not so eager to assert that their institutions and conditions are unique. There can, of course, be no precise identity between the institutions and situations of peoples widely separated in space and time; but where analogies exist it seems reasonable that they should be emphasized if this helps to strip the institutions or situations of a false glamour of uniqueness or oddity. Some analogies between the economic situation of Japan to-day and that of Great Britain in the early nineteenth century have already been suggested. Although many Japanese think that the survival among them of the small unit in industries which are conducted on a large scale in the West, is to be attributed to some essential and enduring peculiarity of their own social organization, actually the situation is just what might be expected to exist in their country in her present stage of industrial development. Capital is relatively scarce, and industrial labour, through the high rate of increase of the population and through migration from the land, is abundant. In these circumstances it naturally pays to employ industrial processes which require a large amount of labour and little capital. In the first half of the nineteenth century, when similar conditions existed in Great Britain, most of the British industries of the type corresponding to the present small-scale trades of Japan were conducted in small workshops and were organized in the same way. Even the co-existence of a few large factories amid a multitude of small workshops, which so impresses the casual observer of modern Japan, is not unique. One may recall, for instance, the great Soho foundry of Boulton and Watt, which, along with a few other great businesses, stood out in contrast with multitudes of small workplaces in the Birmingham area at the end of the eighteenth century. Or, to move to a very different setting, one may find other analogies from the industrial development of Imperial Russia. There, as in Japan, in the early days of industrialization large factories for providing equipment and goods needed for national security were first established by the State or by persons to whom the State gave special privileges. These factories were in contrast with the small units typical of the majority of industries; and after foreign capital came into the country towards the end of the nineteenth century and some huge businesses were established in the heavy industries, the contrast became more striking than ever. At that time, as in Japan to-day and in all countries where capital is in a few hands and initiative not widely diffused, the concentration of economic power was far greater than in the older and richer countries. Moreover, the same kind of paternalism existed in the early Russian factories as in the Japanese factories at the present time. The employers were accustomed to house and feed the workers and to provide welfare facilities for them, from the same motives as have guided the Japanese employers. Although many of the details of Japanese economic development and conditions are peculiar, yet in essentials we find that most other industrial countries have had a similar experience at some time or other.

Peculiarity is also claimed for certain features of the political system, and in this connection the influence exercised by the Army and Navy over Governmental policy is often stressed. Yet, to take examples only from recent times, a very similar influence was exercised by the Army in Imperial Germany and in Spain. Again, the history of political myths can provide us with plenty of examples of doctrines of national development that are identical with those now popular in Japan. For instance, old-fashioned historians used to show that power passed from one race to another as they waxed or waned in virility and military efficiency. This interpretation of the course of history is now popular in Japan. England and France, it is said, were once great nations, but are now decadent. Not only will power pass inevitably to the growing, vigorous Japan, but it is right that it should so pass. The mere fact that Japan is a "growing" nation justifies her in assuming control of wider areas of the world: it is not merely inexpedient but immoral to oppose her. These views, common in Japan to-day, and dressed in mystical plumage, are no different from those that were held in England in the days of her triumphant imperialism.

The Japanese institution which is held to be unquestionably unique in the world is the Emperor. Among rulers of the present time he certainly occupies a position of peculiar splendour and sanctity. His ancestry is traced to the Sun-Goddess and he himself —*Tenno-Heka* (The Son of Heaven)—is divine. The old mythologies and ceremonies associated with *Shinto* were revivified in modern times for the purpose of mobilizing the patriotic and religious emotions of the whole race behind his person. To-day, Emperor-worship, which is synonymous with Nation-worship, is the first article of the Japanese creed. Now, a modern European has difficulty in understanding or sympathizing with this aspect of Japanese political life. Neither the limited monarchs nor the dictators provide very close resemblances to the Emperor in the position they occupy or the emotions they excite. But if we glance back to the early days of the Roman Principatus, we find an analogous institution. At that time there was an Emperor (Augustus) who professed to trace his descent, like Julius Caesar before him, to the Gods—to Aeneas, son of Venus. He also became the State's religious head (Pontifex Maximus) as well as its secular head, and all types of power were concentrated in him. He was worshipped as a god by his people and formally deified after his death. Even the process by which the Roman God-Emperor achieved his eminence was in many respects similar to that carried out in modern Japan. Decaying religious symbols were given a new significance in Imperial Rome as in post-Restoration Japan, and in both, the revival of the ancient cults was encouraged for nationalistic rather than for strictly religious reasons. Augustus was addressed by Ovid as "Templorum positor, templorum sancte repostor," and the same terms might be applied to the reigning Emperor Showa; for in recent years the policy of rebuilding the national shrines, for which Augustus was praised, has been followed in Japan. There has been, in the latest development of Emperor-worship, the same effort to revive ancient piety and morals as was part of the Augustan policy. Horace, censuring the exotic dances in which contemporary Roman maidens delighted,[1] has his counterpart to-day in the conservative Japanese who sees in the popularity of the dance-halls an indication of the decline of ancient virtue.

The same conflict between Christianity and the State as developed during the pagan revival in Rome is now beginning in Japan. The State, as we have seen, is refusing to tolerate any aloofness on the part of its subjects from the worship of the national deities, and it is insisting that Christianity, if it is to survive there, must make terms with *Shinto*. The subsequent fate of the Roman Empire offers a warning to Japan, no less than to the dictators, against insistence upon this conformity. As Professor Zimmern has said: "Men must be spiritually free before they can co-operate politically on the highest terms." For good or ill Japan has received a cultural message from the West. Many Japanese have come to value intellectual liberty and have assimilated, in some measure,

[1] *Odes*, III, 6.

Western habits of mind. The whole trend of material development will foster these habits of mind among the people. A policy of preserving, without exact definition, the old ideological foundations of the State, and at the same time of allowing spiritual and intellectual freedom to individuals, would permit the gradual and insensible modification of these foundations as the temper and outlook of the people slowly changed. This policy was, on the whole, being followed down to 1930. But to attempt to base the State unequivocally on what must eventually become outworn symbols and to insist on the conformity of everyone to an ideology which, though for the moment fashionable, cannot forever survive the spread of a scientific attitude of mind, is to invite disaster. Men will, of course, conform for a time, but in conforming they will make mental reservations, and so the whole of public life will become riddled with insincerities. What can be the future of such a State?

It would be misleading, and, indeed, unfair to Japan, to end on this pessimistic note. Throughout her modern history she has been faced with great dangers and moved by powerful external influences. Her course has not been easy to steer, and on several occasions she appeared to be heading for disaster. At one time, a strong outburst of nationalist feeling has menaced kindliness, tolerance, and all vestiges of political freedom; at another time, the popularity of Western institutions and ideas has threatened to engulf the graciousness of the past and the strong aesthetic habit which is, perhaps, Japan's most valuable quality. Yet these impulses have always been restrained before it was too late. Up to now Japan has been skilful in avoiding extremes in her social, political, and cultural life, and experience should warn us against the assumption that the present disastrous trends will continue indefinitely. Her future course will depend in some measure on the policy of Western Powers, and it must be remembered that the clumsy treatment which she received from them in the past has helped to foster the present national temper. Abhorrence of Japan's current policy ought not to cause us to withhold sympathy from her in the difficult problems with which she is faced.

APPENDIX

AN ESTIMATE OF THE ECONOMIC EFFECTS UPON JAPAN OF THE SINO-JAPANESE WAR

THE view has been expressed that Japan, in spite of her military superiority over China, will be unable to fight a long war because of her financial weakness and the shallow economic foundations upon which her power is based. In my opinion this is a rash judgment. The capacity of Japan's industrial system, immature though it may be, is underestimated by those critics who are so mistaken as to imagine that the small size of the technical unit in many industries is necessarily an indication of inefficiency or of inability to provide the equipment needed for war. The remarkable development of the metal and engineering industries during the last decade and the improvement in the quality of the product of those industries must not be neglected. Further, there seems no likelihood that foreign suppliers of raw materials and finished products which Japan cannot produce for herself, will refuse to sell to Japan. In spite of boycotts abroad and rising costs at home there is every probability that Japan will be able to sell a sufficiently large volume of exports to enable her to buy the foreign materials essential for the prosecution of the war, however much she may be forced to economize in her purchases of other things. Her Empire is almost self-sufficient in the staple foodstuffs. Finally, the experience of other countries suggests that financial difficulties alone would not cause Japan to stay her hand before her political ambitions have been satisfied. Countries in far worse financial straits than those in which Japan now finds herself have continued to fight without loss of military efficiency.

There can be no doubt, however, that the war, if protracted, will impose a serious strain on Japan's economic system, and that she will emerge from the conflict in a weakened condition. The nature of the strain may be indicated by a brief reference to foreign trade and finance during the last fifteen months. The exchange value of the yen, as we have already seen, was tending to depreciate towards the end of 1936. The weakness in the currency was associated with the slowing-up of the export boom which Japan had enjoyed ever since 1932, and this, in turn, was to be attributed partly to the increasing restrictions imposed on Japanese exports by other countries, and partly to the rise in Japanese prices produced by a long series of unbalanced budgets. To counter this tendency for the yen to fall, in January 1937 the Government introduced strict foreign exchange regulations, together with an import-licensing scheme. These regulations were tightened in July 1937, and after that month traders had to obtain the permission of the Ministry of Finance for import transactions of which the monthly total amount was in excess of 1,000 yen. Later, the Government was empowered to restrict, or, if necessary, prohibit the import of certain classes of materials, and this power was extensively used in the latter part of 1937 with the result that a shortage of important industrial materials, such as raw cotton, appeared. Consequently, schemes for rationing the supply of raw materials had to be introduced into a number of export industries. In the meantime the Government had written up the Bank of Japan's gold reserves approximately to their market value, and it proceeded to export large quantities of gold in payment for the war materials it required. In the course of 1937, 830 million yen of gold was exported. This was roughly equivalent to the profit realized by the Government as the result of revaluation. There now remains only a small "free" gold stock, other than the 801 million yen counted as a currency reserve. Numerous other measures of control over economic life have also been instituted. For instance, before any new capital issues can be made, permission now has to be obtained from the Government, and this power has been used to direct capital into the war industries. The tendency has culminated in the passing in March 1938 of the National Mobilization Act, which provides the Government, in an emergency, with almost unlimited powers over national resources. Naturally the main effect of State intervention has been to divert capital, materials, and labour to the munition industries, and this diversion has been to the disadvantage of the export trades as well as of industries that cater for everyday domestic needs.

The foreign trade returns for 1937 seem to indicate that the immediate result of the war was not the curtailment of exports but a large expansion of imports. Compared with 1936 exports in 1937 rose by 18 per cent. and imports by 37 per cent.; while the import surplus reached 644 million yen compared with 111 million yen in 1936. The growth of foreign trade is, in some

Year	Domestic Exports (in million yen)	Retained Imports (in million yen)
1936	2,641	2,753
1937	3,132	3,776
Dec. 1936–Feb. 1937 (inclusive)..	704	872
Dec. 1937–Feb. 1938 (inclusive)..	635	665

degree, attributable to higher prices; for it is estimated that exports and imports rose by only 4 per cent. and 6·1 per cent. in volume.[1] Nevertheless, the figures do suggest, at first sight, that the import restrictions in 1937 were not of any considerable practical importance. It must be remembered, however, that Japan was importing greatly increased supplies of war materials during the earlier part of the year, and that a large growth in imports as a whole is not inconsistent with the existence of restrictions on imports of materials not required for war purposes. Towards the end of 1937, moreover, a marked deterioration in the foreign trade set in and this tendency persisted in the early months of 1938.

As the import-controls further reduce the supply of materials available for manufacturers, the difficulties in the way of maintaining exports will be increased. This will have a cumulative effect.

[1] *Mitsubishi Monthly Circular*, March 1938, p. 5.

Unlike the Allies in the Great War, Japan is unable to borrow from foreign capital markets and she has no large reserves of gold, foreign exchange, and foreign securities. Thus, every fall in her exports at once reduces her capacity to import. As, in consequence of the Governmental regulation of trade, the reduction in imports is being concentrated upon materials not required for munitions manufacture, the damage to other industries is likely to be considerable.

The effect of the war on the national finances is brought out by the following figures (in million yen):[1]

Financial Year	Expenditure	Revenue (excluding receipts from loans)	Revenue Raised, or to be Raised, by Bond Issues
1936–37 (actual) ..	2,282	1,762	610
1937–38 (Budget estimates)	5,475	2,081	3,394
1938–39 (Budget estimates)	8,364	2,903	5,461

In an interpretation of these figures it should be realized that the amounts for 1937–38 and 1938–39 are Budget estimates, and that whether the huge expenditure provided for is actually necessary will depend on the progress of the war. Up to the end of March 1938 the actual issue of national bonds was about 900 million yen less than had been authorized by the Budget of the financial year 1937–38.[2] According to the explanation afforded by a Japanese economist the military and naval authorities had large stocks of war material on hand when the conflict began, and so were not obliged immediately to make use of their Budget appropriations. Up to the present, then (March 1938), the war has not imposed on Japanese national finances the strain that the Budget figures suggest. But it is evident that the Government anticipates a long and expensive war, and in that event the financial position may become very serious, for only a small part of the

[1] *Mitsubishi Monthly Circular*, April 1938, pp. 7–9.

[2] *Japan Weekly Chronicle*, April 7, 1938, p. 423.

increased expenditure is likely to be covered by taxation. Even as it is, the national debt has risen steeply in the course of the last year, and the service of this debt will create a difficult problem for future Ministers of Finance. The rapid expansion of the note issue is another symptom of the inflationary conditions that are appearing.

The inflationary policy is leading to a sharp rise in prices. Even

National Debt

(In million yen)

Year	Internal	External (valued at par)	Total
1931 (March)	4,675	1,479	6,154
1936 (March)	8,976	1,332	10,308
1937 (December)	10,585	1,308	11,893

Bank of Japan's Note Issue

(Daily average for December of each year, in million yen)

1935	1,462
1936	1,562
1937	1,936

before the war began Japanese prices were beginning to move out of line with those of other countries, and since July 1937 the upward movement in Japan has continued, although abroad the trend has been in the opposite direction. This growing divergence between Japanese and foreign prices is obviously unfavourable to the maintenance of the export trade.

The effect of inflation on the standard of life is already making itself felt. The retail price index which was 157 in January 1936 (July 1914 = 100) had moved up slowly during that year and stood at 163 in December 1936. In the early months of 1937 the rise was rapid and the index reached 171 in June 1937. Then it mounted rapidly and in February 1938 it reached 190. Although actual money earnings also increased, they did not keep pace with the movement of prices, so far as can be judged from the available indices; and this fact, together with the heavy fall in the turnover of the departmental stores, seems to show that the standard of life has fallen. As in other countries in which the State exercises considerable control over economic affairs, the extent of the inflation

Index Number of Wholesale Prices

1929 = 100

Year	Japan	Great Britain
1935 (Average for Year)	**84**	**74**
December ..	87	77
1936 (Average for Year)	**90**	**79**
June ..	88	75
December ..	98	86
1937 (Average for Year)	**108**	**89**
June ..	108	91
July ..	109	92
August ..	107	90
September	109	88
October ..	108	86
November ..	108	83
December ..	110	84
1938 January ..	112	83

has been disguised by the fall in the quality of the goods provided. Substitutes for natural materials are now being extensively introduced. Municipal employees and students are being dressed in staple-fibre uniforms; while the cotton industry is compelled to use a large proportion of staple-fibre in manufactures destined for the home market. Economies in expenditure on the heating of schools and other public buildings are also being effected, and all these devices must tend to depress the standard of life, even if for a time the hardships are willingly borne by people buoyed up by patriotic enthusiasm.

The damage that the war is inflicting on the economic strength of Japan and on the standard of life of her people is not, at this early stage, considerable. But it has already become sufficiently marked to justify the conclusions put forward. With the prolongation of the war it is likely to be serious, and even when the war is over, and on the assumption that Japan is victorious, she will be faced with heavy expenditure in the conquered territories and with the problem of adjusting her economic life to normal conditions. This last problem alone will be difficult enough to face; for Japan's resources will be maldistributed from the standpoint of peace-time needs, and her price- and cost-structure will have become distorted. The prospects are all the more unfavourable for her because she began the war with her finances in an unsound condition. For five years her munitions and metallurgical industries had been expanding under the impetus of heavy Governmental expenditure financed by internal borrowing. A return to a balanced Budget, which sooner or later must be the alternative to uncontrolled inflation, will be difficult to achieve without bringing about a very serious depression. At the same time her strength as an exporter of manufactured goods is being undermined by the institution of controls designed to foster the war industries and to increase the military power of the country. Yet, in view of her growing population and her shortage of industrial raw materials, a failure to expand the export trade must inevitably lead to a fall in the standard of life. Territorial expansion and the development of a flourishing export trade are, to some extent, alternative policies for Japan, and the realization of this has been one reason why the business classes have looked with dread on the Army's adventures in Asia. It is difficult to believe that Japan is strong enough to pursue both of these policies successfully, and she now seems to have trusted her fate to the former. A complete success in the war might enable her ultimately to obtain profitable investments and valuable markets in China; but these benefits could not be reaped quickly. Furthermore, her ability to exploit any territory that she might conquer would depend, largely, on whether she could borrow capital from abroad. All these conclusions are necessarily tentative, since the duration and the outcome of the present struggle cannot be foreseen. But it seems clear that while Japan's economic position is not so vulnerable as to lead to a collapse of her military effort, the war is likely to be very costly for her, and even victory would leave her economic strength seriously impaired.

GLOSSARY

Japanese Term	*English Equivalent*
Banto	An assistant, a manager, company official
Daimyo	Feudal Lord, before the Restoration
Fusuma	An opaque sliding screen with a frame of lacquered wood, used to provide the interior walls of a Japanese house
Geta	Wooden footwear
Genro	Elder statesman
Hakama ..	A skirt of formal male dress
Kaisha ..	Business company
Kimono ..	Japanese dress
Sake	Alcoholic drink distilled from rice
Samurai ..	A member of the military class in feudal Japan
Shogun	The military governor of the State during the period when the Emperor himself remained aloof from administration
Shoji	A sliding screen consisting of an unpainted wooden frame covered with translucent paper and used both as a kind of external wall and as a means of dividing a Japanese house into rooms
Suki-yaki ..	A Japanese dish, much liked by foreign residents.
Tatami	A thick mat made in standard size of straw overlaid with rushes and used as a floor-covering in all Japanese houses (*see* illustration facing p. 72)
Tokonoma ..	Alcove or ornamental recess (*see* top left of illustration facing page 72)
Zaibatsu	Money cliques or plutocracy
Tokugawa Era ..	1603–1868: the House of Tokugawa ruled Japan during this period as *Shogun*
Meiji Restoration	The restoration, in 1868, of the Emperor to his former position as *de facto* as well as *de jure* head of the State

Meiji Era ..	Reign of the Emperor Meiji, 1868–1912
Taisho Era ..	Reign of the Emperor Taisho, 1912–26
Showa Era ..	The present reign, 1926 to date
Yen	1s. 2d. at present rate of exchange
Sen	A hundredth part of yen

INDEX

For Product Safety Concerns and Information please contact our EU
representative GPSR@taylorandfrancis.com
Taylor & Francis Verlag GmbH, Kaufingerstraße 24, 80331 München, Germany

www.ingramcontent.com/pod-product-compliance
Lightning Source LLC
LaVergne TN
LVHW011118300926
849160LV00008B/437
9780415852357